Jewish Gangsters
of Modern Literature

King Alfred's
Winchester

Martial Rose Library
Tel: 01962 827306

Jewish Gangsters
of Modern Literature

Rachel Rubin

University of Illinois Press

Urbana and Chicago

Library of Congress Cataloging-in-Publication Data
Rubin, Rachel.
Jewish gangsters of modern literature / Rachel Rubin.
p.   cm.
Includes bibliographical references (p.) and index.
ISBN 0-252-02539-3 (alk. paper)
1. American fiction—20th century—History and criticism.
2. Jewish criminals in literature.
3. Babel', I. (Isaak), 1894–1941—Characters—Jewish criminals.
4. American fiction—Jewish authors—History and criticism.
5. Ornitz, Samuel, 1890–1957. Haunch, paunch, and jowl.
6. Fuchs, Daniel, 1909–   —Characters—Jewish criminals.
7. Gold, Michael, 1894–1967. Jews without money.
8. Gangsters in literature.
9. Jews in literature.
I. Title.
PS374.J48R83   2000
813'.540935203924—dc21   99-6761
CIP

C 5 4 3 2 1

In memory of my brave mother

When a gentile is a thief, they hang the thief. When a Jew is a thief, they hang the Jew.

—Yiddish proverb

We are coming Father Abraham! The boys of the Jewish persuasion are getting heavy on muscle.

—Isadore Choynski

Gangsters, entertainers, shysters, communists, troublemakers.

—Barbara Rosenblum

The social organization most true of itself to the artist is the boy gang.

—Allen Ginsberg

Contents

Acknowledgments

Although I was unaware of it at the time, my father, Larry Rubin, who grew up tough in the Bronzeville neighborhood of Brooklyn in the 1910s and 1920s before becoming a CIO organizer for more than two decades, provided me with my earliest hints that the historical and emotional truths about Jewish street life and Left politics might have something to do with each other. He accomplished this, among other ways, by encouraging me to give the dolls sent by my mother's Southern Methodist family names like "Lefty the Rat," "Moksl Coksl," "Big Stinker," and "Little Stinker," while singing me to sleep with "Solidarity Forever" and "Banker and Boss Hate the Red Soviet Star." To top it off he was my favorite writer; my first thanks, as always, must therefore go to him, as well as to the many people—both Russians and Americans—who shared, with pride and sheepishness, great stories about bootleggers and *shtarkers* in their own family trees.

I am grateful to friends and acquaintances in Russia and Ukraine, especially Konstantin Ustinov, who cheerfully sent newly available materials by mail. On the American side, David Maisel has been a steady fount of knowledge about Yiddish language and culture.

I have valued the kind responses of scholars who met with me, commented on my drafts, and shared materials and advice. I am especially thankful to Barbara Foley, Alan Wald, Matthew Jacobson, Werner Sollors, Alan Trachtenberg, James Bloom, Benjamin Harshav, Jenna Weismann Joselit, and Gregory Freidin. Katerina Clark's extraordinarily sharp insight pushed me to clarify my thinking on a variety of levels, ranging from my understanding of Soviet literary history to murky formulations in my own writing. And I cannot overestimate my debt to Michael Denning, who hung in there as "advisor" for as long as it took, and who continues to be an important academic model for me.

I have benefited endlessly from support and encouragement from colleagues and co-workers at UMass-Boston, especially Judy Smith, Lois Rudnick, Shauna Lee Manning, Jason Loviglio, and Reebee Garofalo. Others also stood at the ready with pep talks and advice, and thanks are due to Tim Buckley, Robert Johnston, Linda Dittmar, Jim Keane, and Daniel Boudreau.

Others have left their mark upon this book in various ways. Gerald Horne affirmed my conviction that gangsters are significant cultural players. Michael Brandon helped me greatly with the daunting task of getting citations in order. The members of the editorial collective of *Radical Teacher* furnished me with role models.

A Junior Faculty Development Grant from UMass-Boston, and a generous grant from the Longfellow Institute for the study of Literatures of What Is Now the United States (LOWINUS), provided me with the opportunity and space to think about what the categories "Russian" and "American" have meant to each other in literature.

My friends and family have been very supportive. Cindy Weisbart has taught to me be unstinting in all endeavors; her indelible stamp is on this book, as it is on my character. Susie Ringel, Geoffrey Jacques, and David Hershey-Webb fed my love of literature and popular art. Alex Liazos demonstrated the ways that scholarship and social engagement can motivate each other. My brothers Josh and Larry knock me off my high horse if ever necessary. I've been lucky to have an extended collection of "in-laws" (Melnick, Swimmer, Smethurst, Cannon) to whom I owe a lot; Ludlow Smethurst and Bill Smethurst in particular have given me years of generous encouragement and challenging conversation. And I am indebted in more ways than I can enumerate to Jim Smethurst—co-parent, friend, and ideal reader.

My son, Jacob Rubin, has reminded me hourly of what really counts—and has developed my ability to answer the question "Why?" more than any living person. My daughter, Jessie Rubin, whose first year marked the process from dissertation to book, kept me smiling besottedly through it all.

Finally, I am grateful to Jeff Melnick for reading every word and engaging every concept, for providing enthusiasm and countless insights, and for giving me endless moral and physical support. This project is also his.

A Note on Transliteration

I have followed the British MHRA system of transliteration from the Cyrillic alphabet because I believe it is the most comprehensible to English speakers not accustomed to the Russian alphabet. I have adapted my occasional transliterations from Hebrew characters according to a similar system. Exceptions in transliteration have been made when there is a familiar English equivalent (usually of proper or place names).

Jewish Gangsters
of Modern Literature

Introduction:
Reading, Writing, and the Rackets

Here, on the roof, he saw the dream of his kingdom.
The flapping sheets on the lines
Were his plains . . . .
—Jacob Glatshteyn, "Sheeny Mike"

Did'ya ever see George Raft dance?
—the gangster Cheech in *Bullets over Broadway*

Woody Allen's film comedy *Bullets over Broadway* (1994) finds a prim young playwright of the 1920s mired in his own flaccid dialogue. His absurdly stilted play is doomed to aesthetic failure—his actors cannot say their lines convincingly. Salvation arrives from an unlikely quarter: a sullen gangster with a handful of murders to his credit, who has been hanging around the play's rehearsals as the reluctant bodyguard of his boss's "actress" girlfriend. In an unlikely chain of events, the gangster begins to moonlight as secret script editor; in short order, he manages to save the play by injecting some vitality into the script. The gangster accomplishes this artistic feat by teaching the Jewish playwright to use the vernacular.

With this help, and with the accidental inclusion into the play on opening night of the gunshots that kill the gangster, Allen shows a Jewish writer combining dialogue based on how people "really talk" with an act of violence; the vernacular is pushed into the public sphere even as the messenger is killed. Allen's movie pivots upon a special relationship between Jewish writers and gangsters that I propose to take quite seriously. That special relationship is the occasion for this book.

Woody Allen is hardly the first (nor the last) to explore questions of artistic power through the surprising figure of the gangster. The title of this introduction is borrowed from the Jewish poet Kenneth Fearing, who uses the phrase "Reading, Writing, and the Rackets" to name the foreword he wrote to a collected edition of his poetry, thereby hinting at important connections between the American literary experience and organized crime.[1] Fearing wrote a poem about a Jewish gangster named Louie Glatz in 1926; in "St. Agnes Eve," vernacular language and violence merge on the page as they do on the stage in *Bullets over Broadway:*

> But dangerous, handsome, cross-eyed Louie the rat
>
> Spoke with his gat
>
> Rat-a-tat-tat
>
> Rat-a-tat-tat
>
> And Dolan was buried as quickly as possible.[2]

This book explores the cultural work performed by fictional gangsters like Fearing's Louie the rat, as the aggressive gangster—who possesses (among other things) secrets of language—becomes a double of, and possible model for, the Jewish writer in search of a useful posture. Because of this high level of self-consciousness in play when the gangster hits the page or screen, it is probably more accurate to state that this book is about metaliterary gangsters, rather than literary gangsters.

The attraction of the Jewish gangster as a site for "high-literary" self-contemplation dates from the interwar years, first taking shape during the period of artistic experimentation known broadly as modernism. At the turn of the twentieth century, the literary gangster escapes from the ghetto where hitherto his story had been told. He now takes on special meaning as a manifestation of artistic choices facing Jewish writers during the 1920s, when a collapse of cultural certainty characterized the artistic arena.

Much has been written about the host of literary movements that flourished during the 1920s, ranging from Italian and Russian futurism to Anglo-American imagism to German expressionism. One element that seems to have been part of every modernist credo was an irregular, multidimensional "kaleidoscope" technique. Traces of Henri Bergson's notion of "simultaneity" informed all theories of avant-garde art. Expressionists, for instance, noted that being true to the world demanded no less than chaos. In the Yiddish journal *Albatross* (Warsaw, 1922), Uri Zvi Grinberg, who had been a soldier and deserter in World War I, wrote:

> This is how things are. Whether we want it or not. We stand as we are: with slash-lipped wounds, rolled up veins, unscrewed bones, after artillery bombardments

and cries of "Hurrah," after gas-attacks; after bowls filled with gall and opium and daily water: disgust. And the foam of decay covers our lips.

Hence the atrocious in the poem.
Hence the chaotic in the image.
Hence the scream in the blood.

... It is imperative to write such poems. Atrocious. Chaotic. Bleeding.[3]

Along the same lines, the Italian and Russian futurists called for the breakdown of artificially imposed temporal and spatial boundaries; the Dada poets staged cacophonies of competing voices and noises, some human and some not. The writers treated here found the intersecting planes of influence, the chaos, within the fluid identity of the Jewish gangster, whose violence, transgressiveness, and ongoing internal conflict fix him as an important symbol of modernity.

Interestingly, these high-literary, highly theorized gangsters appear most often in the work of writers who considered themselves to be communists of some variety (or were at least supporters of the Russian Revolution), whether they ever joined the Communist Party or not. Following the Russian Revolution of 1917, a new way of conceptualizing the purposes and strategies of culture was taking shape in Russia and the United States. The "Soviet experiment" galvanized radical Jews especially, and great excitement gathered steam in the conscious development of a new literature to serve idealistic ends. This idealism emerged in the face of extreme economic hardship: in the United States, the "prosperity" of the 1920s had never reached New York's Lower East Side, and the new Soviet Union struggled with severe shortages and economic disorder following the Russian Civil War in 1921. Powered by the ideals of socialism, and committed to wresting art from its position as a diversion for the elite and returning it to the daily life of the working masses, a remarkable variety of American and Soviet writers turned their attention to the ways in which literature could be relevant to collectivism, modernization, and the demands of a new historical moment. In the midst of this focus on contemporariness and populism, radical writers in the United States frequently looked to "the Soviet experiment" for inspiration while writers in the Soviet Union often considered the United States, with its skyscrapers and suspension bridges, an icon of the modern world.[4] This cross-inspiration resulted in a working concept of "modern art" that drew not only upon the formal complexities that have come to act as a shorthand definition for it, but also upon the leftist ideas and philosophies behind the Russian Revolution and the early structurings of the Soviet government.

It is easy to see why the figure of the criminal provides, for socially oriented writers, an excellent way to interrogate "the system" and to locate a work of literature within a political economy. There is, in fact, a long-standing literary tradition of "inverted kingdoms" of criminals, stretching back at least to Shakespeare (especially Falstaff's role-playing in the Henriad); a familiar example is the "little kingdom" of Fagin—another Jewish criminal—in Charles Dickens's *Oliver Twist*. Such inversion calls into question, and by definition criticizes, existing social hierarchy. High-literary representations of gangsters during the 1920s and 1930s participate in this type of commentary, in addition to expressing the subjectivity and irregularity of the "modernist" aesthetic.

I am interested in bringing writers who are generally classed as "writers on the Left" (and thereby, in many cases, promptly dismissed) into the canon of modernism via their interest in the literary gangster.[5] This in turn should enlarge the possibilities for what sorts of aesthetic experimentalism may be anointed with the term "modern" by retrospective readers. To this end, I will focus on aspects of the fictional representation of gangsters that cause these two spheres, "modernist" and "communist," often vehemently differentiated by critics, to overlap. I approach the gangster's nonstandard speech (inflected by Jewishness and criminal street slang) as a study of urban polyvocality. I explore the masculinist concerns of the communist and the Jewish male in relation to the sexual politics of modernism. I highlight the extraordinarily intertextual, dialogic nature of these works as a multivalenced form of metacommentary, focusing in some detail on the nature of this intertextuality, which is cross-continental and encompasses the high and low (ranging from the plays of Schiller to Hollywood movies). Finally, I consider the socialist aesthetic in literature as a "modern" experiment in its own right, with its prominent self-mythologizing, its conscious break with bourgeois cultural traditions in favor of a radical content grounded in the present, and its emphasis on the ritual and the iconographic, updated and transformed by revolutionary politics.

This study ultimately focuses on the development of the Jewish gangster as an important literary trope for American Jews. But the progenitor of this genealogy of self-consciously drawn literary gangsters is the Russian Jew Isaac Babel, and because Babel's writing was so important to left-wing Jewish American writers, a study of modern literary gangsterism must start with his work. Babel's Odessa tales (written between 1921 and 1933) portray the Jewish underworld in Odessa; his gangsters, led by the indomitable Benya Krik, are bold, strong, and flamboyant. Babel's gangsters are part of an obsessive quest by the author for an intellectual Jewish militance (as opposed to a bookish Jewish passivity). This defining quest of Babel's would be immediately taken up by a number of Jewish American writers, such as Michael Gold, the putative founder of American proletarian writing. Babel and Gold, in their preoccupation with the revolutionary potential of Jewish masculinity, voice a communist revision of the Zionist Max Nordau's call in 1902 for new "muscle Jews" (Muskeljudentum), which urged Jews to develop pride in physical prowess.[6]

Concern with defining a new Jewish manhood for a new age helped to establish the Jewish gangster as a consequential player in the creation of national identity. This simultaneously heroic and marginalized figure was fluid enough to be used as a vehicle through which to consider assimilation into, and difference from, "mainstream" culture at a moment when the United States and the Soviet Union were preoccupied with "national questions." As the Bolsheviks consolidated their state, Lenin's famous assertion that the revolution should lead to a freeing of the inmates from the Russian Empire's "prison-house of nations" made questions of ethnic culture under socialism (questions that had already emerged among Jewish intellectuals in the years before the revolution) a high priority for Soviet theorists. These early Soviet explorations of the "national question"—the difference between revolutionary nationalism and bourgeois or feudal nationalism, for instance—in turn wielded a huge influence on cultural explorations of ethnicity and nationality in the United States, particularly within its literary Left. Meanwhile, the enormous impact of the so-called new immigration from Eastern and Central Europe on all aspects of American culture was being furiously debated by a wide range of cultural critics, public officials, social workers, racial anthropologists, and educators.

Anxiety over these population shifts was in part articulated through a heightened discussion of Jewish criminal activity on both continents. The notorious report by New York police commissioner Theodore Bingham in 1908 had alleged that Jews constituted at least half of that city's criminals. Though Bingham ultimately retracted much of his article, the notion of a thriving Jewish underworld remained a live concern inside and outside the Jewish community. The issue was foregrounded in 1912 after the shooting of Herman "Beansey" Rosenthal, a gambler who was a friendly witness for the New York district attorney's office in an investigation of police corruption. While most of the mainstream press focused its coverage of the murder on issues of police and municipal corruption, the Jewish press was far more concerned with the fact that twelve Jews were implicated in the crime, including the victim and nearly all the gunmen who committed the murder. Newspapers from the ultrareligious *Judisches Tageblatt* to the socialist *Jewish Daily Forward* were determined to unearth causes for what everyone wanted to think was a departure from the Jewish historical experience.[7] The New York Jewish community, as Jenna Weissman Joselit puts it, became obsessed with the question of "what, then, had gone awry? How was one to reconcile the promise of America with the reality of a Lefty Louie?"[8]

This apparent chasm between gangland and promised land narrowed somewhat in 1928, when New York became preoccupied by the murder of the powerful Jewish gangster Arnold Rothstein, allegedly by Jewish gunmen (although the case was never solved). The resulting uproar revived the question of whether crime was a Jewish or an American problem. Unlike the hapless Rosenthal, however, Rothstein was eulogized in both the Jewish and mainstream press as an urbane "American" criminal who was one of the founders of the new "business-type" gangsterism.[9] A year after Rothstein's murder, the journalist Donald Henrick Clarke published a book called *In the Reign of Rothstein* that is almost unseemly in its admiration of its ruthless subject.

Rothstein's sensational death was not the first event to thrust his name into the national press. The most infamous incident connected to Rothstein was his alleged responsibility for the fixing of the 1919 World Series. Although it now appears that Rothstein was not involved in the plot, the press accused him of masterminding the entire "Black Sox" scandal. Henry Ford seized upon these stories and used them in a series of articles in his *Dearborn Independent* with titles such as "The Jewish Degradation of American Baseball" and "Jewish Gamblers Corrupt American Baseball" to represent a larger cultural construct—the foreign Jew corrupting America: "The only fact of value brought out of all the trouble is that American baseball has passed into the hands of Jews. If it is to be saved, it must be taken out of their hands. . . . If it is not taken out of their hands, let it be widely announced that baseball is another Jewish monopoly, and that its patrons may know what to expect."[10]

Americans still love to tell the story of Rothstein's alleged corruption of baseball—Rothstein's appearances in the second half of the twentieth century include Eliot Asinof's book *Eight Men Out* (1963) and John Sayles's movie version with the same name (1988); Harry Stein's novel *Hoopla* (1983); and Eric Rolfe Greenberg's novel *The Celebrant* (1983). But the *locus classicus* for artistic representations of Arnold Rothstein is F. Scott Fitzgerald's *The Great Gatsby* (1925). Fitzgerald's Meyer Wolfsheim, a gambler, is identified by Jay Gatsby as "the man who fixed the World Series back in 1919."[11] Though Fitzgerald obviously bases his character upon Rothstein, he makes Wolfsheim appear far more "foreign" than Rothstein, who grew up on New York's Upper West Side, not the Lower East Side. Although Rothstein was known for his "good looks, polished manners and 'abundant personal charm,'"[12] Wolfsheim speaks in a caricature of Yiddish-influenced English, jabbering, "It was six of us at the table, and Rosy had eat and drunk a lot all evening. . . . I understand you're looking for a business gonnegtion. . . . He went to Oggsford College in England. You know Oggsford College?"[13] While Rothstein was a handsome and dapper play-boy who moved comfortably in "high" society—years after Rothstein's death, the Italian mobster "Lucky" Luciano recalled that "he taught me how to dress"[14]—Wolfsheim is unappealingly described as "a small, flat-nosed Jew" with "a large head."[15] Fitzgerald also dwells upon Wolfsheim's profusion of nose hair. For Fitzgerald, Wolfsheim—and by extension Rothstein—is not merely a particular man who "fixed" the World Series, but rather *the* generic Jew, both alien and repulsive, who attacked an important icon of American life: "The idea staggered me. I remembered, of course, that the World's Series had been fixed in 1919, but if I had thought of it at all I would have thought of it as a thing that merely happened, the end of some inevitable chain. It never occurred to me that one man could start to play with the faith of fifty million people—with the single-mindedness of a burglar blowing a safe."[16] In the context of Ford's populist conception of the Jewish gangster as an embodi-ment of the foreign pollution of American culture, and similar "high-culture" representations (most notably in *The Great Gatsby*), any writer using a Jewish gangster was engaging a polemic that surrounded this question of corruption: were Jewish criminals spoiled *by* America, or spoilers *of* it?

At the same time, in the new Soviet Union, the very conception of Jewish criminality acquired fresh meaning as a new economic system outlawed specu-lation and profiteering, the "middleman" professions traditionally associated with Jews.[17] (Ironically, a similar discussion has reasserted itself with the end of socialism in the former Soviet Union; the spread of Jewish gangsterism in Odessa has once again become a pressing subject of discussion, suggesting that for some, Jewish criminality is still an index of social change.) As the country quickly industrialized during the 1920s, and Russians started moving in large numbers to the cities during the 1920s and 1930s, anxiety over changes in the nature of work—and competition over who would find themselves doing which new jobs—magnified this tendency to invoke Jewish criminality to ex-plain social transformation, pressing the Jewish gangster into service as a sym-bol of modernization, with its own attendant paradigm shifts, in much the same way that he came to be an important symbol of literary modernism during a time of loss of cultural certainty. A clear literary portrait of this is Yurii Libedinskii's "Nedelya" (A week; 1922), which pictures a weak, asthmatic Jew-ish druggist whose shop has been collectivized by the Bolsheviks. The phar-macist, filled with resentment, longs for the pre-Soviet days when he could profiteer unhindered; according to the new system, acting upon his class alle-giances would be not only contemptible but criminal.

Such negative portraits of counterrevolutionary Jews were in fact relatively few during the early postrevolutionary period for at least two compelling reasons. In the first place, it was well known that Jews in large numbers had avidly supported the revolution from the beginning. Furthermore, the defeat of anti-Semitism was recognized as an indispensable part of the Bolsheviks' plan for social reorganization. But a fair number of Soviet writers—among them some pillars of Socialist Realism—took up, and then carefully refuted, the idea that Jews would rather steal money than work for it. These literary assurances that Jewishness is *not* equivalent to criminality obliquely indicate what kinds of ongoing discussions writers considered themselves to be engaging. For instance, in the Nobel Prize–winning novelist Mikhail Sholokhov's *Tikhii Don* (And quiet flows the don; 1928–40), a young Jewish woman joins a machine gun unit and has the following conversation with her group's leader:

> "It's good that you are with us."
> "Why?" she inquired.
> "Well, it's like this. The Jews have a reputation, and I know that many workers think so, you see, I am a worker myself"—he added in passing—"that the Jews only like to order everybody and never go under fire themselves. That is incorrect, and you are the best proof that this view is unfounded."[18]

At the same time, anti-Soviet forces had sought to discredit communism by identifying it with Jewish criminals. Bernard Weinryb cites the archives of the city of Smolensk from 1917 to 1938, that show peasants resisting the communist government because they felt it would make them vulnerable to Jewish parasites.[19] There was widespread belief that Jewish communists planned to steal money from the Russian Orthodox Church. In these seemingly contradictory systems—Jews as parasites as anti-communists or Jews as communists as parasites—a "natural" Jewish criminality is used to organize a conception of the infant Soviet Union.

Simple either/or constructions of the gangster (corrupted by or corrupter of; communist or anti-communist) are confounded by the writers I discuss in this study. On many levels, these writers—Isaac Babel, Samuel Ornitz, Michael Gold, and Daniel Fuchs—saw their endeavors as akin to those of their gangster protagonists. Actively "knee-breaking" or "black-marketeering" their way into an exclusive literary canon, they are outcasts and rebels who still "do business" with the system—indeed they need to, and must demand their right to do so. This attitude was cleverly articulated by Gold's mentor, the socialist writer, editor, and gentile Max Eastman, who described his circle of left-wing experimental writers in the 1920s as a "fraternity of disturbance," casting the group as a kind of artistic version of a criminal gang.[20] The writers under consideration here were born between 1890 and 1909; they published their accounts of fictional gangsters between 1921 and 1937. Of the four, only Babel has been generally established as an accomplished literary artist: indeed, one aim of this study is to recuperate Gold, Ornitz, and Fuchs as ethnic modernists of merit.[21]

The profundity for ethnic writers during the interwar years of the gangster's aggressive social mobility—outside the mainstream, he uses whatever tools he can to break into it—is articulated in the 1936 movie *The Petrified Forest,* in which a tough-talking actor named Humphrey Bogart took to the screen the gangster persona that had already made him famous on Broadway. During a tense hostage scene, a benign, elderly character called "Pops" defends Bogart's character, the fugitive criminal Duke Mantee, against the charge that "he's a gangster and a rat." Pops clarifies sagely, "He ain't no gangster, he's one of them old-fashioned desperadoes. Gangsters is foreigners, and he's an American."

This association of gangsters with foreigners may be what Rich Cohen and David Singer are responding to in their calls for Jews to reclaim the gangsters in their ancestral closets. In his article "The Jewish Gangster: Crime as 'Unzer Shtik'" (1974), Singer acclaims Jewish gangsters as ones who made sure they were "able to do their own ethnic thing."[22] And for Jews—who, conventional wisdom dictates, had never been allowed to be comfortable anywhere—there is a particular piquancy to having that freedom. Again Hollywood provides an instructive example: Jewish actors who anglicized their names for professional reasons clearly did not feel allowed to "do their own ethnic thing." But those who became prominent screen gangsters—and in the cases of Edward G. Robinson (born Emanuel Goldenberg) and Paul Muni (born Muni Wisenfreund), lastingly defined filmic gangster mannerism through a display of identifiably Jewish affect—could sublimate their Jewishness in these roles, with the result that on screen, actors were frequently Jews hiding as gangsters. (In an interesting tribute to the success of these actors, two fairly hard-boiled African American writers, Amiri Baraka and Ishmael Reed, have expressed passionate admiration for John Garfield [born Julius Garfinkle], another Jewish screen gangster who starred in more than thirty movies, because Garfield seemed to be "doing his own ethnic thing" in a manner so uncompromising and rugged.)[23] Furthermore, as the generic elevation of the hard-boiled suggests, gangsters boast an irreproachable masculinity. In other words, to paraphrase Singer, the Jewish gangster has also been able to do his "own male thing."[24] Thus the powerful Jewish gangster, who operates conveniently outside of the overdetermined annals of "legitimate" history, allows marginalized men of letters to invent for their own purposes powerful men of action.

Benya Krik: Gangster and Father of Gangsters

Irving Howe, in his influential anthology *Jewish-American Stories* (1977), explained his seemingly curious decision to include a story by Isaac Babel by making a claim for the enormity of Babel's influence on the American writers whose stories he chose for inclusion.[25] Of the American writers treated in this study, only Daniel Fuchs appears in Howe's anthology, although certainly the veracity of Howe's claim is evident in the work of Ornitz and Gold as well. Babel's proclivity for juxtaposing on the page Jewish intellectuals with virile "men of action" is probably what has most captured the attention of American writers, a fascination that has not been limited to Babel's contemporaries. More recently, the novelist Daniel Pinkwater uses Babel's Odessa stories as a lens through which he might understand his own father's shady and uncompromising past. Ehud Havazelet, writing about growing up in a bookish Jewish family in Brooklyn, interweaves events in his own childhood with events from Babel's stories. Rich Cohen invokes Babel's "brutal, farcical" characterizations to aestheticize the adventures of American Jewish hoods. And the U.S. poet laureate Robert Pinsky probes the immigrant psyche of his own grandfather through the instructive example of Babel's criminal Odessans.[26]

Babel's writerly obsession with the contrast between active violence and passive introspection evolved from life experiences—as Gregory Freidin notes, Babel's work is "dominated by the figure of the autobiographical narrator-protagonist" whose over-intellectualism is his bane.[27] Born in Odessa in 1894, Babel grew up in a family that emphasized scholarship at the expense, Babel felt, of physical hardiness and knowledge of the natural world. In 1917 Babel joined the Red Army at the Rumanian front, serving under Commander Budenny and alongside uneducated Cossacks, the historical makers of pogroms against Russian Jews. For many readers, this seeming incongruity symbolizes the essential conflict that structures Babel's writing.

The Russian Jew's bespectacled gaze, with which Babel himself observed the violent Cossacks, shaped not only the three cycles of short stories upon which his renown rests (*Red Cavalry, Odessa Tales,* and *Childhood*) but also dozens of his other stories, a few plays, and many newspaper articles. Babel became famous quickly by publishing stories in *Krasnaya Nov'* (Red virgin soil) and *Lef* (an abbreviation for "Left Front of Art"), two of the most influential outlets for the "new" Soviet literature. He continued stalwartly to claim art for the revolution by trying to make it part of everyday life. But by 1925, Babel (like Samuel Ornitz and Daniel Fuchs later) took up the writing of film scripts in order to support himself, and sank heavily into debt by refusing to meet deadlines with manuscripts he felt were not ready. The 1930s found Babel hounded in the Soviet press for his failure to produce appropriate material. He was eventually murdered during the Stalinist purges.

Benya's Literary Progeny

Samuel Ornitz—plump, gentle, nearsighted, highly educated, and described by his cohort without exception as mild-mannered and bookish—was in many ways the picture of the kind of manhood Babel's gangsters are set against. In his own writing, though, Ornitz created the meanest, most unredeemed literary gangster in this study. Ornitz was born in 1890 on New York's Hester Street to a merchant family that, like Babel's, lived in comparative comfort. He dated his political commitment to a transformation at the age of ten; by twelve he was a soapbox orator like the one invoked in the well-known final scene of Michael Gold's novel *Jews without Money* (1930). After a couple of years in college Ornitz became a social worker; he began moving in literary circles through an involvement in left-wing theater companies. But he didn't write his first novel, *Haunch Paunch and Jowl* (1923), until he was thirty-two years old, when he reportedly poured it out over the course of three feverish months.[28] *Haunch Paunch and Jowl* became a foundational work of Jewish American fiction, predating and prefiguring Jerome Weidman's *I Can Get It for You Wholesale* (1937) and Budd Schulberg's *What Makes Sammy Run?* (1941) in establishing a type of mercantile Jewish protagonist who is completely repugnant and entirely unmystified.[29] For this Ornitz received his share of critical allegations of anti-Semitism and self-hatred, including such an insinuation in the supposedly objective *Encyclopaedia Judaica*.[30]

Ornitz remained an activist his whole life. When he moved to Hollywood in 1928 to write for films, it was mostly to support himself and his family while he conducted antifascist organizing (Ornitz helped to found the Hollywood Anti-Nazi League). Ornitz left Hollywood several times before he finally settled there, and, although he worked on a number of films, he never really distinguished himself as a screenwriter. In fact, Ornitz is most remembered neither for his novels nor his screenplays, but for his role as a member of the Hollywood Ten, the legendary group of "unfriendly" witnesses who refused to answer questions posed to them by the House Committee on Un-American Activities (HUAC) about their membership in the Communist Party of the United States (CPUSA) and the Screen Writers Guild. For refusing to cooperate with HUAC, Ornitz was sentenced to a year in prison in 1950. He was ill when he entered prison and he never fully recovered, dying in 1957. Ornitz never renounced his affiliation with the Communist Party; despite cold war repression, despite revelations about Stalin's activities, and despite fierce party infighting, he chose to associate himself with the communist Left that had framed his lifelong activism. Perhaps Ornitz believed steadfastly in the Communist Party—warts and all—and perhaps, unlike fellow Hollywood Ten writers Alvah Bessie and Dalton Trumbo, who publically left the CPUSA in this period, he did not want to appear to cave in to redbaiters. Most likely Ornitz was motivated by a combination of these two.

In his own uncompromising way, Michael Gold mirrored Babel's idealistic bid to claim art for the revolution, exhorting young American writers to "Go Left!" as he attempted to define the "proletarian" aesthetic. As noted above, a major component of that aesthetic was revealed for Gold in Isaac Babel's lifelong quest for intellectual militance. Gold met Babel (whom he admiringly called a "frenzied poet") in Paris in 1935, at a meeting of the International Congress of Writers in Defense of Culture.[31] The two spent a day together wandering around Paris's Jewish quarter. Gold wrote of their stroll, "I told him about the East Side and he told me about Odessa."[32] It would have been fascinating to eavesdrop upon their conversation, the language of which would have been Yiddish, which Gold grew up speaking in New York's Jewish ghetto. Gold was born there to immigrant parents in 1893; they named him Itzok Isaac Granich, and his earliest writings were signed Irwin Granich (Irwin being an anglicized form of his first name). He took the name Mike Gold during the Palmer Raids of 1919–20 to protect his identity, and the pseudonym, which he borrowed from a Civil War hero of his, stuck.

Gold's political life began at a demonstration of unemployed workers at Union Square in 1914, when he apparently dedicated himself to revolutionary politics. His literary life began shortly thereafter at the socialist journal *Masses,* under the tutelage of Max Eastman and Floyd Dell. But Gold indubitably came into his literary own at the radical journal *New Masses,* of which he was a founding editor, and where he first published *Jews without Money* in serial form. Gold's vituperative attacks in *New Masses* and in the Communist Party's *Daily Worker* on writers he considered to be enemies of the working class have made him notorious. He remains America's most famous literary communist. For his leading role in defining a new literature to be written by the working class for the working class, and for remaining unwavering and outspoken in his commitment to literary communism until his death in 1967, his literary executor Michael Folsom confers upon Gold the title "pariah of American letters."[33]

Gold himself, it must be admitted, participated in his popular definition as obnoxious. He took pains to fashion himself as a miscreant. His contemporaries recall him spitting upon carpets, ignoring conventions of dress, going about unwashed, and generally playing the role of the reprobate. Gold's early mentor Max Eastman wrote in his autobiography *Love and Revolution* that "Mike was a dark-eyed, handsome social mutineer with wide lush lips, uncombed hair, and a habit of chewing tobacco and keeping himself a little dirty to emphasize his identity with the proletariat."[34] Far more interested in attracting attention than in theoretical consistency (which is hardly an unusual stance for a newspaper columnist), Gold tended to attack extravagantly—rudely, many felt—in print. One result, as James Murphy has astutely noted, of Gold's "inclination toward the sweeping, provocative statement" is that it is "relatively easy to find one quote or another to demonstrate his alleged rejection of everything bourgeois"; in short, Gold's provocative style has allowed critics to oversimplify his actual positions.[35]

What is most interesting, however, is how frequently Gold's decided obstreperousness has been connected to his Jewishness. For instance, Claude McKay, with whom Gold shared leadership on the successor to the *Masses,* the *Liberator,* describes their disagreements in his autobiography *A Long Way from Home* (1937), complaining that "when [Gold] attacked it was with *rabbinical zeal.*"[36] More recent, and more subtle, is Douglas Wixson's elevation of a "native" midwestern radical literary tradition at the expense of the supposedly imported radicalism of New Yorkers such as Gold (shades of Jewish-Communist conspiracy!).[37] Thus, Gold's "badness" in terms of behavior, politics, and literary achievement tends to be conflated with his Jewishness. In *Jews without Money,* Gold enfleshes—and enshrines—the notion of the disobedient Jew in the figure of the Jewish gangster.

For the less idealistic Daniel Fuchs, the gangster represents not the disobedient Jew but rather the manipulated and institutionalized one; his books, appearing last in the cluster I am treating, are written against Babel's romanticized portraits, although no less in their shadow. Fuchs's Jewish gangsters are put forth as victories of assimilation: as before, they are brutal men, but now they also seem somehow docile in terms of their social function. Rather than challenging the status quo, they exemplify it; rather than demanding their place from outside the mainstream, they have been brought thoroughly into the thriving circle of American consumer capitalism. Fuchs's contribution to the gangster story makes plain how far the fictional Jewish gangster managed to travel during its years as an important literary trope: from folk and popular literature to avant-garde literary experiments; from Europe to the United States; from grand or shrewd actor to everyday tool.

Fuchs was born in 1909 on Manhattan's Rivington Street (which Meredith Tax uses for the title of her historical novel of Jewish gangsters and labor organizers). When Daniel was five years old, the Fuchs family moved across the bridge to Williamsburg, an ethnically mixed area that was beginning to attract a good number of New York's poor immigrant Jews such as Fuchs's parents. Like Mike Gold, Fuchs recalled a neighborhood in which young boys fashioned themselves into juvenile street gangs; these juvenile gangs find their way into Fuchs's first novel, *Summer in Williamsburg*.

After graduating from college, Fuchs worked for six years as a permanent substitute teacher in Brooklyn's Brighton Beach. The boardwalk culture of Brighton Beach—coupled with the amusement park at the next subway stop, Coney Island—provided material for the fictional Neptune Beach in the novel *Low Company*. But the poverty of the teacher's lifestyle prompted Fuchs to accept an offer to write for the movies, where, unlike Ornitz, he had a successful career as a screenwriter, even turning one of his own novels, *Low Company*, into a film called *The Gangster*.

Although Fuchs spent an impressive thirty years as a screenwriter, movies had begun to shape his artistic vision long before he went West. From the point of view of his fiction, perhaps the most important fact about Fuchs's biography is that he entered adulthood amid the release of the first talkies. Gangster movies in particular were part of his youthful landscape: in 1930, when Fuchs turned twenty, twenty-five gangster movies were released, fully one-third of the output for this genre during the entire decade.[38]

Fuchs was much more politically active in California than he was able to be as a public school teacher in New York, when he was writing his novels. His visible activism appears therefore to have started after his career as a writer was already launched; although Fuchs connected with the left-wing writers in California, he could not be said to have emerged from the radical New York literary circle that produced Gold and Ornitz (whose Hollywood career coincided with Fuchs's).

Although only some of the writers introduced above knew each other personally, all of them tried to use the fictional Jewish gangster to dispense with rigid or reductive positions of Jewish ethnicity, so that they could begin to sketch out routes for the Jewish writer in the new landscape of revolutionary poetics. The figure of the gangster allowed them to connect their writing to both Jewish and non-Jewish, American and European, "high" and popular works. The gangster functions as a transnational and cross-cultural figure, at once locally rooted in Odessa or the Lower East Side and broadly functional as a character who questions the most basic terms of identity and artistic creation. Isaac Babel draws his gangster-king of Odessa, Benya Krik, large enough to contain all this meaning. Benya Krik is a king of kings, and as he grows in stature, his story becomes the stuff of legend.

1

Imagine You Are a Tiger

A New Folk Hero in Isaac Babel's *Odessa Tales*

> And Benya Krik had his way, for he was passionate, and
> passion rules the universe.
> —Isaac Babel, "The King"

Isaac Babel's colorful Odessan gangsters loom larger and wilder than life, and the responses of his readers at home and abroad have tended to refect this. "Babel's Odessa is a fairyland," writes Andrey Sinyavsky, "where local images and national traits are surrounded by a halo of legend." James Falen agrees: "Everything about the gangsters is exaggerated and fantastic." Frank O'Connor quips, "if I were dependent for my idea of reality on the Odessa gangsters of Babel I should be in a bad plight indeed."[1] These glorious bandits tower above the cramped Jewish ghetto, liberated from its deprivations by the brilliance of their iniquity.

If the resplendence of their deeds exceeds the credible, the aplomb of these gangsters is not out of proportion with the impact of these stories upon the literary world. Babel wrote seven short stories—totaling around sixty pages—about Benya Krik (Benny the yell), passionate "gangster and king of gangsters."[2] These few pages—though frequently overshadowed critically by Babel's longer and better-known story cycle *Red Cavalry*—were groundbreaking for a host of diverse writers, including those to be treated in this study. The effect of their publication upon the literary world, recalled Konstantin Paustovsky, author of several affectionate memoirs of Babel, was like being hit in the face with a stream from a siphon.[3] The story of the literary gangster must start here, in the Jewish ghettos of prerevolutionary, cosmopolitan Odessa.

With *Odessa Tales*, Babel inaugurated the Jewish gangster theme into "high" literature, although stylized Jewish criminals had certainly inhabited popular and folk forms in Russia and the United States.[4] By taking the folk character of the social bandit and investing his experience with complex motivations, political immediacy, and modern ambivalence while allowing him to remain glorious, Babel created a character with unusual allure for Jewish intellectuals in the New World of America as well as in the new Soviet Union. In order to trace the important figure of the Jewish gangster in modern American prose, one must first look to Babel's rogue heroes.

Babel's elevated portraits nourished a fascination on the part of European and American writers with modern underworld figures. Most important, his treatment of Jewish gangsters as ideal studies in social, artistic, linguistic, and political modernity remains influential for writers on both continents. The reminiscences of Robert Pinsky, in addition to hinting at the remarkable geographic and temporal range of the stories' impact, disclose exactly what so many Jewish writers found compelling about Benya Krik. Pinsky connects indulgent memories of his own grandfather, a New Jersey gangster, with a readerly appreciation of Babel's gangsters, noting that "one of the many things that interest me . . . is the process of mythologizing and glamorizing." Of shady gangster toughness—a blow in the face of Jewish tradition—Pinsky contends, "the point . . . is not assimilation but something like assurance."[5]

For Pinsky, Babel's creations signal a healthy bravado, spelling an "attractive counterforce" to the typical Jewish underdog. But most interesting is the self-consciousness in Pinsky's blueprint; his emphasis on the *process* of mythologizing points to a *rhetorical invention*—the image of the gangster—who will serve the needs of a marginalized Jewish writer. The connection between writer and gangster proposed by this study starts with Babel's Odessa tales. These stories are the first to pair the two as artistic foils, turning the gangster from a literary device into a metaliterary device: if the writer were more like the gangster, the stories suggest, he or she could respond effectively to anti-Semitism, craft a hardy Jewish identity, and be at home in the polyvocal modern city (not only its Jewish ghetto), whether Odessa or New York.

This relationship between artist and killer was emphasized by the New York intellectual Lionel Trilling, who in 1955 wrote a short introduction to a major English translation of Babel's short stories. Trilling's introduction would become a cornerstone of Babel's American reception and an important meditation upon the place of the Jewish intellectual in America. Trilling, whose admiration for the stories cannot always cloak a certain squeamishness, writes what amounts to a summary of Babel's first American reception (even invoking his own experience reading Babel's stories twenty-five years earlier). Trilling recalls how to those American writers and artists whose attentive eyes were fixed on the "Russian experiment" came the complicated Isaac Babel, who always "speaks of art with the language of force."[6] In Babel, Trilling sees a Jewish artist torn between peace, which is associated with the memory of Babel's father groveling before a Cossack soldier, and war, which is associated with the gangster Benya Krik, who creates his own future.

Whatever expectations about Soviet art may have circulated, Babel's violent stories closed a chapter in shtetl-centered portrayals of Jewish life, while establishing new categories for other writers to contend with. Drawing heavily from the seminal Yiddish writers Sholem Aleichem and Mendele Moykher-Sforim, known for their humorous chronicling of Russian Jewish life at the turn of the century, Babel attaches elements of satire and dissonance: he thereby not only produces the shock of his own Odessa tales, but also insists upon a look below the charming surface of the earlier texts. *Man without a World,* a fake "lost" Yiddish film by the American filmmaker Eleanor Antin, captures this well in an aside: an explanatory "scholarly" note scrolls across the screen at the beginning to explain that the film's backers had rejected Babel as a possible screenwriter because they desired a shtetl film, pure and simple, without any of the lurid or bizarre complications for which Babel was well known.

Babel's grim adaptation of Yiddish idiom to Russian and the modern experience shaped another generation of Yiddish writers across the ocean in America. For instance, Jacob Glatshteyn's poem "Sheeny Mike" (1929), which tells of the rise and fall of a dead Jewish gangster in a New York neighborhood, is noticeably indebted to *Odessa Tales.*[7] The escapades of Babel's gangsters seem to inspire not only the subjective introspection of Glatshteyn, but also the sardonic humor of Ornitz, the offhanded cruelty of Fuchs, and the heightened pathos of Gold. The most striking aspect of this band of criminals is how truly they resist old categories. This fluidity perhaps more than anything else indicates the true stamp of Babel's imagination.

Like his unruly gangsters, Babel has continued to evade critical templates. During his life and posthumously, during his peak of productivity and during the years when he was practicing what he termed the difficult genre of "silence," Babel has worn too many provocative and seemingly contradictory hats to allow anyone to be completely at ease with him. He has been hailed and reviled as the first real Soviet writer; as the first integrated Russian Jewish writer; as the literary ancestor of the score of younger Russian writers who began under his impress; as a martyr to Stalinism; as a devoted Bolshevik and even Chekist (the Soviet Secret Police, later called the KGB); as an uncompromising chronicler of the horrors committed by *both* armies in the Civil War; as a celebrator of Jewish folkways and collective identity; as a self-hating Jew who rejects and ridicules the world of his parents and commits the mind-boggling trespass of admiring that ancient enemy of the Jews, the Cossacks.[8]

Babel's reception at home and abroad has reflected an ambivalence corresponding to the complexity of the author's own position. Like many of his contemporaries, Babel was arrested during the Stalinist purges (in 1939, which was relatively late) and ultimately executed; predictably, the content of his writings emerged as a component of his indictment. He was officially rehabilitated by the Soviets in 1954 during the process of de-Stalinization and cleared of all charges, but a specter continued to haunt his reputation in the Soviet Union. Those of Babel's works that were republished in the Soviet Union following the clearing of his name were issued in tiny printings and in sharply edited form; suppressed diaries, correspondence, and the like continue to surface in archives in the former Soviet Union. Even able critics from outside the Soviet Union are frequently more comfortable explicating Babel's accomplishments as existing *in spite of* his politics, rather than considering methodically how Babel's political philosophy contributed to the formation of his inimitable aesthetic. Although superlatives are commonly linked to his name, a full critical biography of Babel remains to be written.

Babel himself has contributed to this elusiveness: his autobiographical stories are typically misleading. Even his often-anthologized two-page scrap of an autobiography ("Avtobiografiya") contains several misleading or inaccurate descriptions. One thing Babel is straightforward about is his trickiness. The boy-narrator of "In the Basement" tells the reader directly, "I was an untruthful child," effectively warning the reader not to confuse artistic truth with fact.[9] Likewise, the narrator of "Moi pervyi gonovar" (My first fee) cites lying as his first professional venture as a writer: he entertains a prostitute with a fabricated life story and elicits her sympathy; she returns his money.[10]

It is precisely from these lacunae of indeterminacy, however, that some of the most relevant truths about Babel emerge. Isaac Emmanuelovich Babel was born in Odessa in 1894 into a secular, lower-middle-class Jewish family. Although his autobiographical writings indicate that he spent his entire childhood in this Black Sea port city, his biographers assert that shortly after his birth, the Babel family moved to nearby Nikolayev, where Babel's sister was born; they did not return to Odessa until 1905. This immediate discrepancy, unremarkable enough for any writing tossed into the vexed category of autobiographical fiction, is consequential in two ways: it indicates Babel's obstinate tendency toward the enigmatic; and more specifically, it manifests his relentless privileging of the port city of Odessa.

Tales of Odessa

Even the most cursory biographical or critical sketch of Babel must also be a portrait of his beloved Odessa. The Odessa of Babel's day was the most cosmopolitan city in Imperial Russia. Odessa was an important port town founded shortly after Peter the Great established his capital of St. Petersburg; its population (until the devastation of World War II) consisted of a substantial mix not only of Russians but also Ukrainians, Jews, Greeks, Moldavians, Poles, Germans, Turks, Karaites, Bulgarians, Armenians, French, and Italians.[11] By the time Babel was born, Odessa had become the largest Jewish settlement outside of Poland, the population of Jews having grown from 246 in 1795 to 152,634 in 1904.[12] Odessa boasts a mild climate (especially compared to the frigid Russian winters pictured by Dostoevsky and Pasternak), bathing beaches, and a variety of available delicacies such as fresh fruits and vegetables. This appeal, coupled with the attraction of its ethnic diversity, has always given the city a remarkable drawing power and reputation as charmingly "exotic" among tourists, artists, and writers. Patricia Herlihy writes that by the 1880s Odessa's image as "an El Dorado for Jews and gentiles alike had flashed throughout the Pale."[13] Maurice Friedberg, in his study of Odessa during the last twenty-odd years (the title of which, *How Things Were Done in Odessa,* is borrowed from Babel), maintains that in recent times "Odessa appears to have retained more color, more spunk, more irreverence than most Soviet cities."[14]

Babel's warmth toward his hometown is a constant force in his writing. Besides providing the milieu for the adventures of Benya and his gang, Odessa is the setting of some deeply moving childhood stories ("Pervaya lyubov'" [First love], "Awakening," "Story of My Dovecote," and others) and numerous less famous works. Additionally, Babel wrote several discursive pieces dealing with Odessa, and in his personal correspondence frequently refers to its appeal and color, especially in terms of language.[15] His wife, Antonina Nikolaevna Pirozhkova, recalled that in Odessa Babel would coach her to listen for typically Odessan phrases.[16] Although the formalist theorist Victor Shklovskii is credited with later identifying a discrete Odessan literary tradition, Babel remarked on more than one occasion that Odessa was uniquely capable of producing the kind of writer that the changing world was awaiting.[17]

In his essay on the emergence of modernism, Raymond Williams cites the "miscellaneity of the metropolis" as a key factor in the production of formally experimental literary works. Williams connects aesthetic innovation with the collision of different native languages or traditions and the shedding of provincialism that occurs in the complex metropolis: the sophisticated social environment produces a heightened self-consciousness, and as a result language is "more evident as a medium—a medium that could be shaped and reshaped—than as a social custom."[18] (The Jewish American short-story writer Grace Paley more simply and graphically described a "lucky composting" that began for Babel in Odessa.[19]) Babel frankly declares the diverse and changing cultural milieu in Odessa to be the source of his own inspiration, especially his attention to language. In an early essay on Odessa, he explicitly connects regionalism with linguistics, ethnicity, history, literary power, and law:

> Odessa ochen' skvernii gorod. Eto vsem izvestno. . . . Mne zhe kazhetsya, chto mozhno mnogo skazat' xoroshego ob etom znachitel'nom i ocharovatel'nyeshem gorode v Rossiiskoy Imperii. Polovinu naseleniya ego sostavlyayut evrei. . . . Bednykh evreev iz Odessy ochen' pugayut gubernatory i tsirkulyary. No sbit' ikh s pozitsii nelegko, ochen' uzh starodavnyaya pozitsiya. Ikh i ne sob'yut i mnogomy ot nikh nauchitsya.

> Odessa is an awful place. Everybody knows how they murder the Russian language there. All the same, I think there's a lot to be said for this great city, which has more charm than any other in the Russian Empire. Half the population consists of Jews. . . . Poor Jews in Odessa are very confused by provincial governors and official forms, but it's not easy to get them to abandon positions they took up a very long time ago. You can't get them to do that, but you can learn a lot from them.[20]

This early jibe marks a connection between language and difference that is an important reason for creating fictional gangsters. In the opening lines of the essay Babel concretizes this connection textually, giving two pithy examples of the "nasty" (*skvernii*) way Odessans speak. The first example underscores the notion of difference: instead of saying "a big difference," Odessans say "two big differences" ("vmesto 'bolshaya raznitsa' tam govoryat 'dve bolshie raznitsi'").[21] The second example invokes place or regionalism: Odessans, Babel claims, mispronounce the phrase "here and there."

Babel responds directly to critics of Odessan speech, such as the novelist Yevgeny Zamyatin, who was innovative and unconventional in his own prose but oddly resistant to what he considered to be "contamination" of the Russian language. Zamyatin writes:

> In the Western provinces, the Russian language has been corrupted by Byelo-russian and Polish influences; in the provinces of southern Russia, by admixtures of Polish, Ukrainian and Yiddish. The use of southern and western provincialisms in dialogue is, of course, entirely legitimate. But it would be a gross error to introduce them into the text, into the author's comments or descriptions of landscape. This fault is especially pronounced in the works of southern writers, since the worst adulteration of the language has occurred in the south and particularly in Odessa.[22]

The threat of language contamination seems to be a common way of articulating and deflecting anxiety about other blendings—in particular, miscegenation. (I discuss this deflection at length in chapter 3, on Mike Gold.) In this light, the highest tribute paid in the stories to Benya Krik—that he could spend the night with a Russian woman and she would be satisfied—perhaps vocalizes a fear on the part of anti-Semites as well as an internalization of this fear as desire on the part of the Jewish narrator.

Babel, on the other hand, makes the case for language blending as the way to achieve literary excellence.[23] To do this, he mimics in his essay the "charm" of this integrated city in the language he uses. He interjects frequently in French (the language in which, at fifteen, he wrote his first stories)—Odessa possessed important trade connections with France—but translates the Yiddish word *luftmensch* into Russian, rendering it literally as *chelovek vozdukha,* or "person of the air"; in short, he uses a Yiddish idiom to coin a new Russian phrase.[24] Not only is *luftmensch* a Yiddish idiomatic expression referring to someone insufficiently grounded in daily reality, but the figure of the luftmensch is a standard of Jewish folk and "high" literature that is invoked by a myriad of Jewish writers, including Babel.[25]

Whether Babel's notion of an Odessan "literary messiah" is an overstatement may be open to debate.[26] But the halls of the Odessa Literary Museum show inarguably that the city has produced some of the most important Russian writers, as well as Yiddish and Hebrew ones: Babel himself, of course, and also Konstantin Paustovsky, Yurii Olesha, Valentin Kataev, the team Ilf and Petrov, the poet Eduard Bagritsky, and Mendele Moykher-Sforim, the undisputed founder of both modern Hebrew and modern Yiddish literature; the list could also include important work done in or about Odessa by Anton Chekhov, Alexander Kuprin, Ivan Bunin, and Sholem Aleichem.

The work of these writers, taken together with historical accounts, indicates that Odessa also excelled at the production of criminals. As critics have noted, "high" writers of Babel's generation seemed to be obsessed with criminal or near-criminal types, and Odessa supplied ready material: according to Konstantin Paustovsky, there were two thousand professional criminals in the Jewish Moldavanka district of the city, which was "one of the shabbier quarters [of Odessa]. . . . It was dirty, poor, noisy, overcrowded, and dangerous."[27] Leon Trotsky called Odessa "perhaps the most police-ridden city in police-ridden Russia."[28] Paustovsky opens his volume of memoirs of Odessa with a chapter headed "Forerunners of Ostap Bender"; by describing the city's criminal population in terms of a literary character, Ilf and Petrov's rogue hero from *The Twelve Chairs* and *Little Golden Calf,* he makes an imaginative link between gangsters and writers. Paustovsky goes on to testify to the fascination these characters had for his group of young writers, which included Babel:

> What has made me think of him [Ilya Ilf] and his hero, the fearless racketeer Ostap Bender, is that even in those grim days racketeering flourished in Odessa. Even the most spineless caught the infection. They, too, came to believe in the

ancient law of the junk-market: "If you want to eat, know how to sell the sleeves of a waistcoat."

In time, the rackets infiltrated even our literary and journalistic milieu.[29]

Despite the grip that the actual gangsters had upon the public imagination of Odessa, it is no accident that the linguistically fastidious Babel, known for the obsessive attention he paid to the choosing of each word in his stories, named his cycle of stories after Odessa rather than after the gangsters. Babel's text mirrors the heterogeneity and turbulence of the city: a host of different vernacular voices present themselves, frequently without narrative mediation; clichés and banalities are passed off as high drama; literary conventions ranging from the folkloric to the epic are invoked and then abruptly undercut. For instance, an astute reader might recognize "Laugh, Clown" as the aria from Leoncavallo's *Pagliacci*, but will be startled to hear it belted out by the horn of a gangster's bright red car. Of course, the Russian formalist critics had already coined the term *ostranenie*, or defamiliarization, to describe this quest for the frisson of novelty.

Babel relies upon *ostranenie* to make topical points about the status of Jews, and the Jewish writer, in Russia. At the same time that Babel was beginning *Odessa Tales*, the Jewish writer and critic Lev Lunts groped toward a definition of the Russian Jewish identity, writing in a letter to Maxim Gorky, "I'm a Jew, staunch, loyal, and glad to be one. And I'm a *Russian* writer. But I'm also a Russian Jew, and Russia is my homeland, which I love more than any other country. How does one reconcile these?"[30] Babel uses the textual instability he models upon the commotion of Odessa to recreate in the reader a sense of anxiety and paradox that mirrors the position of the Jews in Imperial Russia.

Most important, however, Babel's stories create a climate of estrangement, in which familiar situations are frequently not what they seem to be or what they used to be. Estrangement is necessary to his portrayal of a society on the cusp of shattering technological and political changes.[31] This overarching sense of estrangement situates Babel's poignant self-consciousness as a product of a way of life that is about to end—one that Babel himself, when he joined the revolution, was actively working to end. A number of other modernist writers in "great power" countries were at this time acknowledging their own untraditional use of language as a rebellion against themselves as products of their imperial nations. For instance, in his account of the "lost generation" of the 1920s, Malcolm Cowley recalls his circle of intellectuals as thinking that "life . . . is joyless and colorless, universally standardized, tawdry, uncreative, given over to the worship of wealth and machinery." Confronting this problem, Cowley writes, "the intellectuals had explored many paths; they had found no way to escape; one after another they had opened doors that led only into the cupboards and linen closets of the mind." The closest thing to an answer for young writers in the twenties, according to Cowley, was a belief in "form, simplification, strangeness."[32] This account of the modernist impulse, with its sense of pathos and impotency in the artists' intellectual hatred of themselves as well as their culture, speaks to Babel's own sense of distance and alienation, even as he joined forces with the Bolsheviks.[33]

This keenly felt alienation might be Babel's greatest literary obsession. The works in his *Childhood* stories focus on a Jewish disunion from the natural world.[34] His *Red Cavalry* tales thrust a lone Jewish intellectual into the company of uneducated Cossacks. The stories in *Odessa Tales* address the sense of alienation by setting up a highly visible system of insider/outsider paradigms that are constantly in flux. By using gangsters, as James Falen has aptly remarked, Babel managed to create characters who are "*in* but not *of* the ghetto."[35] Because of their "profession," the gangsters represent an assault on traditional Jewish values and folkways as surely as the Bolshevik Revolution does in *Red Cavalry*.

At the same time, however, the gangsters are useful to the Odessa community. They are able to move among worlds in a way that others cannot, thereby bridging many realms: legal with illegal, Jewish with non-Jewish, ghetto with mainstream. The ambiance of the wedding Benya Krik hosts for his sister Deborah attests to the gangster's role as sui generis diplomat:

Nezdeshnee vino razogrevalo zheludki, sladko perelamybalo nogi, durmanilo mozgi i vyzyvalo otryzhku, zvuchnuyu, kak prizyv boevoi truby. Chyorny i kok s "Plutarkha", pribyvshego tret'ego dnya iz Port-Saida, vynyos sa tamozhennuyu chertu pusatiye butylki yamayskogo roma, maslyanistuyu maderu, sigary s plantatsii Pirponta Morgana i apel'siny iz okrestnostei Ierusalima. (Ko, 243)[36]

Wines not from these parts warmed stomachs, made legs faint sweetly, bemused brains, evoked belches that rang out sonorous as trumpets summoning to battle. The Negro cook from the Plutarch, that had put in three days before from Port Said, bore unseen through the customs fat-bellied jars of Jamaica rum, oily Madeira, cigars from the plantations of Pierpont Morgan, and oranges from the environs of Jerusalem. (K, 207–8)

This ritual meal is truly a feast of the gods, attended by Jews as well as their friends. Konstantin Paustovsky recalls Babel remarking:

"You remember Blok—'I see the enchanted shore, the enchanted distance.' [From "The Unknown Lady" (Neznakomka).] He got there all right, but I won't. I see that shore unbearably far off. I'm too sober. But I thank my lucky stars that at least I long for it. I work till I drop, I do all I can because I want to be at the feast of the gods and I'm afraid they'll throw me out."

He took off his glasses, and wiped his eyes on the sleeve of his patched jacket.

"I didn't choose to be born a Jew," he said suddenly. "I think I can understand everything. Only not the reason for that black villainy they call anti-Semitism."[37]

Taken together, these two passages show the gangsters as having a unique ability to overcome "that black villainy."

The special capacity of urban transgressors to unite is crucial to the story "Froim Grach," which details the death under socialism of Ephraim Rook, the old-style gang leader who gives Benya his underworld start. An officer of the Soviet intelligence agency says of Grach, "He's a fantastic fellow . . . you will see the whole of Odessa in this man" (FG, 13). Grach is described as "huge as a house" (FG, 13), an image establishing him as connecting many discrete rooms that could have very different inhabitants. His ability to encompass so much is facilitated by his outlaw position as someone heedless of convention. The tale of the modern city is the tale of the glorious gangster.

Benya's Yell

What does a criminal do to rules of language? Babel's king of gangsters, Benya Krik, occupies the same transgressive space linguistically that he does legally, speaking an unforgettable admixture of Russian, Yiddish, Odessan jargon, and thieves' argot. In other words, he commits crimes in speech; Benya Krik might have been who Babel was thinking of in his essay "Odessa," when he made the facetious observation that Odessa is a terrible place because of the way people speak there. Babel was eventually condemned by Stalinist critics for this very crime: violating the Russian language through an assault on its "purity" evinced largely by his use of vernaculars.[38]

Indeed, scholarship about Babel has tended to appropriate with admiration this notion of assault from Babel's Soviet detractors; James Falen, for instance, comments that Babel "murders in art," while V. I. Pritchett asserts that he "was a man who hit one in the belly."[39] In such descriptions, Babel becomes the Jewish gangster, as grand in his way as Benya Krik.

The "assault" represented by Benya Krik's vernacular Russian is what makes him an important gangster in the world of the stories, and also to the writers in Europe and America who came under Babel's influence. Acts of physical violence or terror occur in each of the Odessa tales. But Benya is a gangster of language more than anything else. His acceptance by the gang, recounted in "How It Was Done In Odessa," is couched in terms of extraordinary speech acts. When, with forceful and colloquial eloquence, he demands that Ephraim Rook take him into his band of thieves, Ephraim responds appreciatively to Benya's words *as such,* remarking that "Benya says little, but what he says is tasty. He says little, and one would like him to say more" (H, 213). In "Justice in Parentheses" the narrator closely echoes Ephraim Rook's assessment of Benya's speech, saying, "The king speaks and he speaks politely. This frightens people so badly that they never ask him to repeat" (JP, 256).

These descriptions seem to indicate how the laconic Babel, whose revisions of his stories apparently consisted largely of obsessively cutting any words that could be considered extraneous, would have measured his own literary success. In his reminiscences of Babel, Paustovsky has him frequently performing excruciating revisions: "Babel would go up to it [his manuscript] and stroke it gingerly like a half-tamed beast. He often got up at night and reread three or four pages by the light of a wick-lamp, hemmed in by thick dictionaries standing on their sides. Every time he found a few more unnecessary words and triumphantly crossed them out. 'Language is clear and powerful,' he used to say, 'not when there is nothing more you can add to a sentence, but when there is nothing more you can cut out.'"[40]

By gifting Benya with the realization of Babel's own creative ideals, Babel equates initiation into gangsterhood with the highest achievement as a writer. The gangsters are inventive and daring; moreover, they have found a way to be semantically forceful. Benya's gangster nickname, *krik*, means yell. On more than one occasion, Babel drew connections between the ability to shout and the ability to write well. Paustovsky remembers Babel saying: "Writing! I've got asthma and I can't even shout properly, but a writer can't mumble—he has to shout at the top of his voice. You can bet Mayakovsky didn't mumble; and then there was Lermontov, slamming his verse into our faces."[41] Benya Krik, a masterful Jew whose very name is "shout," must then represent an exemplary Jewish writer.[42]

Indeed, Benya Krik makes ample "professional" use of his literary abilities. During his first raid as a member of Ephraim Rook's gang—before he has earned the nickname "King"—Benya passes the time while the money is being placed into a suitcase by telling stories—stories *about Jewish life:*

> Nervnyi Solomon skladyval v chemodan den'gi, bumagi, chasy i monogrammy; pokoinik Iosif stoyal pered nim s podnyatymi rykami, i v eto vremya Benya rasskazyval istorii iz zhizni evreiskogo naroda. (Kak, 250)

> The nervous Solomon was packing cash, securities, watches, and monograms in a suitcase; the late Joseph stood before him with his hands in the air, and at that moment Benya was telling anecdotes about the life of the Jewish people. (H, 217; translation altered)

Engaged in a crime, the gangster becomes chronicler for the Jews. In fact, here it is precisely Benya's actions as a Jewish criminal that have provided the occasion (not to mention the audience) for him to act as Jewish "writer."

Throughout this story, Babel's equation of Jewish speech with Jewish gangsterism is explicit. During the raid, the clerk Joseph is killed, and Benya—who feels responsible although he was not the one who fired the shot—arranges a lavish funeral. The elder Arye-Leyb recounts how Benya—who, he takes pains to point out, was not yet called the King—came to the front of the gathering:

> —Chto khotite vy delat', molodoi chelovek?—podbezhal k nemu Kofman iz pogrebal'nogo bratstva.
> —Ya khochu skazat' rech',—otvetil Benya Krik.
> I on skazal rech'. (Kak, 254)

> "What have you in mind, young man?" cried Kaufman of the Burial Brotherhood, running over to him.
> "I have it in mind to make a funeral oration," answered Benya Krik.
> And a funeral oration he made. (H, 221)

Benya's oration is compelling through its evocativeness rather than anything resembling logic. He arrives in his red car, which trails smoke and flame and plays an aria from *Pagliacci*. Stretching forth his arms toward the people and standing upon a mound of earth, he speaks in seeming non sequitur that nonetheless captures the bleakness of ghetto life—a bleakness that Benya has overcome partly through his verbal flamboyance.

> "Gospoda i damy. . . . Vy prishli otdat' poslednii dolg chestnomu truzheniku, kotoryi pogib za mednyi grosh. . . . Chto videl nash dorogoi Iosif v svoei zhizni? On videl paru pustyakov. Chem zanimalsya on? On pereschityval chuzhie den'gi. Za chto pogib on? On pogib za ves' trudyashchiisya klass. Est' lyudi, uzhe obrechennyie smerti. I est' lyudi, eshchyo ne nachavshie zhit'." (Kak, 254)

> "Ladies and gentlemen and dames. . . . You have come to pay your last respects to a worthy laborer who perished for the sake of a copper penny. . . . What did our dear Joseph get out of life? Nothing worth mentioning. How did he spend his time? Counting other people's cash. What did he perish for? He perished for the whole of the working class. There are people already condemned to death, and there are people who have not yet begun to live." (H, 221)

When Benya has departed in his improbable automobile, it is his oration, rather than an act of physical prowess, that earns him the name "King." After Joseph's murder, Benya Krik and Joseph's former employer, Tartakovsky, clash dramatically over how much of a pension Tartakovsky will award to the dead man's mother—but, as Falen observes, "the battle here . . . is a thing of words."[43]

The high social stakes of Benya Krik's battles can be best understood through an intertextual reading of "Sunset" with an event from Babel's childhood that he fictionalized in two stories, "The Story of My Dovecote" (1925) and "Pervaya lyubov'" (First love; 1925). Each story revolves around a generational conflict; to resolve it, the young generation is called upon to create its own meaningful cultural arguments. Ultimately, the gangsters emerge as the only Jews with the resources to rectify the traumas of Babel's Jewish childhood.

In "The Story of My Dovecote," an adult narrator recalls his experience as a boy in the 1905 pogrom in Odessa. The Odessa pogrom was part of a large wave of pogroms that year, affecting more than 650 Jewish communities (including Odessa) during the course of a single week. At least three hundred of Odessa's 160,000 Jewish residents were killed; thousands more were wounded, and forty thousand were financially ruined. It was not unusual for Russian soldiers to participate in these attacks.[44]

The narrator of "The Story of My Dovecote" relates that all his life he had longed to own a dovecote. It is not until the age of nine that his wish is realized: after frenzied studying, the boy is admitted to secondary school (despite suffocating quotas on Jews and discriminatory examinations) and his father rewards him with the wherewithal to buy wood to build a hutch and three pairs of pigeons to stock it with. But while the boy is still in the marketplace, a pogrom breaks out, and a mob forms to kill the boy's grandfather. Grandfather Shoyl is brutally murdered, and although the boy and his parents are hidden by gentile neighbors and go unharmed, a cripple who had been beloved by children smashes the boy's pigeons against his face. This moment is the horrifying dramatic climax of the story:

> Ya lezhal na zemle, i vnutrennosti rasdavlennoi ptitsy stekali s moego viska. Oni tekli vdol' shchek, izvivayas', bryzgaya i osleplyaya menya. Golubinaya nezhnaya kishka polzla po moemu lbu, i ya zakryval poslednii nezaleplennyi glaz, chtoby ne videt' mira, rasstilavshegosya peredo mnoi. Mir etot byl mal i uzhasen. (Is, 46)

> I lay on the ground, and the guts of the crushed bird trickled down from my temple. They flowed down my cheek, winding this way and that, splashing, blinding me. The tender pigeon-guts slid down over my forehead, and I closed my solitary unstopped-up eye so as not to see the world that spread out before me. This world was tiny, and it was awful. (SD, 262)

"Pervaya lyubov'" takes place later the same day; the boy is taken to the gentile neighbors where his parents are hiding. The emotional crux comes when the boy, still splattered with feathers and blood, witnesses his father groveling before a Cossack on horseback during the pogrom. The sympathetic female neighbor, about whom the boy has previously had disturbing erotic visions, washes the blood and feathers off his face and kisses him on the lips.

This bloody smashing of the pigeons remained an affecting memory-image for Babel into adulthood; Paustovsky recalls him weeping, "I came safely through a Jewish pogrom as a child, only they tore my pigeon's head off. Why?"[45] The opening lines of "Sunset" invite an intertextual reading with the pogrom narrative. Mendel Krik's younger son, Levka, has fallen in love with a girl named Taybel, and Taybel, as the story's narrator reminds us repeatedly, is Yiddish for dove (pigeon). When Levka tells his abusive father of his infatuation, Mendel verbally destroys her:

—Ty polozhil glaz na pomoinitsu,—skazal papasha Krik,—a mat' ee bandersha. (Z, 280)

"You have taken a fancy to a slut," said Papa Krik, "and her mother keeps a whorehouse." (S, 141)

For this symbolic pigeon-crushing and for other acts of cruelty, Mendel has been nicknamed by the town "Mendel Pogrom."

Unlike Babel's weak intellectual father, who grovels before the Cossack officer, or the boy, who is unable to save his pigeons or even understand their destruction, Benya Krik responds with decisive action. He galvanizes his brother and sister to kill their father. The three siblings (with Benya standing "on the left by the dovecote" [S, 147]) severely beat Mendel, the pogrom.

The parallel is suggestive in two ways. In the first place, Jews like Benya—violent, illicit, potent—appear to be the ones who can react usefully to the anti-Semitism that Babel told Paustovsky he cannot comprehend. In the second place is the casting of the father in the role of the pogrom: to save themselves from victimization, Jews must reject the filiopiety and pacifism that is associated with them, and murder the world of their fathers. It is tragic, but ultimately necessary.

"Sunset" does not end with the beating of Mendel. The story goes on for some pages to evoke pity for, or even partially to redeem, the old man. It is fitting that Levka, the brother whose dove is crushed, should be the one overcome with grief for his defeated father:

—Benchik,—skazal on,—my muchaem starika. . . . Sleza menya tochit, Benchik. (Z, 290)

"Benchik," he said, "we are tormenting the old man. . . . It makes me cry, Benchik." (S, 153)

It may be necessary to dispose of one's Jewish parents to avoid becoming the helpless boy who comes home covered in bloody feathers, but the psychic cost is great.

The significance for the Soviet artist of this outlaw shedding of generational and cultural baggage is conveyed in a minute but compelling image in "Sunset." The night following the beating of Mendel, an unseen phonograph starts to play Jewish songs. These songs—written, no doubt, in a minor key—drift through a tawdry and malevolent night in which a keen ambivalence regarding the death of lyricism is projected onto the very landscape:

> Zvezdy rassypalis' pered oknom, kak soldaty, kogda oni opravlyayutsya, zelenye zvezdy po sinemu polyu. (Z, 287)

> Stars—green stars on a dark-blue background—were scattered in front of the window like soldiers relieving themselves. (S, 150)

Almost immediately, the music, a lovely but atavistic cultural production of Mendel's generation, ceases. It is a grand Babel success that the whole trajectory is accomplished in one sentence: "A phonograph started playing Jewish songs, but then it stopped" (S, 150).

The Odessa tales not only establish gangsters as consequential cultural actors, the stories directly—and favorably—compare their creative abilities to the skill of writers. A professional writer, who acts as an educated framing narrator for the folk narration of the elder (*starik*) Arye-Leyb, is introduced into the text of "How It Was Done in Odessa." This young writer discovers that he could learn much about his own craft by observing the successes of Benya Krik.

The literate narrator begins the story with a series of questions about Benya's ascent. But it is the silver-tongued Arye-Leyb who understands and relates what really transpired. Arye-Leyb is an elderly Jew who earns his living praying for the dead (consequently he is often to be found in the cemetery, the cemetery wall being his usual vantage point). As James Falen observes, Arye-Leyb is associated with the biblical Aaron, whose stature derives from his speaking abilities; he accompanies his stuttering brother Moses ("little lisping Mose" in the stories) before the Pharaoh to negotiate freedom from slavery for the Jewish people. A profound separation exists between Arye-Leyb and the writer-narrator of "How It Was Done in Odessa," in terms of their speech habits and their ability to understand the workings of Moldavanka. Although the writer-narrator establishes a relationship with Arye-Leyb (if nothing else they are both observers and tellers), he speaks standard Russian where Arye-Leyb's Russian is noticeably Yiddish-inflected. (For instance, Arye-Leyb uses the article *ob* [preposition] exclusively—akin to using "an" exclusively in English—but the unnamed narrator does not.) His standard speech marks him as an outsider, and he seems unaware or uncomprehending of events that shook the whole town.

The literate narrator is tormented by an impotence that seems to result from his overintellectualism. His effeteness is counterpoised to the character of the vibrant gangsters. The writer-narrator, it is made clear, will never be called "the King" as Benya Krik is called, for he has "spectacles on his nose and autumn in his heart":

> Chto sdelali by vy na meste Beni Krika? Vy nichego by ne sdelali. A on sdelal. *Poetomu on Korol', a vy derzhite figu v karmane.* (Kak, 127; emphasis added)

> What would you have done in Benya Krik's place? You would have done nothing. But *he* did something. *That's why he's the King, while you make a fig in your pocket.* (H, 212; emphasis added; translation altered)

Since Benya, who "did something," has earned the nickname "King" by distinguishing himself verbally (at Joseph's funeral and in his "business" negotiations), the implied comparison is linguistic. Dispensing with the sort of writer who "does nothing"—whether he partially or fully represents Babel's own sense of self—represents a break from the literary past and acknowledges the exhaustion of lyricism as a viable literary mode. The masturbatory, furtive image of the milquetoast writer "making a fig in his pocket" adds to the picture of the inadequate artist as possessed of a frustrated masculinity. Arye-Leyb's formula that the writer can do nothing because he has "spectacles on his nose and autumn in his heart" would resonate deeply among American readers. For example, in Daniel Fuchs's bitter novel *Summer in Williamsburg*—which also ponders whether gangsters are the ones truly able to accomplish great deeds—a young aspiring writer, whose character presents a mockery of frustrated Jewish masculinity, paraphrases the words to read, "I have pimples on my face and tears in my eyes." Likewise, Philip Roth, a writer as concerned as anyone with the intersections among ethnicity, masculinity, and creativity, picks up on Babel's "definition" of a Jewish writer in his novel *The Ghost Writer* (an irreverent, obtrusively Jewish romp through modernist literary history), adding to it "and blood in the penis."[46]

This contrast between the intellectual's sterility and the gangster's power prompted Stephen Marcus to complain in the *Partisan Review* that "Babel respected Jews only when they answered the violence done to them with violence. . . . These stories of Odessa seem to me unpalatable."[47] It is worth pointing out that within Marcus's reproach resides an acknowledgment that Babel had created in the gangster a Jew who was not a victim.

Taking the "Mama" Out of *Mama-loshen*

With Benya's yell as a possible model, the Odessa tales grope toward a powerful new definition of the Jewish writer that is both potent and activist. Babel posits this ideal in a visibly masculinist rhetoric:

> Tak vot—zabud'te na vremya, chto na nosu u vas ochki, a v dushe osen'. Perestan'te skandalit' za vashim pis'mennym stolom i zaikat'sya na lyudyakh. Predstav'te sebe na mgnoven'e, chto vy skandalite na ploshchadyakh i zaikaetes' na bumage. Vy tigr, vy lev, vy koshka. Vy mozhete perenochevat' s russkoi zhenshchinoi, i russkaya zhenshchina ostanetsya vami dovol'na. (Kak, 246)

> Forget for a while that you have spectacles on your nose and autumn in your heart. Cease playing the rowdy at your desk and stammering while others are about. Imagine for a moment that you play the rowdy in public places and stammer on paper. You are a tiger, you are a lion, you are a cat. You can spend the night with a Russian woman, and satisfy her. (H, 212)

Here a bold solution is offered to the writer's torment of impotence: by envisioning himself as a gangster—even for a moment—the Jewish writer can redeem his own masculinity. This would turn out to be one of Babel's literary legacies, one that a number of Russian and American writers would find deeply compelling. In a number of ways, they would explore how this vision of the writer as gangster translates into creative literature.

Battling literary impotence was a driving force behind many modernist artistic techniques, according to Sandra M. Gilbert and Susan Gubar in their seminal work, *No Man's Land: The Place of the Woman Writer in the Twentieth Century*. Gilbert and Gubar offer a fascinating analysis of the sexualized linguistics of modernist and postmodernist writing. Their compelling discussion of male modernist fantasies regarding "what they *as men* could do with that common language" is extremely suggestive in terms of Babel's various literary toughs—especially the Jewish gangsters.[48] Ultimately, Benya Krik and his company appear to be engaged in the same enterprise as moderist writers like James Joyce: the "parabolic wresting of patriarchal power from the mother tongue."[49]

Babel's grotesque portraits of actual maternal bodies (such as the awesome Lyubka Cossack, with her enormous, milkless breasts) have been noted by critics; it is more fruitful for my purposes to consider his use of motherhood as a theoretical construct implying generational continuity and what Nancy Chodorow calls sociofamilial "relatedness"—a line that Babel seems eager to interrupt. It is through the mother that Jews inherit their Jewishness and babies acquire language. Walter J. Ong points out: "Our first tongue . . . is called our 'mother tongue' in English and in many other languages, and perhaps in all languages is designated by direct or indirect reference to mother. There are no father tongues—a truth that calls for deeper reflection than it commonly commands."[50] The concept of motherhood (and its intimate connection to language) provides the key to the writerly reason for Babel's creation of Jewish gangsters: a de-domesticization of the mother tongue.

Historically the Yiddish language has been dogged by its association with the mother (it is known to Jews as the *mama-loshen,* a cozy form of mother tongue) and the banalities of everyday life; as a vehicle for Jewish culture, it was degraded at the expense of the holy tongue, Hebrew. Prayer books for women were the only ones in Yiddish. The "grandfather" of modern Yiddish literature (first named so by his admirer Sholem Aleichem), the Odessan Mendele Moykher-Sforim (Mendele the book peddler), saw it as his job to transcend the trite history of Yiddish: "In my time, the Yiddish langugage was an empty vessel, containing naught but gibes, nonsense, and fiddle-faddle, the jabber of fools who had nothing to say. *Women and vulgar folk* read it."[51] Identification of the Yiddish language as female was characteristic before Mendele "forge[ed] it into a modern Yiddish literary instrument."[52] Sholem Aleichem's contemporary critics hailed him for raising Yiddish literature above the level of a "kitchen language" and for nursing the mother tongue to adulthood. Sholem Aleichem drafted a pamphlet, "Shomar's Mishpot" (Shomar's trial), condemning Yiddish writers of romances and serial novels, which were associated with women readers.

Benya Krik's task is to take the Yiddish language further away from the passive Jewish mothers. In this light the slaughter of milk cows in "How It Was Done in Odessa" is of great significance: it indicates Benya Krik's need to murder domesticity in order to establish his control over the vernacular. While Benya and his gangsters kill the passive cows, conventional womanhood becomes the greatest threat:

> Vo vremya naleta, v tu groznuyu noch', kogda mychali podkalyvaemye korovy i telki skol'zili v materinskoi krovi, kogda fakely plyasali, kak chernye devy, i baby-molochnitsy sharakhalis' i vizzhali pod dulami druzhelyubnykh brauningov,—v tu groznuyu noch' vo dvor vybezhala v vyreznoi rubashke doch' starika Eikhbauma—Tsilya. I pobeda Korolya stala ego porazheniem. (Ko, 241–42)

> During the raid, on that dreadful night when cows bellowed as they were slaughtered and calves spilled and slithered in the blood of their dams, when the torch-flames danced like dark-visaged maidens and the farm-women lunged back in horror from the muzzles of amiable Brownings—on that dreadful night there ran out into the yard, wearing naught save her V-neck shift, Tsilya the daughter of old man Eichbaum. And the victory of the King was turned to defeat. (K, 206)

Not only are the cows dying pathetically, but their calves are slipping around in their mothers' blood, a painful inversion of the Jewish law that accounts for the "milk" and "flesh" categories: an animal should not be cooked in its own mother's milk. Jewish law also specifies how an animal must be slaughtered (which in addition to the kind of animal is what qualifies meat as kosher). Benya, therefore, kills Mosaic law.[53]

Benya Krik's masculine victory over Jewish domesticity is demonstrated by the passage's overtly gendered symbology. Benya and his men appear in Eichbaum's yard at night holding aloft poles and brandishing phallic guns, knives, and fists. They terrify not only the dying cows but also the dairymaids (*baby-molochnitsy*) and farm women (*rabotnitsy*). And when Tsilya runs across the yard and turns Benya's thoughts to love of women and marriage, it constitutes a "defeat." Love of a woman as the road to defeat would become a convention of Jewish and non-Jewish gangster stories (and hard-boiled detective fiction).

Babel facetiously gestures toward the Jewish marriage impulse as interfering with creativity and adventurousness in an early introduction to a never-published collection of stories by young Odessan writers:

> Tut vse delo v tom, chto v Odesse kazhdyi yunosha—poka on ne zhenilsya—khochet byt' yungnoi na okeanskom sudne. I odna u nas beda,—v Odesse my zhenimsya s neobyknovennym uporstvom.

> The whole point of this book is that in Odessa every youth—until he marries—wants to be a cabin-boy on an ocean-liner. We have only one problem: in Odessa we are unusually insistent upon marrying.[54]

Like other Odessans, Benya Krik is certainly unusually insistent upon marrying; in the four Odessa tales he is shown marrying two different women. In order that marriage not spell the defeat of the King, Benya Krik must prevent the female voice from retaining control of the mother tongue. In "Justice in Parentheses," he has to silence his pregnant wife to conduct business with the narrator:

> Takoe u menya bylo mnenie. I zhena korolya s nim soglasilas'.
> —Detka,—skazal ei togda Benya,—ya khochu, chtoby ty poshla otdokhnut' na kushetke. (Sp, 257)

> Such was my opinion. And the King's wife agreed with it.
> "Child," Benya said to her then, "I want you should go and rest on the couch."
> (JP, 255)

Somewhat chillingly, the wife's pregnancy serves to connect her viscerally with the cows murdered in the presence of their calves in "The King." The gangster's success depended upon killing the cows; the writer can approximate this success by muting the woman.

Viktor Shklovskii measures Babel's artistic success on the terms set up by Babel himself. Shklovskii, perhaps responsible for the most astute characterization of Babel's style—"[his] principal device is to speak in the same tone of voice of the stars above and of gonorrhea"—feels sure that Babel could spend the night with a Russian woman and satisfy her, because a Russian woman loves a good story.[55] In other words, Shklovskii feels that Babel has taken his own advice and envisioned himself as a gangster while he is writing, the result being that he has overcome the aspects of Jewishness debilitating to an author's manhood.

While this equation of penis and pen is an old one, Babel's reinvestment of the *mama-loshen* with a masculine, immediate tone associates him with leading modernists worldwide who were experimenting with a multiplicity of voices and a corresponding multiplicity of language forms. Babel scholars have tended to trace the origins of his vernacular technique to Russian ornamentalist writers such as Andrei Remizov (1877–1957) and Nikolai Leskov (1831–95). But as Gilbert and Gubar's work indicates, Babel's attempt to reinvent Yiddish needs to be placed into a context of formal and thematic radicalism that characterized literature (and the other arts) during the period surrounding World War I.

This radicalism demonstrated the breakdown of the dominance and absolute assurance of nineteenth-century Western European bourgeois aesthetics (foreseeing an end, or at least a realignment, of the total political and economic domination of the great powers of the nineteenth and early twentieth centuries). Some modernist writers, notably T. S. Eliot, lamented this passing of cultural certainty, but many "ethnic" writers saw instead a widening of artistic possibility, an opportunity for them to find what William Boelhower calls a possible ethnic cultural space.[56] For these writers, there was room for celebration of the liberality of the movement, in which multiple languages could interact on something like equal ground. For instance, the American poet William Carlos Williams, in *Spring and All* (1923), explores forms of American English, advertisement language, official and quasi official language, parodies of literary language, and much vernacular speech, including some African American language as poetic material. Williams's use of the vernacular underscores the poems' thematic digs at the stiffness of the standard literary language from which the speakers deviate.

Babel makes a kindred case for the newly achieved literary potential of the vernacular in his story "Guy de Maupassant," in which a Jewish woman makes a pallid translation of de Maupassant's work into Russian because the Russian she uses is too pure, "the way Jews used to write Russian." The implication is that now—as the male narrator realizes—there are more possiblities. Revising her translation, he understands that in good literature, "all kinds of weapons may come into play" (GM, 331). The idea of style as a weapon—implied here is Jewish style in particular—invokes once again the act of powerful Jewish writing as assault. The American writer Raymond Rosenthal recognized that Babel "was not simply a Jew writing in the language of Turgenev and Dostoevski, . . . he was a genius who spoke with a new inflection."[57] In the Odessa tales, the modern frisson of Yiddish is both amplified and embodied in the forcefulness of its speakers, who are violent criminals.

Ultimately, in these stories, the "othered" language appears more "authentic" than the standard; Babel's move away from the domesticity of the vernacular is also a move away from the condescension to the vernacular on the part of the standard. His reinvention of Yiddish in gangsters' mouths marks a rejection of nineteenth-century romantic uses of "dialect"—characterized, for instance, by Ivan Turgenev's representations of Russian serfs or Harriet Beecher Stowe's representations of African American slaves. This move once again associates Babel's language experimentation with the work of leading modernist writers outside of Russia. James Joyce in *Ulysses* lampoons the nineteenth-century sentimental condescension of the official literary language for the vernacular:

> —Do you understand what he says? Stephen asked her.
> —Is it French you are talking, sir? the old woman said to Haines.
> Haines spoke to her again a longer speech, confidently.
> —Irish, Buck Mulligan said. Is there Gaelic on you?
> —I thought it was Irish, she said, by the sound of it. Are you from the west, sir?
> —I am an Englishman, Haines answered.
> —He's English, Buck Mulligan said, and he thinks we ought to speak Irish in Ireland.[58]

Benya Krik's Yiddish is not textually patronized; on the contrary, the underpinning of Yiddish in Benya's words is the source of Babel's literary "assault" in the Odessa tales.

We receive Benya's words in Russian, but they destabilize that language, inflected as they are with Yiddish idiom, hyperbole, and sardonic tone:

> Vyshla gromadnaya oshibka, tetya Pesya. No razve so storony Boga ne bylo oshibkoi poselit' evreev v Rossii, chtoby oni muchilis', kak v ady? I chem bylo by plokho, esli by evrei zhili v Shveitsarii, gde ikh okruzhali by pervoklassnye ozera, goristy vozdukh i sploshnye frantsuzy? Oshibayutsya vse, dazhe Bog. Slushaite menya ushami, teotya Pesya. Vy imeete pyat' tysyach na ruki i pyat'desyat rublei v mesyats do vashei smerti,—zhivete sto dvadtsat' let. (Kak, 252–53)

A terrible mistake has been made, Aunt Pesya. But wasn't it a mistake on the part of God to settle Jews in Russia, for them to be tormented worse than in Hell? How would it hurt if the Jews lived in Switzerland, where they would be surrounded by first-class lakes, mountain air, and nothing but Frenchies? All make mistakes, God not excepted. Listen to me with all your ears, Auntie Pesya. You'll have five thousand down and fifty rubles a month till you croak—you should live a hundred twenty years. (H, 219; translation altered)[59]

Benya's outburst is strongly evocative of the Tevye stories by Sholem Aleichem (the first of which appeared in 1894). The embattled Tevye endlessly and intimately wrangles aloud with God over the state of his world. In one memorable harangue in the story "Today's Children," Tevye bemoans the fact that he must work endlessly serving the rich in order to earn his paltry living. What he wants to know—given that there is no shame in working for a living—is "where does it say in the Bible that Tevye has to work his bottom off and be up at the crack of dawn every day when even God is still snoozing away in bed?"[60]

Babel's literary involvement with Sholem Aleichem is extensive. He did his own translations of Sholem Aleichem into Russian because he felt that previous renderings were poor, and he translated some works that had not been previously translated. Babel also wrote a screenplay based on Sholem Aleichem's novel *The Adventures of Menachem-Mendl*. According to Babel's wife, he said that he worked on Sholem Aleichem "to feed his soul."[61]

The complicated relationship of Babel's Odessa tales to works by Sholem Aleichem, particularly the Tevye stories, is worth some attention. Babel's invocation of the quintessential Yiddish writer indicates a self-awareness on Babel's part of the relationship of his Jewishness to his own cultural work and a resultant desire to place himself in a literary ancestral line that included Jewish writers as well as Russian ones like Turgenev, to whom Babel also pays homage.[62] The presence within Babel's Russian text of Sholem Aleichem's Yiddish text manifests a subversive approach to the Russian language itself, one that carries Babel's well-documented use of vernacular above the level of stylization and demonstrates the historical and ideological depth of Babel's polyphonous aesthetic.

Babel's famous obsession with temperament, particularly Jewish temperament, owes much to Sholem Aleichem's Tevye. Tevye is a milkman; his job is delivering milk, cheese, and butter to the wealthy people who summer nearby. But the word Sholem Aleichem uses to describe Tevye (*milkhiker*) does not literally mean milkman. In fact, the word is a coinage on Sholem Aleichem's part, created not from the Yiddish word for milk (*milkh*) but from the word *milkhik,* which refers to a dietary category: according to kosher law, milk and flesh cannot be combined, so a meal consists of foods from either the *milkhik* group or the *fleyshik*.

Sholem Aleichem uses these kosher dietary categories to establish two temperamental types. Tevye the milkman is frequently contrasted with more worldly, aggressive, and financially successful butchers. He is concerned about giving his eldest daughter in marriage to the successful butcher Lazer-Wolf not only because he is old enough to be her father, but because he is a butcher: "'A diamond,' I say, raising my voice, 'and twenty-four carats too! You'd better take good care of her and not act like the butcher you are.'" Tevye not only hesitates to engage his daughter to Lazer-Wolf, he refuses to sell him his cow, lamenting, "It's just a sin to hand over a poor innocent beast to be slaughtered. Why, it says in our holy Bible...."[63]

Despite the fact that Tevye's innocence and benevolence cannot triumph, Sholem Aleichem treats him lovingly. Although Tevye's rebellious daughters are generally vindicated in their strivings to direct the course of their own lives, often against the wishes of their father, it is the gentle Tevye who commands the reader's sympathy precisely because of his utter lack of bitterness. The metaphor of milk and milkiness was one that Sholem Aleichem would return to on several occasions during his lengthy career, taking pains to place himself squarely in Tevye's camp.

Babel, on the other hand, is appalled by the tendency of Jews to possess the "milky" temperament. The problem of milkiness is a repeated theme of *Red Cavalry:* for example, a Cossack comrade scolds Lyutov for riding into battle without any cartridges in his revolver, telling him, "you're a Molokan [a member of a pacifist sect that took its name from the Russian word for milk], one of them milk-drinkers.... I've got a law written down about Molokans that says they ought to be wiped out. They worship God."[64] There is also the story of Matvei Pavlichenko, a dreamy herdsman whose problem, as he voices it in the story's opening lines, is that he smells dreadfully of milk: "As for my heart—you know what it's like, Natasya; there isn't nothing in it, it's just milky, I dare say. It's terrible how I smell of milk." Matvei ultimately solves his problem of milkiness by trampling his master to death "for an hour or maybe more." He goes on to become a Red General.[65] Unlike Sholem Aleichem, Babel privileges the fleshy, active world. The vibrancy of his gangsters is elevated at the expense of bookish introspection.

Babel, as he establishes his typology, returns again and again to images of milk or milkiness. The female presence among the gangsters, Lyubka Cossack, who runs a brothel and smuggler's hangout, is a potent and awesome figure. She reigns wholly over her inn. Her nickname reflects the vitality and force that drew Babel toward the Cossacks in *Red Cavalry.* Lyubka is also a mother—not only a mother, but the mother of a child with a king's name: David. This powerful and untamed figure is unable to produce milk for the baby:

> Mal'chik potyanulsya k nei, iskusal chudovishchnyi ee sosok, no ne dobyl moloka. (LK, 149)

> The child strained toward her, bit at her monstrous nipple, but achieved no milk. (L, 239)

While Tevye the milk(ish)man cannot bear to think of slaughtering a milk cow, Benya the gangster, in the pivotal scene discussed earlier, arranges a mass slaughter of milk cows. Benya writes a series of letters to Zender Eichbaum, who owns sixty milk cows, demanding that he leave twenty thousand rubles in the entrance to an Odessa building or else "something unusual will happen to you" (205). When the letters go unanswered, Benya acts:

> Benya otbil zamki u saraya i stal vyvodit' korov po odnoi. Ikh zhdal paren' s nozhom. On oprokodyval korovu s odnogo udara i pogruzhdal nozh v korov'e serdtse. (Ko, 241)

> Benya beat the locks from the door of the cowshed and began to lead the cows out one by one. Each was received by a lad with a knife. He would overturn the cow with one blow of the fist and plunge his knife into her heart. (K, 206)

The scene is a gruesome one, with the pathetically lowing animals falling in gore at the feet of Benya Krik, king of gangsters and killer of cows.

The resolution of Benya's challenge to Eichbaum represents a final inversion of the Tevye stories. Benya's raid ends when Eichbaum's daughter Tsilya runs across the yard in her shift, and Benya falls in love with her. No longer concerned with the twenty thousand rubles, he wants to marry Tsilya. Marriage of the daughters is the organizing principle of the Tevye stories (which have even been translated under the name *Tevye's Daughters*). Tevye has seven daughters, and his biggest concern is finding them appropriate husbands; his fall is measured by the growing *in*appropriateness of each successive union. By having the violent Benya Krik force his way into a wedding with the milkman's daughter, Babel turns him into another traditionally inappropriate husband and Eichbaum into a less lovable—but also defeated—Tevye. (The name Tsilya sounds quite a bit like Tseitl, the name of Tevye's eldest daughter.) Thus, Benya Krik comes to represent the end of Tevye's world.

But Babel the revolutionary must welcome the end of Tevye's world, and even find a kind of harsh and tragic beauty in the inevitability of its demise. *Odessa Tales* often revisits the theme of "today's children" who find it necessary to annihilate the ways of their parents. As often as not, it is the kind of passivity represented by Tevye that they are rejecting. Benya's father Mendel, a drayman, is associated also with Tevye, who always appears in a cart behind his horse. In Babel's later story "Sunset," Benya and his siblings overthrow their father in a violent and righteous acting out of the dilemma of "today's children." If the Tevye stories represent a version of Turgenev's *Fathers and Children* from the point of view of the father,[66] the forward-looking Benya Krik stories, seizing upon this same filial conflict, display an underlying tension of Babel's oeuvre: the sometimes tragic need for young generations to destroy and devour the past:

> [Benya] razognal lyudei palkoi, on ottesnil ikh k vorotam, no Levka, mladshii brat, vzyal ego za vorotnik i stal tryasti, kak grushu.
> —Benchik,—skazal on,—my muchaem starika. . . . Sleza menya tochit, Benchik. . . .
> —Sleza tebya tochit, otvetil Benchik, i, sobrav vo rtu slyunu, on plyunul Levke eyu v litso.—O nizkii brat,—prosheptal on,—podlyi brat, razbyazhi mne ruki, a ne putaisya u menya pod nogami. (Z, 290)

> [Benya] scattered the crowd with a stick and drove them back to the gate, but Levka, his younger brother, took hold of him by the collar and began to shake him like a pear tree:
> "Benchik," he said, "we are tormenting the old man. . . . It makes me cry, Benchik. . . ."
> "It makes you cry, does it," Benchik replied, and collecting all the spittle in his mouth, he spat in Levka's face. "Oh, lowdown brother," he whispered, "vile brother, free my hands and don't get in my way." (S, 153)

The question that remains for Babel is what role Yiddish will play after it has been divested of the traditional Jewish "milkiness."

Babel's revisions of Sholem Aleichem's seminal Yiddish texts are part of his continual exploration of the role Yiddish language, literature, and culture might play in the radically reorganized world of the Soviet Union. (Babel's Jewish American counterparts would be moved to consider this same question in an American context.) To understand how Babel envisions Yiddish functioning in the Soviet context, it is helpful to take a broader look at his systematic use of vernacular forms, a technique called *skaz* (from the Russian root "say"), to represent collectivity and Marxist materialism. Definitions of *skaz* by formalist critics in the 1920s tended to posit a classical (or Hegelian) dialectic, wherein the literary or standard language acts as a thesis, the *skaz*

voice forms an antithesis, and whatever artistic resolution occurs is the synthesis.[67] This system demands a rather rigid presuppostion of one official and one unofficial language within a *skaz* work.

Babel, however, takes more from the Marxian dialectic, which is not as straightforward. Although Marx's model is primarily bipolar, in that he indicates two major contending forces (the bourgeoisie and the proletarian classes), he also allows for the existence of other classes, such as peasants or petite bourgeoise, that do not fit neatly into a two-part paradigm.

This notion of the collision of a number of forces sheds light on Babel's use of *skaz,* which emphasizes a plurality of Russian voices rather than the duality suggested by Bakhtin's description of *skaz* as "double-voiced." Babel seeks to convey the different speech patterns of Cossacks, peasants, Jews, Ukrainians, and street criminals. It is important to expand the definition of *skaz* beyond the traditional two-part official/unofficial schema, because the various language forms Babel uses may have entirely different subtextual meanings.

Yiddish becomes emblematic of the Marxian model of social evolution, for it is by nature a language of fusion. Its very composition—with elements of vocabulary, grammar, pronunciation, and syntax cobbled together from German, Hebrew, Russian, Polish, and later, English—reveals the history of Jews' interactions with other cultures. According to Benjamin Harshav, the irony implicit in this layering is "the meaning of Yiddish": "The vocabulary of Yiddish is rather poor in comparison with English or Russian, but each word has an aura of connotations derived from its multidirectional and codified relations not just within a semantic paradigm, as in other languages, but to parallel words in other source languages, to an active stock of proverbs and idioms, and to typical situational clusters. . . . Since each word may belong to several heterogeneous or contradictory knots, ironies are always at hand."[68] The presence of Yiddish in the stories, with its "contradictory knots" of influence, helps to position Jews as particularly able to represent "all of Odessa" (as the gangster Froim Grach did for the Cheka officer).

The transgressor/bridger role of the gangsters, owing to their particular location as Yiddish speakers and criminals, is evident in Benya's eloquent demand that Efraim Rook accept him into the gang:

Grach sprosil ego:
  —Kto ty, otkuda ty idesh' i chem ty dyshish?
  —Poprobui menya, Froim,—otvetil Benya,—i perestanem razmazyvat' beluyu kashu po chistomu stolu.
  —Perestanem razmazyvat' kashu,—otvetil Grach,—Ya tebya poprobuyu.
  I naletchiki sobrali sovyet, shtoby podumat' o Benye Krike. (Kak, 247)

Rook asked him:

"Who are you, where do you come from, and what do you use for breath?"

"Give me a try, Ephraim," replied Benya, "and let us stop smearing kasha over a clean table."

"Let us stop smearing kasha," assented Rook. "I'll give you a try."

And the gangsters went into conference to consider the matter of Benya Krik.

(H, 213; translation altered)

"Kasha" as Benya uses the word dovetails with a Russian idiomatic expression for convoluted talk or making trouble.[69] But the word "kasha" also occurs in Yiddish to represent a thorny or perplexing question—and not as one of the 20 percent of Yiddish words that entered Yiddish from Slavic languages. The "kasha" in Yiddish is an Aramaic word that comes from descriptions of rabbis arguing "difficulties" of Talmud scholarship.

Babel's emphasis on the signifying nature of Yiddish suggests that Jews possess the tricky combination of ethnic culture and internationalism that Lenin called for, and therefore should naturally be successful at creating a new working-class culture. Lenin asserts in his "Critical Remarks on the National Question" (1913) that "our slogan is: the international culture of democracy and of the world working class movement," but also maintains that "it is true . . . that international culture is not non-national."[70] The Yiddish of the Odessa tales encompasses both of these mandates: it interacts with Russian, enacting an ipso facto internationalism, and yet it remains powerfully and identifiably Jewish.

But Babel still needs gangsters to act as his integrationists: he was, as I have noted, keenly aware that Jewish participation in the cultural fund will be resisted. The elderly Arye-Leyb, who recounts the rise of Benya in "How It Was Done in Odessa," expresses this sense of exclusion from the Russian cultural fund by darkly inverting a familiar convention of fairy tales. Russian fairy tales frequently end with a "validating" formula, such as, "How do I know? Why, I was there, and I ate and drank and danced until dawn." Arye-Leyb borrows this formula, but instead points out that he was *not* present, that he was excluded—a sly move he uses more than once.

Arye-Leyb's subversive use of storytelling convention is an example of how Babel deliberately thwarts his reader's literary expectations; to borrow Jonathan Culler's terminology, Babel's tales demand of their reader a high level of literary competence, but having established what seems like a familiar pattern (in this case the fairy tales), Babel frequently yanks out the rug of convention. For instance, in "The King," Arye-Leyb describes how the gangsters shot into the air because "if you don't fire into the air, you may kill someone" (K, 206). Although James Falen overdignifies this joke as indicative of the gangsters' underlying "bourgeois respect for caution and tradition," he does recognize the deflating effect of this one-liner on the gangsters' supposed daring.[71] Actually, what Arye-Leyb does is pass off as humane or prudent an old joke—or rather one of a whole category of jokes—about Jewish "schlemiels" attempting either to avoid or to survive conscription into the tsar's army. Ruth R. Wisse repeats several variants on this theme in her book *The Schlemiel as Modern Hero:* "On the battlefield he cries: 'Stop shooting! Someone might, God forbid, lose an eye!'"; "A Jew . . . was suddenly arrested by the challenge of a border guard: 'Halt, or I'll shoot!' The Jew blinked into the beam of the searchlight and said: 'What's the matter with you? Are you crazy? Can't you see that this is a human being?'"; and so forth.[72]

The myriad jokes on this subject (Babel's included) were a way for Russian Jews to confront a problem that was both serious and severe. According to regulations set up by Nicholas I, a specified number of Jews over the age of eighteen were to be drafted into military service for a period of twenty-five years (children of twelve could be taken for several years of training before the twenty-five-year term). Since parents whose sons were forced into the army could assume they would never see them again, extreme measures were taken to prevent this from happening: young men fled into the woods, swapped names and identities with the dead, and submitted to mutilation such as blinding to render them undesirable for conscription. The association of the seemingly invincible gangsters with the desperation and pathos of ordinary Jews reminds the reader of the cultural vulnerability from which such extraordinary Jews as Benya Krik had sprung.

The cultural vulnerability of the Jews in Moldavanka is mirrored in the author's relationship to the standard literary language. Babel's community language was Yiddish; his earliest language of scholarship was Hebrew; and standard Russian was something he associated with formalized institutions of learning, an association burdened with duress and discrimination: "I was only nine, and I was *scared stiff* of the exams. In both subjects, *Russian language* and arithmetic, I couldn't afford to get less than top marks. At our secondary school the *numerus clausus* was stiff: a mere five percent."[73] Rather than being entirely native either to the world of the folk or to the world of standard usage—a dichotomy frequently used to describe the motivation behind *skaz*—Babel is alien to both: his Jewish background divides him from the literary language, and his revolutionary politics and relatively cosmopolitan education distance him from the "folk." Therefore, the most useful way of looking at language choice in Babel is not in terms of "official" versus "unofficial" speech. Leiderman's fluid categories of "translated" and "translating" verbiage are more appropriate.[74] These categories are neither as fixed nor as valanced as "official" and "unofficial"; instead, the counterpoised languages define each other's status according to which form controls a given situation. Leiderman's system allows not only for the presence of multiple voices, but also for the language forms to occupy *either or both categories in different contexts,* which is crucial for Babel. In the Odessa tales, Yiddish and other vernaculars are sometimes translated and sometimes translating, demonstrating shifting balances of linguistic power, and frequently an intentional subversion of literary hierarchies that leaves the standard, educated form on the bottom. For instance, when the narrator of "Sunset" explains that "Taybel is Yiddish for dove," the educated Russian reader is placed in the position of not having been able to understand without the assistance of someone who speaks Yiddish. This sense of upheaval accounts for the unusually bifurcated tone of the story "Froim Grach," in which the lens through which events are understood switches midstory from the consciousness of the gangsters to the consciousness of a troubled, sincere agent of the secret police who is grappling with questions about what the Soviet collective requires.

The intensely personal nature of Babel's chronicling of a struggle for collectivity is perhaps the most poignant aspect of his work. Writing during the thick of the civil war that consolidated the power of the Soviet government, Babel had to wrestle with the position of art within that new society. Multiple *skaz* voices help him to be an artist of the collective, to get away from the intimate "I" of earlier literature, and to avoid the limitations of what came to be called *meshchanstvo,* or petty, cowardly individualism. The vernacular voices make their own conclusions, judgments, and observations, operating as a kind of class-conscious Greek chorus in their independent commentary:

... Papasha Krik lezhal borodoyu kverkhu.
—Kayuk,—skazal Froim Grach i otvernulsya.
—Kryshka,—skazal Khaim Drong, no kuznechnyi master Ivan Pyatirubel' pomakhal ykazatel'nym pal'tsem pered samym ego nosom.
—Troe na odnogo,—skazal Pyatirubel',—pozor dlya vsei Moldavy, no eshche ne vecher. Ne videl ya togo khloptsa, kotoryi konchit starogo Krika....
—Uzhe vecher,—preval ego Ar'e-Leib, nevedomo otkuda vzyavshiisya,—uzhe vecher, Ivan Pyatirubel'. Ne govori "net", russkii chelovek, kogda zhizn' shumit tebe "da." (Z, 285–86)

... Old man Krik was lying with his beard in the air.
"Curtains," said Froim Grach and turned away.
"It's all over," said Chaim Drong, but Pyatirubel the blacksmith wagged his forefinger under Chaim Drong's nose:
"Three against one," said Pyatirubel. "What a disgrace for the Moldavanka. But it's not night yet...."

43

"It is night," interrupted Arye-Leyb, who had suddenly appeared from nowhere. "It is night, Ivan Pyatirubel. Trust a Russian to say no when life is crying out yes." (S, 148)

The materialist quality of *skaz* provides the stories with a semblance of plurality.

A product of Babel's renunciation of the intimate is the objectification of language as a thing-in-itself, possessing cultural or moral meaning of its own. This objectification is foregrounded in "Justice In Parentheses." The primacy of language itself, and its multiplicity of function (as medium, character, artifact, setting, and so forth), are established immediately, in the story's opening lines:

> Pervoe delo ya imel s Benei Krikom, vtoroe—s Lyubkoi Shneiveis. Mozhete vy ponyat' takie slova? Vo vkus etikh slov mozhete vy voiti? (Sp, 256)

> The first deal I had was with Benya Krik, the second, with Lyubka Shneyveys ["Snow-white"]. Can you understand the meaning of such words? Are you able to penetrate the flavor of such words? (JP, 254; translation altered)

In this story as well as each of the others, Benya's utterances (especially his two letters, "reproduced" without mediation in "The King" and "How It Was Done in Odessa") seem suspended on the page in a way that is extraordinary in dialogue. Benya's unforgettable language becomes not only a means to express an experience but also a self-conscious part of that experience, and therefore a concrete artistic artifact:

> —Idite k svoemu semeistvu, Tsudechkis,—obrashchaetsya ko mne korol',—v subbotu vecherkom, po vcei veroyatnosti, ya zaidu v "Spravedlivost'." Voz'mite s soboi moi slova, Tsudechkis, i nachinaite idti. (Sp, 257–58)

> "Go back to your family, Tsudechkis," the king says to me. "On Saturday evening, in all probability, I'll pay a visit to Justice. Take my words with you, Tsudechkis, and go." (JP, 256)

Here Benya's words are gifts that Tsudechkis can carry with him; shortly thereafter, Tsudechkis compares Benya's words to a boulder.

"Justice in Parentheses" is littered with instances of words as things, starting with the naming of the collective the gangsters plan to rob as "Justice." The word "justice" is ironically concretized in the existence of the collective, but it is once again underscored as language by the story's title, which, by placing it "in parentheses," forces the reader to picture it on the page.

This concretizing of language ultimately calls attention to every speech act as *art*. The chatty, persistent narrator of "Justice in Parentheses" refers to his tale not as *"istoriya"* but as *"rasskaz,"* which usually refers to a written form, even as he reinforces the folksy orality of the tale, warning his reader, "It's better not to carry this story into the side-streets" (256). Along the same lines, language becomes a major national product in the conclusion of "Lyubka Cossack:"

> I na sleduyushchii den' Tsudechkis prishel za funtom neobranderolennogo tabaku iz shtata Virginiya. On poluchil ego i eshche chetvertku chayu v pridachu. A cherez nedelyu, kogda ya prishel k Evselyu pokupat' golubei, ya uvidel novogo upravlyayushchego na Lyubkinom dvore. On byl krokhotny, kak ravvin nash Ben Zkhar'ya. Tsudechkis byl novym upravlyayushchim.
>
> On probyl v svoei dolzhnosti pyatnadtsat' let, i za eto vremya ya uznal o nem mnozhestvo istorii. I, esli sumeyu, ya rasskazhu ikh vse po poryadku, potomu chto eto ochen' interesnye istorii. (LK, 269)

> And the next day Tsudechkis looked in for his pound of unbonded tobacco from the State of Virginia. He received it, and a quarter pound of tea into the bargain. And a week later, when I called on Yevzel to purchase some pigeons, I saw the new manager in Lyubka's yard. He was tiny, like our Rabbi Ben-Zkharya. The new manager was Tsudechkis. He stayed in the job some fifteen years, and during this time I heard many a tale about him. And if I am able I will tell them all one after the other, for they are very entertaining tales. (L, 242)

The tea, the tobacco, the pigeons, and the gossip about Tsudechkis are linked as fine products: goods are imported and stories exported in a reasonable exchange.

The last of Babel's gangster stories, "Froim Grach," could be described as a conclusion to the Odessa tales: if the previous stories celebrate the gangsters' linguistic victories, this one shows their final silence. The story relates how the venerable old gang leader Froim Grach, huge, one-eyed, and scarred, goes alone and unarmed to the Cheka building to speak in defense of his "boys," who are being wiped out by the new Soviet regime. A Cheka interrogator, Sasha Borovoi, receives him and leaves briefly to gather all the interrogators and commissars in town so that they might listen to this "legend" who "was the real boss of Odessa's 40,000 thieves" (FG, 14). But when Borovoi returns, he finds Froim Grach's body sprawled under a tarpaulin. The head of the Cheka, who understands that Borovoi is upset, presses his hand compassionately but asks him:

> —Otvet' mne kak chekist,—skazal on posle molchaniya,—otvet' mne kak revolyutsioner—zachem nuzhen etot chelovek v budushchem obshchestve?
> —Ne znayu,—Borovoi ne dvigalsya i smotrel pryamo pered soboi,—navernoe, ne nuzhen. (F, 259)

"Tell me as a Chekist," he said after a pause, "tell me as a revolutionary: what good was this man for the society of the future?"

"I don't know." Borovoi sat motionless and stared in front of him, "I suppose he wasn't." (FG, 15)

As a member of the Soviet collective, Borovoi is well aware that an aging thug like Froim Grach has little to offer a socialist society. As an individual, however, he regrets the stilling of the gangster's vibrant voice. Borovoi himself begins to tell the Chekists from Moscow all about the life of Froim Grach, but even as he describes "his cunning and elusiveness, and . . . his contempt for his fellow man," he knows he is marking a loss: the end to "all these extraordinary stories that are now a thing of the past" (FG, 15).

The Jewish Gangster in the Land of the Soviets

While Babel used his Odessa gang to muse upon what Jews could offer to the revolution and what they would have to sacrifice to it, a handful of Russian Jewish writers followed by taking the figure of the Jewish gangster firmly into the Soviet period. Among the most interesting of these is Venyamin Kaverin's novella *Konets khazy* (End of the gang; 1924). Kaverin's Jewish gangster, Shmerl Turetskii Baraban, represents, according to Hongor Oulanoff, "a 'modernized' version of Benya Krik, the superb and generous 'King.' "[75] Babel and Kaverin delineate the same social transformation—the emergence of the Soviet state— and the figure of the Jewish gangster is a crucial transitional figure for both writers. But they are looking at modernization from opposite sides of the cavern, so that Benya, with his pseudorevolutionary graveyard oration and his run-in with the Cheka, barely glimpses the changes that have already come to pass in *Konets khazy*.

Baraban and his gang—Volodya the Student, Sashka Barin, Five-Spot, and Frolov—are indubitably products of their modern, postrevolutionary city. While Benya burns down the local police station and extorts money from a cattle owner who eventually becomes his father-in-law, Baraban and his company calculate how to use advanced technology to break into the GosBank (State Bank, in Sovietese).

Kaverin's gangsters belong in the ranks of the savvy criminals and quasi criminals who populate the literature of the New Economic Plan (NEP), manipulating with varying degrees of shadiness and violence the NEP's relative looseness. Responding to the economic chaos precipitated by the civil war, a chaos described in the opening of *Konets khazy*, the government introduced the plan in 1921, establishing a permissive policy toward small business and manufacturing, and even speculation. As Maurice Friedberg would have it, Jews in large numbers welcomed the chance to reestablish themselves in traditionally "Jewish" professions, and subsequently turned up in a host of anti-Semitic literary portraits as black-marketeers, moneylenders, profiteers, and crooked businessmen.[76] Questionable morality in legal business under the NEP is briefly thematized in *Konets khazy,* too; Sashka Barin and a couple of henchmen organize a raid on the profits of "one NEPer on Mil'onni Street" with even less compunction than usual and with no small amount of implied reader sympathy.[77] They also rob a Jewish jeweler who cries out in cowardly fashion that the money does not belong to him.

Although one cannot but think of Benya Krik when reading Kaverin, the flamboyant Shmerl Turetskii Baraban most resembles a less charming Ostap Bender, the opinionated, self-aggrandizing con man/protagonist of Ilya Ilf and Yevgeny Petrov's humorous novel *Dvenadtsat' stul'ev* (The twelve chairs; 1928), who is probably a Jew.[78] Bender is extremely—perhaps tellingly—coy about his background; the only piece of information he offers about his past is a repeated, enigmatic claim that his father is a Turkish citizen. This claim may even be an oblique reference to Kaverin's gangster, who goes by the trade name of Turkish Drum. At any rate, Baraban is striving for the level of competence and savoir faire that the "smooth operator" Bender claims as his Soviet birthright. Bender's feeling of ease and belonging in the new Soviet society represent the realization of Baraban's dreams. When Baraban and Sashka Barin have entered the sleeping Pineta's apartment, the sarcastic Pineta demands to know who they are. Baraban answers with a gradiose air that is to become characteristic:

—To est' ya khochu skazat', chto u menya na golove est' shishka, iz-za kotoroi ya po nasledstvennosti stradayu ostrym lyubopytstvom. Naprimer, seichas mne ochen' khochetsya uznat', kto zhe vy, chyort vas vos'mi, takie?
Sashka Barin skosil na nego glaza i zakuril novuyu papirosu.
—My nalyotchiki,—ob'yasnil on dovol'no ravnodushno.
—My organizatory,—popravil Baraban,—vy nichego ne poteryaete ot znakomstvo s nami.[79]

"That is, I want to say, that on my head I have a bump, on account of which I suffer by heredity from acute curiosity. For instance, now I very much wonder who, the devil take you, are you?"
Sashka Barin squinted at him and lit up a new cigarette.
"We're criminals," he explained fairly indifferently.
"We're organizers," corrected Baraban. "You have nothing to lose from acquaintanceship with us."

By calling himself an "organizer," Baraban establishes himself as a willing participant in his modernized surroundings, even though his claim is degraded. He has a passion for following parliamentary procedure during criminal huddles and for planning heists "according to the newest system."[80] He even falls in love with a stenographer, the exemplar of the modern working girl. Ostap Bender, created a few years later, has the opportunity to act upon Baraban's comic claim; among other endeavors, he encounters a convention of confidence men and women that parodies Soviet trade unions and congresses and recalls Baraban's eagerness to be a "modern" gangster. Babel didn't get a chance to tell this part of the story, although it seemed that he intended to; before his arrest he had told his wife that he was working on a novella about a Jewish gangster in the age of Sovietism: "I'm writing a novella in which the main character is a former Odessa gangster like Benia Krik. . . . I want to show how this sort of man adapts to Soviet reality. Kolya Topuz works on a collective farm during the time of collectivization, and then he goes to work in a Donbass coal mine. But since he has the mentality of a gangster, he's constantly breaking out of the limits of normal life which leads to numerous funny situations."[81] Although the social context may have changed, Babel continues to picture the gangster as someone larger than life, free from limitations that hobble others, and able to entertain and instruct as a result.

The End of the Gang

Sympathy between writers and gangsters notwithstanding, Babel most likely did not intend to script his own end at the hands of Soviet intelligence in "Froim Grach." Nonetheless, when he was executed at the age of forty-six, his own "extraordinary stories" abruptly became a thing of the past. Reportedly, at his arrest on May 16, 1939, Babel was led off complaining that he had not been permitted to finish.[82] Like the gangster Froim Grach, Babel had more stories to tell.

It is impossible to comment at this point in history upon the tragedy and waste of Babel's murder without sounding banal, especially in light of his undisputed dedication to the ideal of a communist society; but there is something almost fitting in the official mystery that has surrounded his death, the details of which were largely unknown until recently and are still emerging. It is as though Babel's death returns his readers to the indeterminacy with which I began: the enigma he sought to fashion out of his own life. The charges against him were fantastic and purple, but eventually he "confessed" under torture to numerous crimes against the Soviet government, including having provided André Malraux with secrets of Soviet aviation.[83] On January 26, 1940,

Babel's appeals—in which he vehemently rescinded the testimony he had given under torture and urgently requested a lawyer—were answered with a death warrant. The next day he was shot. With the writer's death, his character Froim Grach's final message, which he had come to deliver in defense of his gang, became painfully profound: "Boss . . . who do you think you're killing? You're killing the best. You'll be left with nothing but riff-raff, boss" (FG, 15).

2

A Sordid Generation

Plundering Ethnic Culture in Samuel Ornitz's *Haunch Paunch and Jowl*

> Who could tell, by looking at a group of East Side
> youngsters, which would become a Gyp the Blood or
> Lefty Louie and which a Marcus Loew or Irving Berlin?
> —Eddie Cantor, *My Life Is in Your Hands*
>
> Hey, Ikey the Killer, give us a song.
> —Samuel Ornitz, *Haunch Paunch and Jowl*

Partway through his novel *Haunch Paunch and Jowl* (1923), Samuel Ornitz comes remarkably clean. A character to whom Ornitz has given his own name, Sam, is about to embark upon an artistic endeavor on the stage. Describing his performative technique to his associates, Sam announces: "I'm gonna come out made up as a Jew" (115).[1] He then ignores his friends' hoots and hollers that he hardly needs makeup, and proceeds to don a too-small derby hat, false sidelocks and beard, and an exaggerated Yiddish accent; Sam's act, as it turns out, is a smashing—read lucrative—success.

Ornitz is making an important point about minstrelsy here: more significant than who you are by birth is what performative mask you wear, and ultimately what use you make of the cultural material that constitutes that mask. In *Haunch Paunch and Jowl*, the Jewish Sam Ornitz does indeed "come out made up as a Jew": the book was originally published by Boni and Liveright in the guise of an anonymous autobiography of a recently deceased Jewish judge with gangland connections. Authorial hints about coming out in Jewish makeup notwithstanding, a large number of the book's many readers were willing to accept that it was what it purported to be: an anonymous autobiography, too scandalous to be released until after the author's death. Ornitz wears this makeup—becoming as exaggerated and unsympathetic a stage Jew as one could hope to find—in order to make the most direct observations about the kinds of power that come into play when artists make use of ethnic culture.

Ornitz's "Jewface" act became a bestseller and attracted attention in a variety of forums, to the point of being presented as a sociological authority on the Lower East Side by the 1937 Works Progress Administration guide to New York, which refers to *Haunch Paunch and Jowl* as "a semi-autobiographical novel of the Lower East Side" and cites its expertise on the division of East Side families by a conflict between the old and the new.[2] With a sometimes shocking lack of sentimentality, the book chronicles the rise of Meyer Hirsch, a Lower East Side Jew whose history encompasses a childhood as the pampered only son in an Orthodox family, an adolescence as the "brains" of a tough juvenile street gang, a career as a ruthless and sleazy gang lawyer, and, finally, tenure as a justice of the Superior Criminal Court of New York. By this time, of course, Meyer no longer lives on the Lower East Side; he has moved alongside other "professional Jews" who occupy the portion of Riverside Drive known as "Allrightniks Row" (which serves as the title of Markus Wiener's 1986 reissue of the novel).[3] In his prosperity, Meyer has become so obese that newspapers have started referring to him as "Haunch Paunch and Jowl."

Ornitz's merciless Meyer Hirsch fits well into the rogues' gallery that forms this study of gangsters as transgressive artist figures. But in contrast to the attractiveness of Babel's Benya Krik, in the case of Meyer Hirsch, we, the readers, are not directed to admire him for the boldness of his trespass. Indeed, Meyer Hirsch is so immediately hateful that, even as a metaphor, the notion of gangsters being left to decide questions of aesthetics becomes chilling rather than intriguing.[4] This unsavory gangster is no positive model for a Jewish writer struggling to inject some vitality into a centuries-old habit of dry bookishness. Rather, Ornitz seems to be making a concrete observation about the possibilities for art in a capitalist economy: under this system, literary transactions are necessarily a kind of gangsterism. Even an artist who may be a product of the ghetto will be encouraged to use his vernacular inheritance cynically, in the same way that Meyer, as a crooked lawyer, is willing to profit from the misfortunes of people he knows. Who, Ornitz asks, are these gangsters writing books?

Since the reader is asked to consider Meyer to be the theoretical author of *Haunch Paunch and Jowl,* the criminal uses to which Meyer puts ghetto materials are consequential; in other words, the way he represents his hapless clients in court cannot be separated from the way he represents them on paper. The connections between exploitation and representation—drawn through the figure of the unscrupulous lawyer—provide the key for understanding

Ornitz's use of Jewish gangsters. This chapter explores three ways in which Ornitz treats literary representation as an act of plundering. First, he creates gangsters who are literally involved in the production of minstrelsy. Then, through their activities he examines the fate of language in the marketplace. Finally, Ornitz posits the gangster as exemplary of a dangerously fraught notion of American manhood.

The Poetry of the Gang

The narrative of Meyer Hirsch's rise to power contains a key scene that acts as a primer on how art and crime are envisioned to be mutually defining in *Haunch Paunch and Jowl*. A passage in the fifth period (instead of chapters, Ornitz divides his book into "periods") provides a guideline for reading Meyer's involvement in artistic enterprise. Following his stated philosophy of keeping as many people under obligation to him as possible (183), Meyer rounds up peddlers' votes for the Tammany Hall boss, Big Jim Hallorhan (a thinly disguised version of Big Tim Sullivan, a Tammany Hall boss from New York's Bowery district, who commands the dubious distinction of having been the first to introduce the young Arnold Rothstein to the useful world of politics).[5] Meyer insinuates himself into Hallorhan's good graces in his characteristic way—by coldly exploiting his fellow Eastern European Jewish immigrants. He organizes the struggling pushcart peddlers into a "Protective Association"; from there, he offhandedly comments, he has them sworn in as American citizens "in batches of four and five, sometimes as many as ten" (207).

Meyer's language of mass production folds the process of naturalization into a factory practice that recalls the speedups enforced by his sweatshop-owning Uncle Philip. And the profits are immediate: not only does the association pay Meyer a healthy yearly retainer, but once the peddlers are eligible to vote, Meyer controls a large electoral bloc, which he provides to the machine for a price:

> Big Jim Hallorhan acknowledged my good services, and I asked him a favor for the boys. I wanted to keep the good will of Shimshin and his gang, as well as the unswerving support of Boolkie and his constantly renewed ranks. There was keen competition for the pickpocket privilege of the Brooklyn Bridge terminal, where swirling, pushing crowds made pocket-picking easy and lucrative. Detectives were assigned to see that the regularly designated pickpockets operated without interference and to keep out poachers from this fine game preserve. Big Jim awarded the Brooklyn Bridge concession to my district. (208)

The details of this crude business transaction are of manifold metaliterary significance. Meyer has made a business out of the sentimental ideal of becoming an American citizen, an ideal that informed early-twentieth-century rhetoric not only in the political world but also the belletristic.[6]

And what Meyer receives in return for his "speedups" are brigands' rights to that venerable icon of modernization and literary modernism, the Brooklyn Bridge, which has been glorified by such disparate artists as the poets Walt Whitman, A. Leyeles, Vladimir Mayakovsky, and Hart Crane, and the graphic artists Joseph Stella, Walker Evans, Louis Lozowick, and Albert Gliezes, among others.[7] The Brooklyn Bridge as a symbol of modernity was particularly visible the year of *Haunch Paunch and Jowl*'s publication, when much of New York was swept up in a celebration of the bridge's fortieth birthday.

The literary overtones to Meyer's mercenary scam situate him as a negative cultural example, unlike the more admirable Jewish American bandits in *Jews without Money*. Mike Gold, no doubt, would boast that if the literary powers-that-be would not let him have the Brooklyn Bridge any other way, he would steal it; compare, for instance, Meyer's winning of the Brooklyn Bridge with the scene in *Jews without Money* when Mikey's gang steals fragments of tombstones and bones from an old American graveyard.[8] Ornitz, unlike Gold, is not concerned with the bravado of the literary underdog, figured conveniently through gangsters. His concern is to condemn the ones who control the literary Brooklyn Bridge by calling them gangsters.

There is an important moment in the book in which gangsters are more literally immersed in artistic enterprise. This is the gang's involvement with the development and production of ragtime music, which, Meyer tells us during the fourth period, "has the whole country jogging" (146). Meyer depicts ragtime as a musical form of ethnic blending carried out by the brash gangsters: "Al and Sam were busy creating original ragtime songs and dances. O'Brien encouraged them, saying its flexibility offered infinite possibilities. He urged them to make use of the negro plantation, levee and spiritual songs with their pulsating African rhythm and ornament them with Semitic colors and figures" (148). In his book on black-Jewish relations in the American music business, Jeffrey Melnick identifies the blending of "African rhythm" and "Semitic colors" as representing for Ornitz a "utopian moment" in which a "joyous American music" is brought into being.[9] Melnick argues that Ornitz envisions Jews as uniquely suited to enact cultural mergers such as ragtime because of their historical spatial mobility and fluidity of identity. In this light, the added transgressiveness of the criminal would facilitate creative synthesis (in the manner of Babel's Benya Krik, who unashamedly miscegenates languages). Compare, for instance, the entitlement of the gang's musical strategy to that of Hugo Reisenfeld, the real-life "father of classical jazz" according to his many admirers. An interview with Reisenfeld in the *Jewish Daily Forward* from 1924 (one year after the publication of *Haunch Paunch and Jowl*) addresses the question of sources for musical innovation:

> We were talking about "Reisenfeld's Classical Jazz" that has captured the ears and hearts of the Broadway theatre goers.
>
> "Please, mention it and tell your readers that I do *not* take classical music and 'jazz it up.' I would not think of degrading the music of Wagner, of Tschaikovsky, of Beethoven. I am taking the popular music in vogue, and I make it so fine, so melodious that it becomes almost classic. As you can see there is a great difference between the two."[10]

Making a fascinating transition, Reisenfeld moves in a few short paragraphs from this reassurance that he knows enough to leave Wagner alone to a suggestion that Jews could help lessen anti-Semitic tensions by refraining from going where they are not wanted: "We should not go where we are not wanted. I have never yet tried to force myself into a hotel where Jews are not wanted, for just as I have a right to dislike a fellow for some reason or other, some other human being has just as much right to dislike me."[11] Reisenfeld's slippage from the purity of Wagner's music to the intact image of a gentile-only hotel speaks volumes in support of Melnick's vision of ragtime. Meyer's gang certainly (one is inclined to say thankfully) goes where it does not belong; unlike the modest Reisenfeld, Meyer's associates "shout . . . in glee that [they] can twist a blareful, stirring Wagnerian fugue into nigger jazzbo stuff" (160).

But a utopian interpretation of the gangsters' musical project is at odds with the hostile thrust of the novel as a whole. By the time Meyer's gang forms its own ragtime quartet, assigns vocal parts, and the reader is told that "Meyer is bass" (118), the statement barely even constitutes a pun, because the links between his music and his corruption have been made so plain. Indeed Meyer, who has promised to hide nothing in his "autobiography," is characteristically unrepentant about the motivations behind this blending, as well as the differing degrees of comfort enjoyed by the "participants": "The negroes had given America its music. Soon the white man started stealing the negro's music and making it his own. There was money in the negro's music" (146). The criminal's ability to challenge a sterile artistic "purity" within the amalgam of ragtime recalls Isaac Babel's celebration of the vernacular Russian spoken by gangsters. But the balance of power has shifted; here, the gangsters are representatives of the bosses, not the insurgents. The hideous (if commonplace) words they use ("nigger jazzbo," for example) confound any notion of the ethnic merger as anything except a commercial product; the motivation of Meyer and his associates, baldly presented, is profit alone. When Davie Solomon, the neighborhood poet/dreamer, suggests in his starry-eyed fashion that they perform a few classical ballads, he is scornfully howled down: "'Classical ballads, say, where do you get that stuff? Do you want to put a crimp in us? There's only one thing goes in this game,—give the gang what it wants, and if you want to get by, you gotta be better than the next guy'" (125). Shortly thereafter Meyer explicitly connects gangsterism to state power (rather than protesting against it), recalling, "the hoodlums and the police were with us" (177).

Furthermore, the music of Meyer's gang is associated with the two lowest kinds of corruption portrayed in the book: the electioneering of Tammany Hall's political machine and child prostitution. Meyer recalls his gang's participation in "dough day," during the time votes were bought for the machine for the standard price of two dollars: "The price of a vote in those days was two dollars, and to a poor man, who saw no farther than his instant belly needs, this was a lot of money. When I saw the money circulating, I confided to Big Jim that I had a gang of strong-arm men working for me and that they were ready for his orders" (178). It is hard to imagine a scenario more cynical and farther from any utopian sense. In the next paragraph, Meyer and his boys use their newly crafted ragtime to cement their position in the political machine that bought votes from their poorer neighbors for the paltry price of two dollars: "Our band was playing 'A Hot Time in the Old Town Tonight,' and when it stopped our fellows began to cheer under Maxie's leadership. Many cheers were given for Big Jim. Then the name of Meyer Hirsch was cheered. 'Who's the bunch outside?' asked Big Jim, cordially. 'That's my club, Boss,' I told him" (179). Every utterance—the music and even the cheering—is calculated for possible future gain.

After they make money with their music for the first time, Meyer's "boys" spend their profits on prostitutes—and not just any hardened East Side prostitutes: "The girls were young, very young, ten to fourteen years old, and imported, imported by Italian padrones, importers of livestock only . . . and Hymie Rubin, rather sensitive and soft-hearted, turned from them in disgust, saying he minded most the little girls' white, bewildered faces" (70). This connection between the quartet's music and pandering is quite strong, and presently it crescendos. Eventually, Meyer perfects the quartet show at the club Lavelle's to include elaborately staged public spectacles, scripted to heighten the off-color panache of the club. He is now peddling not only "ethnic" music, but fully realized exoticizing narratives as well.

An integral part of one such spectacle is a "little white-faced girl" like the ones described above: "There was a little bit of a girl called Millie the Stray. She had the frame and height of a twelve-year-old girl and a thin face with deep-set eyes that helped along the picture of girlishness. . . . As she passed the

Chinamen's table, one of them leaped up and placed his taloned fingers around her neck . . . and apparently the Chinaman was choking to death a little girl of twelve. It was a good sadistic picture" (153). Since the element that links these two scenes is the ragtime music, the implication is that the gangsters are "pimping" the material as the real-life procurers pimped the girls. Of course, since actual pimping, along with quartet singing, is a major source of income for the gang anyway, the distinction becomes a little fine.

This analogy between pimping and exoticizing is furthered by Ornitz's careful notation of the fact that not only African American musical forms but other ethnic material as well is used in the gangsters' profit schemes. Meyer and the gang also trade in Chinese American ethnicity, selling to their white audience notions of "yellow" as well as "black." Meyer describes how he hires "three Chinamen, with particularly yellow and malevolent faces" to play the part of opium-smoking white-slave traders in the café: "Finally the Chinaman dropped Millie to the floor, where she lay in a convulsed heap. She cried out, 'Don't kill me, Ly Chee, don't kill me. I'll bring you all the money next time.' Ly Chee was an intelligent fellow and could speak a pretty fair English but for this occasion he spoke pidgin English. 'Me killee lou, me killee lou, bling allee timee allee money, no floget, me killee lou'" (153). The point here seems to be that any available cultural stuff will be snatched and sold, in whatever debased form is expedient, as long as a market can be found or created.

Indeed, Meyer is quick to use his talents and position to disrupt the one truly utopian (and positively transgressive) merger that does exist in the book: the marriage of his idealistic friend Davie to the former prostitute Billie. Billie is not Jewish, so the marriage represents a cultural mixture based on love, not profit. Furthermore, Davie's nonjudgmental admiration is easily able to decontaminate Billie's disreputable commercial past. The utopian nature of the union is finally apparent in the nature of Davie and Billie's wedding ceremony: in Davie's unencumbered moral universe, the spiritual rather than the legal side of marriage is most important, and the couple weds by stating aloud their devotion to each other, not by registering at city hall. Once Davie has died, however, Meyer uses his eloquence to deny that the marriage ever existed, satisfying the demands of ethnic segregation and avoiding the scandal that has finally arrived because Davie married outside the Jewish faith. Meyer's behavior in this instance belies his standing as a cultural bridger.

Given the gangsters' jaded approach to culture, they engage in a striking number of rather serious discussions about poetry. Meyer "recalls" in some detail numerous conversations, usually involving Davie Solomon, in which the value and purpose of poetry was debated in a lofty manner that seems more suited to a spiritual meditation like Ruskin's *Sesame and Lilies* than to the suppressed tell-all autobiography of a gangster: "Harry Wotin gets up and looks quizzically at Davie. . . . 'A poet,' says he, 'is a bright-colored weed in a potato patch. . . . Look at Davie. He takes up room and air and nourishment and gives nothing in return but an empty, flashing picture. Let him do something.' . . . Esther speaks softly, 'Harry, you are hard. Because you've been hard at it. . . . But I tell you, Harry, poets are not weeds, useless parasites. They are very important to us. They are our eyes and ears to beauty'" (111). This passage—one of several such conversations—continues for more than a page and a half. In light of the brutal events that make up the novel, these fanciful discussions are nothing short of bizarre. At very least, they are self-conscious to the point of being intrusive; even within the parameters of Ornitz's picaresque approach to plot, the poetry sessions invariably read like set pieces. Nonetheless, the subject of poetry is something with which Meyer is, willy-nilly, very concerned.

The idealistic poet Davie functions on many levels as an alter ego for the gangster Meyer. Although Meyer expresses jealousy toward Davie more than once—for his good looks, for winning the devotion of the girl Meyer desires—and purports to be unable to understand him, the two of them are actually very close. For one thing, Meyer tends to define himself in terms of Davie, or at least in terms of what Davie is not: "I was a mystery to Esther Brinn because her mind was mystified by the poetic and theoretical slants she got on life from the Davies and Avrums, who were getting to be as thick as flies around our way. They pictured a world that wasn't or couldn't be, and I was trying to get something in the world—that is . . . poets are a mystery to me" (76). Meyer is a mystery to Esther Brinn, a neighborhood girl he idealizes for her "purity," and Davie is a mystery to Meyer. Meyer's language equates his position vis-à-vis Esther to his own position vis-à-vis Davie. This linguistic echo invites the reader to use Esther's feelings for Meyer—which could best be described as a fairly straightforward dynamic of attraction/repulsion—to "map" Meyer's relationship to Davie and, by extension, to poetry, also a complicated and doomed dynamic of attraction/repulsion.[12] It is necessary to consider the gangster and the poet not as foils but rather as sides of the same coin, related components of Ornitz's consideration of art under capitalism.

Meyer includes in his haphazard narration a poem of Davie's in its entirety—rather incredibly, given the novel's ostensible form as unmediated recollections jotted down from memory many decades later. The almost absurd unlikeliness of such a recitation makes a closer look at the poem worthwhile, especially regarding its relationship to Meyer's own aesthetics. The poem, which Davie reads to the whole "bunch," has no title:

Silence.
Not of the cloister cell,
Sunless place of souls enslaved to fixed fear.
. . . .
Nor of the tomb, stark symbol of formal sorrow,
Decadent with the dust of tears,
Foul-sweet with the sighs of expiring flowers;
. . . .
Nor of the dungeon,
Charged with clamorous quiet,
Where swarm the vermin of melancholia;
And time's a conscious treadmill;
. . . .
No.
I mean
Silence—
Silence—
Amidst the world's moil
The struggle, the clash, the roar, the rush, the lust of money and flesh
The silence
That suspends you in timeless space:
When first
Truth flames across your heaven,
When first
Beauty is revealed,
When first
Love lives. (110)

It is difficult to imagine that Ornitz's readers are supposed to judge Davie's poem to be good, as tortured phrases like "vermin of melancholia" or clichés like "the lust of money and flesh" ensure. But if it is bad, the poem is deliberately constructed by Ornitz as a mishmash. Although Avrum vaguely classifies Davie's poetry—he calls it "the new kind"—the poem fairly bursts with exaggerated elements of widely varying styles: the romantic ("Decadent with the dust of tears") jostles the sweatshop ("time's a conscious treadmill") and the modernist ("No. / I mean / Silence— / Silence—"). These contradictory elements cause Davie to stand in as generic Poet, rather than representing any one figure or school in particular. Indeed, Davie Solomon is drawn almost gleefully as a type rather than a person: golden-curled, moral above mundane law, spouting hyperbolic love and forgiveness, he proves himself too good for this world, and dies young—like the deliberate cliché that he is—of tuberculosis. Meyer, meanwhile, with his loudly professed ambitions of self-interest, represents the repulsive Modern Man, the antipoetic vulgarian running the world in Eliot's dismal formulation.[13]

In various ways, Meyer also becomes an artist in the course of becoming a gangster. Ornitz foreshadows the kind of artist Meyer will become through Meyer's early association (and that of his mentor, Uncle Philip) with the satyr Pan, the earthy musician of Greek mythology. Like Pan, Meyer is half-man and half-goat, for his childhood nickname is Ziegelle, Yiddish for "little goat." When he is around six years old and begins to object to the embarrassing pet name, Meyer learns that it derives from the fact that in steerage to the United States, he was suckled by a goat when his mother's milk dried up and nothing else was available to nourish the child. This detail also ties baby Meyer's steerage experience to the story of Remus and Romulus, the legendary founders of Rome who were suckled by a female wolf, positing the immigrant (and criminal) as a symbolic founder of America. (Mike Gold, in *Jews without Money*, uses gangsters as part of a strategy to appropriate American foundational myths.)

Pan, an ugly but merry minor deity, is famous for his music; satyrs are, of course, generally feared as despoilers of women. Meyer explicitly names the satyr as his inspiration by applying it to his hero and mentor, Uncle Philip, who lies on his deathbed: "A satyr's head: Philip's, his bone-gray hair rumpled into puffs like horns; a carved face with pointed nose and sharp chin" (289). In addition to invoking the satyr as a mythological text, the goat imagery pictures Meyer as too bestial to be fully human.

Through the goat imagery of *Haunch Paunch and Jowl* speaks a whole body of Jewish folklore that centers upon the white kid. Kosher dietary laws forbid that a kid be cooked in its mother's milk. In the biblical story of Exodus, goat's blood is smeared on the doors at Passover to distinguish (and protect) Jewish homes. One of the best-known Passover songs is called "One Little Goat." The concept of the "scapegoat," the sacrifice of which releases a sinner from culpability, is Jewish. Thus, Meyer's namesake is at once a sacrificial figure and a tough survivor.[14]

But the nickname Ziegelle most directly invokes the fantastically popular Yiddish lullaby "Rozhinkes mit Mandlen" (Raisins and almonds), written by the playwright and stage composer Abraham Goldfaden. Ornitz quotes the song in his text, excerpting a few lines that contain the word *ziegelle:*

Unter der veigelle
Shtait ein weisse ziegelle,

Ooh, ooh, ooh—
(Under the little crib stands a little white kid). (24)

For Meyer, a criminal who peddles the materials of art to the highest bidder, the song is particularly resonant. In the song, a mother croons to her beloved baby boy that a little white goat has been sent to the market to buy him raisins and almonds. Ruth Rubin reads the song as only tranquil and pretty; actually, its ambiguous wording (the goat has been sent to trade [*handlen*] for treats for the child) obscures the obvious meaning, that the goat has been sold, its life sacrificed for a good price.[15]

The goat's story, sung to Meyer by his mother in his childhood, parallels his own story. On one level, we as readers might understand Meyer's position the way a child hearing the lullaby might envision the goat: as an actor in the business exchange, who forays out to make a shrewd deal and returns enriched. But the deeper meaning of Meyer's nickname is that he has been sacrificed to the market. The Goldfaden song, sung tenderly in the novel's first period by Meyer's mother, foresees the boy's final ignoble fate.

Lawyer in Three Languages

Meyer's outspoken determination to sell himself is predicated upon a savvy awareness of his audience's presumptions and expectations. With "Raisins and Almonds" he quotes from a song so popular that, although clearly authored, it almost immediately became known as a folk song. In short, he is reasonably counting on the fact that his readers will recognize the song well enough to supply its ending, which the narrator withholds. At the same time, Meyer appears to contradict this expectation in his translation of the song's Yiddish lyrics, presumably for the benefit of a non-Yiddish-speaking readership.

Meyer's translation of Goldfaden's song sets up a pattern he follows throughout his "autobiography": he frequently inserts Yiddish words or phrases and then translates them immediately and intrusively—within the text—in parentheses. The careful and deliberate use of language(s) in the book, and the various kinds of attention paid to it, are an integral part of Ornitz's explorations of the cultural marketplace, presented through the evolution of Meyer's career. That this exploration—what Walter Rideout calls Ornitz's "destructive foray against capitalist society"[16]—takes place on the most micro, linguistic level is not surprising: the fictional man whose memoirs Ornitz ghostwrites is a lawyer, someone who, in effect, sells words for profit. Even before he becomes a lawyer the young Meyer instinctively recognizes the connection between language and ideology; lying awake in bed listening to the adults argue, he hears his uncle introduce two men to each other:

"Barney," says Philip, "you know Finkelstein, but let me introduce you again: this is Benjamin Finkelstein, capitalist."

So—that's the "ist" he is. A capitalist. . . . What in the name of "ists" is a capitalist! (99)

The introduction here of "Benjamin Finkelstein, capitalist," which bestows a Jewish name upon none other than Benjamin Franklin, suggests another kind of translation into "Jewish"—that of the American canon.

Meyer's translations of Yiddish run throughout *Haunch Paunch and Jowl*, chopping up the page: "Lutz, the *shicker goy* (drunken gentile), seated on a box, is laboriously sewing up a rent in his pants. He is the local *Shabbos* (sabbath) fire lighter and lodges with Berel. These two and Yoshke the *Golitzianer* (Galician), a peddler, sleep in this small cellar workroom" (19). Again, Ornitz seems to be assuming at least for rhetorical purposes that the bulk of his readers will not understand Yiddish. His translations create a discomfort, for they interrupt the narrative flow and call attention to themselves. They create a linguistic alienation in the reader, who is immediately positioned as an outsider who needs translation. By positioning Meyer as a tour guide to the Jewish ghetto, upon whom the reader relies for translation, the Yiddish interruptions contribute a feeling of voyeurism to the experience of reading the book: it is as though Meyer Hirsch were driving the bus of slumming tourists that the young Mike Gold and his childhood gang angrily pelt with garbage in *Jews without Money* (see chapter 3). This feeling likens reading the book to being a spectator at Lavelle's and gaping with prurient glee at the scenes Meyer creates there. Both the "autobiography" and the staged dramas are, after all, the openly grasping creations of Meyer.

Indeed, Meyer's explanation of Yiddish words reads and looks a lot like his explanation of thieves' slang:

A thief with a jail term to his credit has the standing of a savant with an honorary degree. Archie now speaks with sophomoric assurance. He says: "Say, we're wised up to a lot of stuff now." The gang listens intently to the wisdom learned in the reform school. How to "roll a lush" (rob a drunken man), how to practice the fine points of "stick up" (highway robbery), how to make a "getaway" under varying circumstances, how to "crack" a small safe, "canopener" fashion, or blow open a big safe with "soup" (nitroglycerine), how to "jimmy" doors, drawers and windows, how to snap a lock, how to use skeleton keys, where to dispose of "swag" and where to buy burglar's tools, how to "fix" (bribe) cops and judges, and many other delightful aids to a happy life of crime and bravado. (89)

There is a long-standing perceived connection between Jewish speech, particularly Yiddish, and the coded language of thieves.[17] Ornitz absorbs the historical link between Jewish language and thieves' language into a form that immediately spotlights the role of the reader in the consumption of both languages, conflating the prurient pleasure of reading about crime with the experience of reading about the Jewish ghetto. The conflation is articulated fully by Meyer, who makes an offhand but crucial comment about "sensationalists who call themselves sociologists" (147). Once this conflation is made, the reader is left unsure about whether the narrative is meant to be considered "real" autobiography, or whether *Haunch Paunch and Jowl* is actually another invention by a professed liar and creator of scandalous histories—one of Meyer Hirsch's staged tavern dramas, crafted in his knowledge of what the market desires. In other words, has Ornitz created a fictional character by drafting that character's autobiography, or has he introduced a fictional character so devious that he would write a fake autobiography if he thought there would be buyers? Indeed, I would posit a real possibility that *Haunch Paunch and Jowl* is intended to be read as another one of Meyer's schemes for personal enrichment: a phony ghetto confessional. At times, the narrative itself playfully calls into question its own implied authorship. In the novel's first period Uncle Philip shows Meyer a notebook he is keeping, titled "Notes upon the education of my nephew, Meyer Hirsch" (17). Since the novel is a kind of dirty education of the naïf, in the manner of Voltaire's *Candide,* Philip's title might easily serve as an alternative to "Haunch Paunch and Jowl." Even more important, though, is the fact that there is no reason to consider that after a lifetime of lying Meyer would suddenly be moved to come clean.

Seen in this context, Meyer's easy promises to be candid and his modernistically self-conscious interpolations of Yiddish words are revealed as brazen trading in Old World cachet. Only in this cynical light does the novel's Yiddish-English linguistic mix suit Meyer, who balks as a child when asked to speak in Yiddish, since to do so would embarrass him on the street. He doesn't hesitate to use the language later, in any instance where it seems expedient. The Old World vernacular *as translated by Meyer* is then infused with a new meaning: a sort of unsavory version of the new poetic occasion members of the literary avant-garde were finding in such materials—for instance, Langston Hughes's use of black American English, William Carlos Williams's recreation of immigrant inflections, Jesus Colon's embrace of Puerto Rican diction, or Carl Sandburg's search for a standard American vernacular. Meyer achieves the same modernist awareness of language as cultural artifact, as a thing-in-itself rather than only a carrier or container of meaning. But in his case, the thingness leads to commodification; for Meyer, the fresh meaning of Yiddish in the American context is simply that it provides something new to sell. Meyer's version of the trilingual literary experimentation of Abraham Cahan is humorously cynical:[18]

Hirsch & Freund

Counsellors at Law

Thus read the large gilt letters on the expansive plate-glass window of the store in which we make our offices. And a swinging yellow and black sign, high above the door, to catch the roving eyes from all points, is more to the point. It bears a one-word legend, in three languages, English, Yiddish and Russian, black gaping out of yellow:

LAWYER. (204)

The sign in "black gaping out of yellow," to "catch the roving eyes," may even refer back to the gang's days as ragtime performers in Lavelle's, when the gang, according to Meyer's descriptions, was battening off yellowness and blackness by presenting debased versions of Chinese and African American culture and physical appearance.

Ultimately, Ornitz's commentary on the avant-garde's experimentation with vernacular forms comes to occupy a singular position: it is both modernist and antimodernist, or rather antimodernist within a recognizably modernist language. The novel's modernist feel comes from the sense of difference and visual discordance created by the nonstop parenthetical interjections. Moreover, Meyer's narrative is so immediately and abidingly shrouded in irony that Walter Rideout was prompted to classify the work as "of the twenties in spirit" despite its occupation with events and circumstances of the period from 1880 to 1910.[19] Ornitz's unconventional formal choices become logical components of a serious assessment of literary modernism, using its own grammar of fragmented and layered meaning for the critique. The division of the book into seven periods instead of chapters is a case in point. Not only does the division represent a break from the traditional novel form by proposing a new way to mark narrative time, but by invoking the seven "acts" on the stage of life set forth by Shakespeare in his "All the world's a stage" soliloquy, the division immediately prepares the reader for a self-reflexive, pointed commentary on the nature and purpose of art.[20]

Ornitz signals his commentary on modernism by invoking texts modernist writers considered originary on account of their self-consciousness, such as Henry Fielding's comic epic *The History of Tom Jones, a Foundling* (1749), in that lurid events propel a rogue hero toward domesticity and self-knowledge, and Laurence Sterne's protostructuralist creation, *The Life and Opinions of Tristram Shandy, Gentleman* (1759), in that Sterne demonstrates his fascination with John Locke's notion of "associated ideas."[21] Although Ornitz borrows details of plot and characterization from these works, his novel's most striking kinship with these sacred texts of modernism is visual: on the page, it looks remarkably like Fielding's and Sterne's. Ornitz indulges in Fielding's sardonic summary titles for each chapter (a device that Fielding claims in *Tom Jones* as his innovation) and Sterne's breathless fragmentation of the narrative by dashes (which Ornitz makes into periods). Peter Quennell's brief description of *Tristram Shandy* in his coauthored *History of English Literature* as "a medley of autobiographical jottings, caustic reflections on life, scandalous anecdotes and strange romantic musings, all thrown together in a lively and eloquent, yet deliberately discontinuous style" could easily serve as an apt and succinct description of *Haunch Paunch and Jowl.*[22]

The literary borrowing from modernists' chosen foundational works calls attention to the structural particularity of *Haunch Paunch and Jowl.* But an antimodernist thrust emerges from the novel's persistent characterization of its own form as distasteful if not downright unethical, as a particularly vulgar way of selling out. This is the chief way in which the gangster works as a negative hero: by ventriloquizing Meyer, Ornitz "allows" him to make his own formal choices, and then to betray his own avaricious motives.

By refusing to speak Yiddish at home, Meyer shows in his youth the immigrant child's archetypal unwillingness to be associated with the language of his parents' past:

> "Gee," I plead in English, "I ain't got time for everything."
> A quick reproving gesture menaces me to silence.
> "Speak to me *momme loschen* (mother tongue) not that nasty gibberish of the streets." (16)

Meyer is a child of the New World, but unlike Abraham Cahan's David Levinsky (with whom he is far too frequently lumped), who sacrifices his shtetl roots for rebirth as an American, Meyer uses the Old World and the New with equal aplomb in order to benefit financially.[23] In this manner Ornitz forbids nostalgia or roots fetishism in Jewish literature. Meyer repeatedly calls the Yiddish language "musical," which not only emphasizes its potential eloquence (as openly argued later by Mike Gold and Henry Roth) but also connects the language question to the gang's profiteering project of writing ragtime songs. Moreover, Meyer presents himself as only using this "musical" language either to deceive potential clients or for purposes of seduction: "I whisper musical Yiddish in her ear. I feel the warm flush of her face, hear her breath coming fast, and know her bust heaves in tumult. . . . She says she cannot understand . . . she cannot believe that I would stoop so low as to be friends with a servant girl . . . particularly, since she is a greenhorn and I, an American college boy" (96). For Ornitz, it is precisely when Yiddish achieves the aggressive masculinity with which Babel sought to furnish it that Yiddish truly becomes the language of thieves.

World of Men

Meyer's gangland domain is buttressed by a language of sinister masculinism. Of the club Lavelle's, the novel's microcosmic representation of New York's mongrel, fast-moving modern society, Meyer declares summarily, "The world came to Lavelle's—*a world of men*" (141; emphasis added).[24] This dangerous, stalking world of men is, for Meyer and his associates, also the artistic world, for here they create ragtime. Thus, the overmasculinized criminal gang becomes a metaphor for a hard-boiled modern art that Ornitz figures as predatory rather than empowering.

Juxtaposed to the predatory masculine is Davie, Meyer's poetic alter ego, who is clearly associated with the feminine. Davie's stage performance is received as female by his audience: "Then Al played an introduction that called for Davie's appearance. He had no makeup on, but his wan beauty and ethereal expression brought cries of 'Oh sister, does mamma know you're out tonight?' . . . 'Hoo, La, La.' . . . 'Sweet baby'" (132). Furthermore, the delicate Davie marries a woman with a man's name: Billie. His early death comes as no surprise, for according to the novel's logic he cannot live: Meyer's ascendancy requires that he bury Davie, who represents the "soft" artistic impulse that runs counter to his own.

Meyer does bury Davie—literally—and in order to do so he unabashedly manipulates the power of language to construct maleness. Meyer arranges for Davie's body to be laid in consecrated ground although he had married a gentile. The absence of a legal marriage certificate, and the fact that Billie disappears following Davie's death, gives Meyer the idea of claiming that Davie was not actually married. Addressing the gathering in the neighborhood temple, he asks rhetorically, "Are we women in the market place that we heed every rumor? No, we are men concerned with actualities and facts" (169). Meyer is able to make use of women's linguistic subordination: no man wants to be accused of being feminine, so his argument easily triumphs. Of course, in this case the "market place rumor" is a good deal truer than the heartless male "facts." By calling the deepest truth of Davie's life a "market place rumor," Meyer is also calling Davie a woman. He then verbally obliterates this truth with male-identified discourse.

Male facts are what Meyer promises at the beginning of the book when he vows to "tell everything. Everything: so that even if I tell pathological lies the truth will shine out like grains of gold in the upturned muck" (13). He then apparently proceeds toward this naturalistic aim, revealing details of his own roguery in a deadpan manner that seems endearingly puckish at first and then becomes merely appalling. Through mastery of language the protagonist of this gritty coming-of-age story designs his own passage into manhood, with that word's full implications of both masculinity and adulthood.

Ornitz's packaging of his ironic novel as a kind of bildungsroman is a wry nod in the direction of a narrative form immensely significant to Jewish American letters: the first-person account of Americanization. Beginning in the 1880s such accounts flourished with Jewish immigration; besides influential full-fledged memoirs such as Abraham Cahan's important five-volume autobiography (1926–31), there were hundreds of essentially anonymous experiential accounts published in journals, newspapers, pamphlets, publications of benevolent societies, and so forth. These accounts, while frequently imbued with the bewildered misery of the impoverished immigrant, generally combine a nostalgia for the shtetl with an eagerness to adapt themselves to the freedom of the New World. With Meyer Hirsch's crooked path to manhood, Ornitz seeks to deconstruct the piety of what in 1923 was already a venerable tradition of Jewish American naturalization tales. Ornitz's literary irreverence is abetted by his invocation and deflation of another sanctimonious and prevalent genre: the vice story (including temperance novels and white-slavery fiction). These stories were composed as titillating personal histories, sometimes anonymously, like *Haunch Paunch and Jowl,* or with names allegedly changed. Like the autobiographical form, temperance novels were designed to seem at once intimate and universal. They were commonly published around this time not only in English but also in Russian and Yiddish, often in cheap, accessible pamphlet form.

In the naturalization tale the newness of America is central, but the notion of Americanness as juvenile was certainly not peculiar to Jewish writers. The year before the publication of *Haunch Paunch and Jowl,* a group of thirty young (white and mostly male) writers—among them Van Wyck Brooks, Harold Stearns, and Ring Lardner—published an important anthology called *Civilization in the United States.* Although the essays observed the condition of American culture from a variety of viewpoints—medicine, sports, humor, science—an area of consensus among the pieces was the extreme youth of the United States.

In this anthology the foregrounding of youthfulness tends to contain a sense of great energy and implicit hope for the future, when the seeds of Americanism will bear the fruit of adult culture. In *Haunch Paunch and Jowl* the child-gangster instead comes into maturity as the metaphorical offspring of capitalism, which seems necessarily to spawn monsters: "The order of the day was—PLAY THE GAME AS YOU SEE IT PLAYED. . . . It was a sordid generation, a generation creeping out of the mud into the murk. Avrum was right about one thing. There was not as yet an American identity. There was yet to

rise up an American standard. . . . It was the time and process of finding our-
selves, a sort of evolutionary process that began as a creeping thing in the scum"
(227). To capture this sense of coming of age, a process Meyer characterizes as
"creeping out of the mud," a child criminal fits the bill perfectly.

The gangster bildungsroman also satirizes the immigrant wisdom that, in
America, the children must act as parents to their mothers and fathers. (In
chapter 3 I discuss Mike Gold's employment of this convention in detail.)
Meyer's Uncle Philip vocalizes this sentiment when he tells Meyer that "we've
got nothing to look back to. It's up to us to be ancestors" (105). Of course, by
the end of the book, Philip, Meyer, and their ilk wind up being the ancestors
of repulsive animals: the overindulged lapdogs and other pets who have, according to Meyer, replaced children for the newly wealthy: "Children romp . . .
but there are so few children. . . . I see plenty of dogs dawdling slack leashes. . . .
Sickening: I wish Gretel wouldn't make such an ado over that miserable
mutt. . . . There is one thing I thought of at Philip's grave. . . . Long ago . . .
that dim time of dreaming and striving . . . he had said we would make our-
selves notable ancestors to be looked back to . . . ancestors . . . to whom . . . lap
dogs . . . lap dogs who whined if they were made to walk across the floor" (288).

Given Meyer's double role as "entrepreneur" and author, it follows that he
must also strive to be his own literary ancestor; as a member of the current
generation of writers, he is also a "creeping thing in the scum." Needless to
say, in light of the warning about begetting a generation of whining, purely
ornamental lapdogs, Ornitz does not seem to foresee that a gangster and a
sweatshop owner (that is, Meyer and Philip) can possibly produce a great generation of artists. Meyer's stage name, Melville Hart, captures the limitations
of his artistic sensibility: the name invokes a landmark novel of commodity
fetishism, Herman Melville's *Moby-Dick* (1851), and connects it to Joseph
Conrad's tale of horrific moral emptiness, *Heart of Darkness* (1902). Meyer's
greed has also caused him to lose the girl he loved, Esther Brinn, whose name
strongly suggests Hester Prynne of Nathaniel Hawthorne's *Scarlet Letter* (1850),
a novel about the wages of sin.

Allrightniks Row

Haunch Paunch and Jowl leaves readers with the misanthropic aftertaste particular to works that have a nasty protagonist. Because of its insistence upon
the impossibility of artistic truth in the capitalist marketplace, the work
Haunch Paunch and Jowl most resembles in spirit is probably Nathanael West's
novel *Day of the Locust* (1939). West, another left-wing Jewish writer who, like
Ornitz and Daniel Fuchs, moved to Hollywood, eventually collaborated with

Ornitz (and Lester Cole) on Ornitz's first movie project, *Follow Your Heart* (1936). The horrifying *Day of the Locust* is apocalyptic in vision, whereas in *Haunch Paunch and Jowl*, gross mediocrity prevails, finally sapping even the negative vitality of the gangster. After indulging in too many rich foods, Meyer has grown so fat that his political enemies have nicknamed him "Haunch Paunch and Jowl." He has been forced to marry his fleshy servant girl to avoid scandal; it is his disadvantageous union ("Gretel was rather crude," says Meyer [294]), not a political defeat, that prevents his career from advancing further. Meyer has become a "Professional Jew" and moved with his wife to a stretch of Riverside Drive known as "Allrightniks Row," populated by newly rich Jews who are entirely given over to ostentatious displays of wealth. In the final passage of James Joyce's masterpiece of modernist literary aesthetics, *Ulysses,* the earthy Molly Bloom offers her husband Leopold her "breasts all perfume" and asserts, movingly and affirmingly, "Yes."[25] In the last passage of *Haunch Paunch and Jowl,* Gretel offers Meyer "potted breast" that "smells good," and he "heaves his great bulk" to accept. Thus, rather than Joyce's moment of return or West's gloriously hideous apocalypse, Ornitz's ending reveals a spiritual death by weary mediocrity: Meyer's demons are, finally, demons of dust. Even the exoticized linguistic blending is hopelessly deglamorized; the obese Meyer waddles off to eat "patate latkes," which he names by pairing an English word for potato (rather than using the Yiddish [*bulbe*]) with the Yiddish word for pancake (*latke*).

Ironically, however, what is revealed in the end is a high degree of idealism on the part of Ornitz, who seems unwilling to compromise his ideals of socialism, under which system the artist would not have to choose between early death and gangsterism. Ornitz romantically displayed this literary idealism, and its outgrowth from realpolitik, when called as an unfriendly witness before the House Committee on Un-American Activities (HUAC) as a member of the Hollywood Ten. Apparently, Ornitz told his fellow defendants that during the hearing they must all be "as brave as the people we write about."[26]

Ornitz does hint in *Haunch Paunch and Jowl* at the existence of less commercialized artistic possibilities—but not under capitalism. In the novel's final pages, Meyer muses upon changes in the political climate of his old stomping grounds: "In the East Side the radicals were making headway. Were they bringing spiritual fare for the spiritually hungry? . . . Who would believe fifteen years ago that the Socialists would carry one of my assembly strongholds as they did last election? . . . In the Ghetto there was a large, growing, fanatic cult of intellectualism . . . a fine frenzied idealism . . . art, literature, music, social science and politics in the pure meaning of the world—calling the new generation" (297). Ornitz carefully connects this projection for the future of politics with the future of literature, suggesting an ideal that Michael Gold would become famous for championing.

In fact, this new artistic potentiality is hinted at early in the novel. Meyer introduces Yetta, a neighborhood girl he describes as plain and unpopular, who goes on to become a suffragist, to organize the girl shirtwaist makers union, to marry a professor of economics, and to write books. Her brief saga identifies her as directly imported from an earlier novel: she is none other than Comrade Yetta of Arthur Bullard's 1913 socialist novel by the same name. In Bullard's novel, though, Yetta must first escape from the clutches of a Jewish gangster who tries to make a prostitute of her. In what by now seems to be typical metaliterary fashion, Ornitz has his Jewish gangster violate Yetta's femininity in writing, by representing her as a failed woman because she is loud in defense of other women and doesn't seem to care about being purely decorative: "but we thought Yetta an extremely dull girl: I guess her hair did not shine. No boy bothered her, but she was busy fighting away boys from other girls" (78). By revealing Yetta's future, however, Meyer has already predicted that she will win. Evading the gangsters' hypermasculine assault on her body, in actuality and on the page, she will organize, change the political realm, and—perhaps most important—go on to write new books, books that will outlast the stolen labor of the gangster, Meyer Hirsch.

3

A Gang of Little Yids

Savage Jews in Mike Gold's *Jews without Money*

> When the Jew breaks from the spiritual heritage of his
> people and his faith, then he becomes a menace; he
> breeds Jewish criminals and Jewish radicals.
> —Morris Lazaron

> Pens must scribble where swords hack'd before.
> —Frederick Schiller, *The Robbers*

> A parrot cursed.
> —Mike Gold, *Jews without Money*

Jews without Money, Mike Gold's autobiographical tenement novel of 1930, opens with self-described chaos, with a seemingly unmediated rush of voices and tawdry images spewed from the narrator's memories of childhood on New York's Lower East Side. As a novel it remains recalcitrant: plotless, loosely cobbled together of numbered fragments, possessed of dubious chronology and obscure destination.

In the midst of this apparent disorder, though, Gold cannily provides throughout the book passages that might be taken as instructions for approaching his meandering novel of "carnival or catastrophe" (14).[1] In an early chapter, for instance, Mikey's "gang of little Yids" (7) chases a sightseeing bus and pelts it with dead cats, rocks, and garbage, asking, "What right had that man with the megaphone to tell them lies about us?" (55). Thus a delinquent gang, led by the future gangster Nigger, manages to challenge and overcome the mainstream narrative of lies about the impoverished Jewish ghetto. Meanwhile, Gold takes a blow at any curatorial, sentimental attraction the ghetto might have held for outsiders (see, for example, Hutchins Hapgood's study

Spirit of the Ghetto [1902]), and also perhaps at any titillation his *own* readers might seek: "What right had these stuckup foreigners to come and look at us?"[2]

Jews without Money, therefore, opens with the twinning of deliberate affront and muscular self-descriptive assertion. Graphically warning the reader against both nostalgia and prurience, Gold enfleshes in the Jewish gangster the notion of an irreverent cultural savior. In a *New Masses* editorial Gold makes explicit this connection between gangsterdom and writing: "The Workers will scorn any vague fumbling poetry, much as they would scorn a sloppy workman. Hemingway and others have had the intuition to incorporate this proletarian element into their work, but have used it for the frisson, *the same way some actors try to imitate gangsters of men.*"[3] Gold posits a kind of logic by which bad writers are to good writers as mere actors are to actual gangsters.

This linguistic movement from gangster to good writer is of great consequence: through language, the behavioral stance of the Jewish gangster as outcast and rebel becomes a literary stance. The literary stance is thematized throughout *Jews without Money.* Early on, in the chapter where Gold for the first time introduces his "gang of little Yids," Mikey describes his battle with a grammar school teacher. The contest is one of words: Mikey has used an obscenity, and the teacher has accordingly called him "LITTLE KIKE" (37).

The primacy of ethnicity in these language battles is plain not only in the name the teacher chooses, but also in the punishment: she washes his mouth out with soap made from animal fat, attempting to coat/cleanse his language source with *treif* (nonkosher food), thus removing or overcoming the "KIKE" in him that she fears and scorns. (Mikey's crime, cursing, is subsequently identified by Mikey's father as a Jewish trait.) The gendering of the passage is explicit in the terms of contempt that the adult Mike uses retroactively for his teacher: "O irritable, starched old maid teacher, O stupid, proper, unimaginable despot, O cow with no milk or calf or bull. . . . O ruptured American virgin of fifty-five, you should not have called me 'LITTLE KIKE'" (22–23). Tellingly, the affair is sexed as well as gendered; by probing Mikey's mouth with soap, the teacher attempts to feminize Mike while masculinizing herself by reversing the roles of penetrated/penetrating in the act of sexual intercourse. Thus, "civilizing" Mikey is equated with silencing him, with feminizing him, and with de-Judaicizing him. The only resolution comes when Mikey's friend Nigger, Jewish gangster-in-progress, steps up and bashes her in the nose.

These two crucial images—a juvenile Jewish gang flinging garbage at liars with megaphones, and a future gangster boldly challenging a genteel tormentor—delineate Gold's agenda in depicting Jewish gangsters. This chapter is divided into three intertwined sections, each of which derives from the chain of resonances set forth above. The first section deals with the gangster as a model for the ethnic writer who bootlegs his way into the American canon, who flings garbage into the face of liars when necessary, who commits acts of violence against authoritative texts, and who through the illicitness of his position is able both to claim the ghetto and transcend its boundaries. In this section I begin to probe the remarkable (yet hitherto slighted) intertextuality of Gold's odd novel. I sketch the relationship of gangsterism to formal aesthetics, particularly the new proletarian aesthetics Gold dedicated his talents to pursuing.

In the second section I focus on the gangster as a meditation upon Jewish masculinity and consider the criminal as an ambivalent projection of the fantasy Paul Breines calls "tough Jews." I locate this fantasy on three planes of meaning for Gold: internalization/revision of received images of male Jewish "difference" in American and European culture; the anxiety about impotence that Sandra M. Gilbert and Susan Gubar demonstrate as dominating modernist literary production; and the valorization of the male working body that characterized Communist Party cultural rhetoric of the 1930s.

The third section organizes the positions of the first two to reflect on something Gold regards as crucial to a discussion of Jewishness: talk. I investigate the web of connections in *Jews without Money* among linguistics, written literature, authority, and gender. In this section I emphasize the book's preoccupation with the figure of Caliban, and look at the relationship of difference to discourse.[4] I also explore how, side by side with his manipulation of high cultural references, Gold is responding to a convention of popular culture that was fairly well established by the time he was writing, and indeed stretches into the present: the reception of Jewish speech as signaling criminality. In addition, I examine the novel's codification of various kinds of speech acts and verbal cultural productions.

Much has been written of Gold's role as an ideologue; indeed, he has maintained his place for decades as the favorite whipping boy for the sins of Communist Party literary dogmatism. He has been called "the party's critical hatchetman," who became "an intellectual robot" and produced "anti-capitalist or anti-Republican war-whoops," while his writing "gave the appearance of having been thought out somewhere in its author's bowels."[5] With few exceptions scholars of the literature of the 1930s continue to pillory him with a doggedness made further remarkable by the fact that virtually no one is willing to take him seriously as a writer. Despite the fact that *Jews without Money* went through eleven printings in the first year of its issue (and remains in print today), what Gold has earned over the years is the dubious distinction of copious "grudging footnotes."[6] In his afterword to the 1965 reissue of the book,

Michael Harrington lukewarmly allows that *Jews without Money* has "a genuine, if modest, claim on our attention as art."[7] It is toward this "genuine . . . claim" that I turn my attention in this chapter; while I include some remarks on the reception of Gold, my resolution to explicate the text as rigorously as possible is a deliberate if ironically old-fashioned move to defamiliarize Gold enough to see him at all.

The People of the Book

> Boston people do not read their Emerson like that.
> —Vachel Lindsey, "The Mountain Cat"

In the midst of recounting two stories his father tells, the narrator of *Jews without Money*, Mikey Gold, reminds his readers that "the Jews have been known as 'the people of the book'" (87). In this moment and throughout the novel, a relationship with letters becomes a sign of Jewish identity. Mikey sets up a genealogy of readership and authorship that stretches twenty centuries, ending with his father—who loves literature and has a passion for the theater in particular—and listing among his favorite playwrights Schiller, Gorky, Tolstoy, and Shakespeare.

Gold's narrator conjoins this love for books to a startling outright claim that there were no Jewish gangsters in Europe: "There never were any Jewish gangsters in Europe. The Jews there were a timid bookish lot. The Jews have done no killing since Jerusalem fell. That's why the Christians have called us the 'peculiar people.' But it is America that has taught the sons of tubercular Jewish tailors how to kill" (23). He makes this declaration despite having read the work of the Russian Jewish writer Isaac Babel, whose Odessa tales chronicle the escapades of Jewish gangsters in the Odessa of the 1910s and 1920s (see chapter 1).[8]

Since Gold must have known not only that there was a flourishing Jewish underworld in Odessa, Warsaw, and other centers, but that there was already a considerable body of folk and art literature on both continents dealing with the subject, his artistic reasons for having Mikey claim otherwise are important.[9] Gold is making a pointed argument for the Americanness of his two key gangsters, Nigger and Louis One-Eye. And through each of these characters, as I discuss below, he energetically engages a number of literary texts within *Jews without Money*, frequently assessing or revising them in terms of Jewish immigrant life. The Jewish gangster operates as a reflection upon the usefulness of the American literary canon.

Although his laboring father reveres books, Mikey comes to the conclusion that literature as it has existed is irrelevant to the struggles of his own life, for it has not belonged to the working people. Mikey graduates early and at the top of his class, but he knows he is heading inexorably toward a factory job. Thus, when his teacher presents him at graduation with a book of Emerson's essays and makes him promise to continue reading, his promise is sullen: "I was trying to be hard. For years my ego had been fed by everyone's praise of my precocity. I had always loved books; I was mad about books; I wanted passionately to go to high school and college. Since I couldn't, I meant to despise all that nonsense" (304). Although the youthful Mikey tosses the volume of Emerson under his bed, an analog to Emerson has already been established in the person of the gangster Louis One-Eye, whose nickname (and the preponderance of eye imagery that necessarily accompanies his presence in the book) is a kind of morbid translation of Emerson's transparent eyeball.[10] Emerson devises the notion of the transparent eyeball to explain a collective wisdom that could come through nature: "In the woods, is perpetual youth. . . . In the woods, we return to reason and faith. There I feel that nothing can befall me in life—no disgrace, no calamity (leaving me my eyes), that nature cannot repair. Standing on the bare ground—my head bathed by the blithe air, and uplifted into infinite space,—all mean egotism vanishes. I become a transparent eyeball; I am nothing; I see all; the currents of the Universal Being circulate through me; I am part or particle of God."[11] Gold slyly positions a gangster as the "eye" through which collective wisdom—about the state—can be attained:

> A keeper once lashed Louis for an hour with a leather belt. The boy had broken some "rule." The flying buckle cracked open an eyeball. The boy screamed in pain. But the insane and legal gangster of the State continued the "punishment."
>
> All that night the boy lay sobbing and bleeding in his cell. He was fourteen years old. In the morning he was quiet. In the morning a cruel and legal "Doctor" of the State snipped out the useless pulp of an eye. (128)

Significantly, Gold not only judges the content of the narrative but, by putting simple words like "rule" and "doctor" in quotation marks, challenges the very language used. He continues the evocative eye imagery every time Louis is mentioned: "His remaining eye had become fierce and large. It was black, and from it poured hate, lust, scorn and suspicion, as from a deadly headlight to shrivel the world" (129).

Gold frequently uses the gangster to approach other texts as he does with Emerson; likewise, his approach to the texts is a kind of gangsterism. He demands them, he creates his own right to take them on his own terms, and he is frequently violent to them. James D. Bloom has succinctly characterized

Gold's allusiveness as "raids on established cultural monopolies"; Gold seems to have learned his approach from the gangsters' style of operation. The knee-breaking style of readership is pictured within Gold's own narrative, in the figure of the saloon goat who lies on the sidewalk outside the bar, lazily munching whatever comes to hand, including scraps of newspaper. As Bloom points out, the goat "obviously and comically . . . exhibits the critical outsider's hunger for culture that characterizes proletarian writing of the thirties, from Gold's *Jews without Money* to Richard Wright's *Black Boy*."[12] But the goat is just as obviously (and comically) performing a slapstick act of cultural resistance, made even more suggestive for the present purposes by the fact that the goat chews up, on the first page of the novel, a copy of the *Police Gazette*. Gold's narrator will state that a certain cop—whom he goes so far as to mention by name—"tipped the balances that swung Nigger into his career of gangster" (29). The goat in turn is identified with the gangster Nigger, who is pictured nimbly "leap[ing] the gaps betwen tenements like a mountain goat" (45), distinctly after the fashion of Samuel Ornitz's gangster protagonist Meyer Hirsch, whose childhood nickname is Zeigelle, or "little goat" (see chapter 2).

The saloon goat, like Gold, is therefore both consuming and pulverizing. The goat represents the vulnerable as well as the resistant aspect of the gangster; in Jewish folklore, a pure white kid is akin to the Christians' sacrificial snowy lamb of God. Furthermore, at that time (indeed, probably to this day) the single most popular Yiddish song was Abraham Goldfaden's "Rozhinkes mit Mandlen" (Raisins and almonds)—a song Gold names as having been his father's favorite.[13] In the song, a mother sings to her child that while he sleeps, a white kid will go to market to bring him raisins and almonds. While it's pretty to think of the animal returning with a basket of goodies over its arm, that's not how goats fetch food: the animal has been slaughtered. Thus, the masticating saloon goat is both innocent sacrifice (to the marketplace) and survivor—it is able to live on cast-off garbage, and breaks the skull of a drunken sailor.

That this whole tension exists in Gold on such a self-consciously literary—and metaliterary—level further indicates the importance of the gangsters to his primary enterprise: contributing practically to the discussion of what kind of writing the "red decade" demanded. By rereading the American canon (from high texts like Emerson to popular ones like *The Police Gazette*) and placing Mikey within established or even revered authors' landscapes, Gold insists upon his own place in American letters—as a Jew, as a ghetto dweller, as a worker, and as a communist. Yet even as he stakes this claim, Gold seeks to disrupt a newly formed academic myth of America evinced by the first generation of American cultural theoreticians (including H. L. Mencken, Van Wyck Brooks, and Lewis Mumford, all of whom Gold excoriated in print).[14]

Sometimes Gold appears to disrupt the seamlessness of the myth of America for the sake of usefully profaning it; after all, he has insisted that cursing is a Jewish trait, and he voices in *Jews without Money* the most well-known Jewish American curse: *A klug tsu Columbus* (a curse on Columbus).[15] But frequently Gold offers an alternative history with Mikey at its center.[16] Finally, the ungentle revisions he offers of his many intertexts, American and European, express ambivalence about Gold's own place in literature—an ambivalence that travels from Mikey's uneasy childhood on the Lower East Side to Gold's uneasy experience of authorship, but which by no means belies the celebration of Americanness that characterizes Gold's work.

The gangster's appropriation of American texts is a major organizing principle of this perversely nonlinear "autobiography." In the chapter called "A Gang of Little Yids," Gold's narrator describes how his unruly band of childhood friends bootlegged American history: "[Our] backyard was a curious spot. It had once been a graveyard. Some of the old American headstones had been used to pave our Jewish yard. The inscriptions were dated a hundred years ago . . . once we had torn up a white gravestone. What an adventure. We scratched like ghouls with our hands deep into the earth until we found moldy dirty human bones. What a thrill that was. I owned chunks of knee bone, and yellow forearms, and parts of a worm-eaten skull" (41). The "old American headstones"—sanctioned texts that have had to give way to the "Jewish yard"—are torn up by the scrabbling hands of the young Jewish readers, who seem equally thrilled by their ability to possess and to destroy these documents. Meanwhile, the "gang of little Yids"—most pertinently the author of the text we are reading—has had access to this (hi)story only by stealing grim fragments of it.

From under the gang's dirty fingernails, so to speak, any number of hallowed "old American" texts can be scraped. The author's own taken name, Mike Gold, represents a self-conscious and self-defining merging of American mythology with Jewishness; it is the name of a Civil War veteran Gold knew and admired as a child. Taking Gold's name served, among other things, to link Itzhok Granich not only to early American history, but to a struggle he could (and did) cast as a liberation, while remaining identifiably Jewish. Moreover, "Gold" as the author of a book called "Jews without Money" affords an ironic level of authorial self-awareness: the word itself is the only gold; language is a richness for Jews otherwise without money.

Mikey's adult voice attests that the tenement houses of the Lower East Side, the tenement houses that Nigger leaps grandly over and Louis One-Eye rules from above, are equivalents of the most sacralized American genesis:

They looked pale and exhausted. They smelled of Ellis Island disinfectant, a stink that sickened me like castor oil.

Around the room was scattered their wealth, all their striped calico seabags, and monumental bundles of featherbeds, pots, pans, fine peasant linen, embroidered towels, and queer coats thick as blankets.

Every tenement home was a Plymouth Rock like ours. (73)

Gold creates for himself and his community a lineage equal to the pedigrees of the citizens Van Wyck Brooks elevated as "hereditary Americans."[17] Brooks, in whom Gold expresses explicit disappointment in his essay "America Needs a Critic" (1926), expressed open dismay that the influx of non-English-speaking immigrants as well as the younger generation of critics from immigrant stock had taken over, supposedly destroying the New England cultural community with their Johnny-come-lately detachment from the American past.

If the Jewish Plymouth Rock is an East Side tenement, then the Jewish father of America is a young gangster. In a neighborhood tavern Mikey's father stands him on a table so that he may breathlessly recite a verse that begins with the line "I love the name of Washington." Earlier in the book, Gold has already invoked the name of Washington. Describing his friends' play, he writes: "Nigger was a virile boy, the best pitcher, fighter and crapshooter in my gang. He was George Washington when our army annihilated the redcoats" (37). Thus, Gold invites us to remember the "name of Washington" as "Nigger"! This backdoor entrance into American myth is emphasized by the presence, on the wall of the tavern where Mikey recites his poem and on the wall of Nigger's dark apartment, of the same picture: a ridiculous but popular chromo showing Teddy Roosevelt charging up San Juan Hill, baring his teeth at the Spaniards.

Even as a gangster's moniker, "Nigger" is particularly resonant, since the "whiteness" of Jews themselves was not fixed in social discourse until the 1930s and 1940s.[18] As the name of Washington, "Nigger" is baldly subversive. The Father of the Country becomes the worker in literal chains. The great progenitor is not the slaveowner but rather the enslaved.

It is at these intricate moments that the mercurial gangster comes into his unspoken role as bridger and boundary crosser. A continuous fluctuation of racial/ethnic identity takes place within Nigger, who is likened variously to an African American, a Gypsy, and an Indian. Through this character Gold also toys with the concept of race in the American family; his friend is called Nigger, but Nigger's sister's name is Lily, as in "lily-white."

Nigger's real name is mostly withheld. The narrator only uses his nickname, which constantly recapitulates a social position. However, Nigger's given name is revealed to be a uniquely rich Jewish name during a brief set piece that has

Mikey bring a gift of stolen eggs to his friend's starving family. Nigger has answered the door, and is standing there sullenly, embarrassed that his family's poverty has been exposed. His mother, who by Mikey's reckoning has been driven crazy by privation, becomes agitated in a mixture of gratitude and despair, and Nigger's father asks his son to bring her a drink.

> "Thank you, thank you, my darling!" she cried, smothering me with hysterical kisses. "May there be better days for all of us! May a fire burn up our enemies! They don't let me sleep at night, but I spit on them! I spit on them!"
> I was appalled and bewildered.
> "Malka," said the tailor quietly to his wife, "you are frightening the child. Abie, give your mother a glass of water. She is excited again." (264)

The name Abie is both the most common stage-Jew name and a grand old American name with a lofty history. For example, Abie served as a name of Jewish caricature at the beginning of the twentieth century in Harry Hershfield's syndicated comic strip *Abie the Agent,* which dealt with a Jewish businessman and ran for years, and in Montague Glass's "Potash and Perlmutter" sketches about two Jewish businessmen named Abe and Mawruss (collected into several books around 1910). The name's seemingly gratuitous presence also connects the gangster to another legendary "father" of America, Abraham Lincoln, toward whom Gold had a strong, long-standing attraction. As James D. Bloom points out, throughout his essays Gold sought to affiliate himself with Lincoln and to redeem Lincoln as a revolutionary hero. The gangster's double naming—as Abie and as Nigger—represents an attempt by Gold to emphasize self-empowerment of African Americans; Nigger is named for the formerly enslaved, and for the one who supposedly did the freeing.

But while insisting on the East Side Jews' place in American folklore, Gold adds a level of bitterness and irony to the story; Nigger and Mikey know that they will never become president, despite Mikey's father's proclamation that "I cannot be the President, Katie, but our little Mikey can" (211). Thus, the next time the name of Lincoln is mentioned in the book, it is loaded down with sarcasm. Mikey's teacher seeks to encourage his studies by reminding of Lincoln's example:

> "It will be difficult to study at night," said Miss Barry in her trembly voice, "but Abraham Lincoln did it, and other great Americans."
> "Yes, Miss Barry," I muttered. (304)

In fact Mikey does eventually "study" at night, but he follows the example of "Abie" rather than Abraham: "I took up with Nigger again. I spent my nights in a poolroom" (309).

Benjamin Harshav's observation about the multidirectional associations of the typical Yiddish utterance (and by extension Jewish experience), wherein each word accumulates clusters of cultural meaning, is useful here in understanding how to unpack the dense significance of Nigger's naming.[19] The character Nigger is associated not only with Washington and Lincoln, but also with the biblical Abraham, who became the first Jew after being released from his promise to sacrifice his son Isaac. Ultimately Nigger is at once enslaved and liberating, sacrificed and sacrificing. He is the Father of Jews and the Father of America. And he is a gangster.

Gold's nonstop cultural blendings produce a novel obsessed with its own belligerently off-color Americanness. As a maturing writer Mikey stands at a complicated American crossroads, as does his companion and double, the maturing gangster. At one point, the child falls asleep in front of his tenement while enjoying the "debauch of patriotism" (142) that is the Fourth of July, that most foundational of American holidays. During the abandon of the celebration, someone throws a firecracker out of a window and it explodes next to Mikey's face. Mikey leaps up shrieking, blood streaming down where the firecracker has torn "a big slice of flesh" from his shoulder (142). For many nights after, he wakes up screaming, reliving the terror and pain of the explosion.

Mikey's wound gives him a troubled claim to Independence Day that is reminiscent of the contradictory impulses in Frederick Douglass's "What to the Slave Is the Fourth of July." It affirms his position as an American: he is war-wounded, the veteran of an incident described as a reenactment of the war itself. "Kids were shooting off toy cannons, firecrackers, and their fingers in every street. The night was lit with a city's bombardment. Grinning Italians shot their revolvers into the sky. Roman candles popped red, blue and yellow balls at the sky. Pinwheels whirled, Catherine wheels fizzed and turned, torpedoes crackled, and rockets flew like long golden winged snakes above the tenements" (142). The passage is particularly evocative of the "rockets' red glare" and "bombs bursting in air" from the most famous American patriotic poem of all, "The Star-Spangled Banner," which was in the process of becoming the official national anthem as Gold wrote his novel. But although the permanent scars on Mikey's mind and body prove his "veteran" status, they also remind him that when he was hurt, his parents, because they were Jews without money, could not afford to send him to the country as the doctor prescribed to cure the nervous disorder he sustained from the incident.

An ambivalent patriotism can be read in Gold's description of the young Mikey's experience on Independence Day. As unsettling as this moment is, its painful intricacies perfectly describe a central undertaking for an American communist at this historical moment: the reconciliation of working-class internationalism with an optimistic Americanism, with "national character," in Gold's case Jewishness, added to the mix. Without falling into the Left-literary nativism of Douglas Wixson (see the introduction), it is also worth pointing out that at this time, the majority of communists in the United States were either foreign-born or first-generation Americans (as in the case of Gold). Their obsession with Americanism and its relation to communist internationalism—particularly where revolutionary ideas were concerned—was practical as well as philosophical.

Isaac Babel, as delineated in chapter 1, was able to use literary explorations of what Benjamin Harshav refers to as the "meaning of Yiddish" to show that perhaps Jewishness (and the Yiddish language in particular), rather than being another wrench in the works, actually held the key to reconciling patriotism with internationalism, combining as it does original ethnic form with historically deep cross-continental experience and influence. Gold's project is a kindred one. By iconizing one suggestive childhood moment, he grapples with this consuming question of the relationship between working-class culture and national culture, a question that would ultimately become canonized in Stalin's famous slogan proclaiming that the new literature should be "national in form, proletarian in content."[20]

Was Huck Jewish?

In 1959 Gold published a series of articles intended, he claimed, as a sequel to *Jews without Money*.[21] One of these articles, "Twain in the Slums," reminisces about "the epoch of Mark Twain in America" and describes Mikey "devouring *Huckleberry Finn* under the gaslight."[22] In fact, "Twain in the Slums" could well have been a subtitle for *Jews without Money*, which reckons with Twain's rural southern bildungsroman from beginning to end.

Twain's books connect the American Mikey to his Romanian father, but they also distinguish the two from each other. Herman chuckles about "*Your* Mark Twain" and compares him to "*Our own* Sholem Aleichem."[23] But the two respond with instinctive identification to Huck's freedom on the raft: "It's just like when I was a boy on our own Danube," Herman gushes, while Mikey insists, "I wish I could live on a raft like Huckleberry Finn."[24]

Gold recalls an event when Twain, on one of his many visits to the Lower East Side, appeared at a Settlement House performance of *The Prince and the Pauper*. He passed among the children, benevolently patting their heads. "My head he also touched," recalls Gold, breaking into Yiddish diction for the first time in the article as he accepts the benediction of the "great man," and perhaps thereby adding the Jewish melancholy that his father found wanting:

"'Your Mark Twain, he understands the aristocrats!' My father chuckled. 'He spits on them, he has a heart of gold! Like our own Sholem Aleichem he wants to help people to laugh. Laughter is healthy, all the doctors prescribe it, says Sholem Aleichem. But I think he also feels the tears of the people. Mark Twain has no tears.'"[25] But Mikey maintains that he still prefers Twain, who after all has a "heart of gold."

One of Mikey's major roles is to illustrate what Huck Finn would be if he did have "the tears of the people." Picking up threads from the quintessential "American boy" narrative, Gold compounds the novel's original morbidity while borrowing for his own purposes the immediate sympathy Huck commands. Like Huck, Tom Sawyer, and their friends, Mikey and the other boys sneak away to swim in the river (it's revoltingly polluted), discover the uses of dead cats (they make good weapons), steal apples (from struggling pushcart vendors), and form a fanciful secret gang, complete with naive blood oath and secret tunnel hideout (they really do draw blood). And when Mikey has his run-ins with the anti-Semitic schoolteacher, he admits perversely that maybe he was a savage, recalling unappealing attempts by the Widow Douglas and Aunt Sally to "sivilize" the resistant Huck Finn.

Like Huck, Mikey pals around with an outcast; his Nigger to Huck's Nigger Jim. (Moreover, the teacher Nigger punches in Mikey's defense is a "teacher for little slaves" [37], a locution that cannot be neutral in a novel so loaded down with Civil War and Emancipation imagery.) Jim's grief when members of his family are sold away from each other speaks to Nigger's rage when his sister Lily, forced into prostitution, is essentially sold away from him.

Most important, though, is Huck's famous resolution at the end of *The Adventures of Huckleberry Finn*—"I reckon I got to light out for the Territory."[26] On one hand, Huck's flight west embodies the move toward the spatial and imaginative freedom that Gold seeks. The expansion and expansiveness implied by the male myth of westering frequently invigorates Gold's discursive writings as well as *Jews without Money*. His clever essay "Go Left, Young Writers!" frames the birth of proletarian literature as an explorative project for literary folk heroes. "The America of the working class is practically undiscovered. It is like a lost continent. Bits of it come above the surface in our literature occasionally, and everyone is amazed. But there is no need yet of going to Africa or the Orient for strange new pioneering. The young writer can find all the primitive material he needs working as a wage slave around the cities and prairies of America."[27] In *Jews without Money*, the Lower East Side is the Wild West's equivalent and the source for "all the primitive material." Mikey describes a childhood fascination with Buffalo Bill—a fascination that comes from reading serial novels about the dashing figure's escapades—and maps

Huck's flight and plans for "howling adventures amongst the Injuns"[28] onto his own landscape:

> I walked down Hester Street toward Mulberry. Yes, it was like the Wild West. Under the fierce sky Buffalo Bill and I chased buffalo over the vast plains. We shot them down in hundreds. Then a secret message was sent us from a beautiful white maiden. She was a prisoner in the camp of the Indians. The cruel redskins were about to torture her. Buffalo Bill and I rode and rode and rode. In the nick of time we saved her. Two hundred cruel redskins bit the dust before our trusty rifles. We escaped with the white girl, and rode and rode and rode.
>
> So why should I fear these Italian boys? (187)

Of course, when *he* ventures into the Indian Territories of Mulberry Street, Mikey has the stuffing beaten out of him by the Italian boys. Once again merging elements of Jewish mysticism with Americana and his own pugilistic masculinism, the young Mikey concludes from the whole incident that "I needed a Messiah who would look like Buffalo Bill, and annihilate our enemies" (190). It is interesting to compare Gold's hyperbole with Babel's desire for a literary messiah, which he felt multinational Odessa was uniquely capable of producing.

As an adult, Gold found one meeting place for Babel's notion of a literary messiah and Mikey's childhood dream of Buffalo Bill (whose advertising posters proclaimed, messianically, "I am coming")[29] in the figure of John Reed, whom he called a "cowboy out of the west" and believed was "the Real Thing." According to Gold's description, Reed's writing appears to be the answer to Mikey's prayers in literary form: "He liked roughnecks, he took himself to queer, far places, he loafed about cities and the underworld. His eyes were keen, his blood boiled with animal joy. The exuberant words leaped in his prose, they swam like laughing athletes, he wrote with broad humor, he exaggerated the bright suns and moons of nature, he splashed the colors on his canvas like a young god. . . . He burst into American writing like a young genius."[30] Connecting young Mikey's ideals with his own adult revolutionary ideals in a search to find and define proletarian art, Gold writes of Reed: "The revolutionary intellectual is an activist thinker. This is what makes him so different from the careful men with perpetual slight colds who write for the New Republic and The Nation."[31]

America, the Thief

Gold's gleeful Americana ranges easily from the popular culture of the "gaudy little paper books" about Buffalo Bill to the highest of highbrow culture. The password used by Kid Louie's gang to communicate that a girl had been brought to their "camp," "Barlow," happens to be the name of a poet considered to be among the first true American writers. Joel Barlow wrote self-described patriotic, political poems about the discovery of America—most notably the heavily annotated, eight-hundred-page *Columbiad* (1807). Invoking his name, however obliquely, in such an obscene context alludes to the common Yiddish immigrant expression *A klug tsu Columbus,* which Mikey's father utters in a moment of despair after vomiting from the paint fumes he breathes all day: "It is all useless. A curse on Columbus! A curse on America, the thief!" (112).

By positing the Jew as damaged by America, Gold sets his text in direct opposition to widespread popular representations of the Jew as foreign corrupter, such as those found in Henry Ford's *Dearborn Independent,* as well as "high" representations of Jews as alien and dangerous, most notably F. Scott Fitzgerald's characterization of Meyer Wolfsheim in *The Great Gatsby* as the squat, repulsive foreigner who fixed the World Series "with the singlemindedness of a burglar blowing a safe."[32]

As I discussed in the introduction, Gold and Fitzgerald were entering a raging public debate about the origins of Jewish crime. Gold pins the blame upon the capitalist system that necessarily positions the Jew in the dual role of outcast and rebel:

> A legend ran that Louis had a violent father. At fourteen Louis saw his father attempt to beat his mother. Louis pushed the man out of a window and almost killed him. For this the boy was sent to a reformatory.
>
> There the State "reformed" him by carefully teaching him to be a criminal, and by robbing him of his eye.
>
> Is there any gangster who is as cruel and heartless as the present legal State? (90)[33]

Mikey's father bemoans "a land where the lice make fortunes, and the good men starve" (79). This assessment is remarkably close to the line taken by the *Jewish Daily Forward* at the time: "Such a society [in which honest workers remain poor while criminals flourish] is neither Jewish nor Christian; neither American nor European. It is capitalist."[34]

Gold at least partially redeems the gangsters by making them into sacrificial offerings to American capitalism. He furthermore allows that, although "one must hate gangsters as one hates all mercenaries" (125), the Jewish criminal can never be in the same circle of hell as the creators of the American class system; the child Mikey, acting as a sort of juvenile Ivan Karamazov, wonders how the supposed God of love could bring into the world bedbugs, pain, and poverty. Mentally comparing God to a beloved neighborhood horse, Mikey feels certain that "a kind horse like my Ganuf would never have done such a thing" (272). *Ganuf* is Yiddish for thief.

Gold doesn't stop at situating the gangsters morally above the system that he claims spawned them. He also avers that gangsters, precisely because of their ability to exist outside of decorum, can act as public servants for meeker Jews. The feared Louis One-Eye rousts some Italian roughnecks who frighten an old Jew by pulling his ritual beard.[35] Mikey's friend Nigger, already headed toward gangsterdom as a schoolchild, is the only one brave enough to punch out the teacher who called Mikey "LITTLE KIKE" (23).

The gangster's ability to function for a broad audience as an ethnic hero received a major boost in popular culture around the time when Gold was writing *Jews without Money,* with the addition of sound to movies in 1927. Around the same time that the talkies were introduced, the gangster film emerged as a dominant genre. Of course, popular crime movies had been made before this time, but the rise of their popularity was meteoric in the early thirties. As several critics have already noted, at the same moment that sound technology was a hugely important innovation, the conventions and elements that would come to demarcate the gangster genre were defined and refined with speech at their core. Because gangster movies, with their promise of street realism and their heavy reliance on urban slang to accomplish it, were able to make such good use of dialogue, critics tend to agree that gangster movies marked the first sustained success of sound technology in films. A result was that now, largely through their speech, the gangsters could be easily marked as ethnic as well as urban.[36] In arguably the three most important classic gangster films of the period—*Little Caesar* (1930), *The Public Enemy* (1931), and *Scarface* (1932)—immigrant Catholic protagonists (Irish and Italian), played in two of the three cases by Jewish actors, rise and fall according to the requirements of the generic conventions and the active censorship boards.[37]

Of course, as David Ruth has pointed out in his fascinating study of the gangster in American culture, for many popular commentators the circulation of images of the ethnic gangster served as a caution to "ordinary Americans," who were besieged by increasing numbers of working-class immigrants and children of immigrants: "The portrayal of the criminal as an exotic, biologically driven alien reflected some Americans' basic values and promoted powerful cultural and political messages. Its conflation of crime and ethnicity argued for the restriction of immigration and for the vigilant oversight of 'foreigners' already here." Ruth points out that many observers went so far as to match people of different nationalities with particular types of crime: "Irish were drawn to crime by alcoholism resulting from an inherited 'unstable nervous organization'; Italians, with their 'highly excitable and emotional disposition,' excelled at kidnapping, blackmailing and crimes of violence; Russians and Poles, at 'gainful crimes such as robbery, larceny, and receiving stolen goods'; Jews, at white slavery and prostitution."[38]

While Hollywood's participation in a popular discourse linking crime with ethnic "others" no doubt bolstered and confirmed xenophobia, as Ruth argues, this alone cannot account for the broad success of gangster movies, which also found a receptive audience within the immigrant communities. Since the gangsters were almost always the most compelling and charismatic characters in the movies, it was easy to root for them instead of fearing the spread of their corruption. To some, their portrayal would be sympathetic, not frightening, because of their ghetto origins; after all, they were able to "make it" (as evidenced by their flashy consumption of clothes, cars, alcohol, and women) on their own terms despite their humble beginnings and despite their exclusion from the world of privilege. In short, they may have been bad guys, and the law-abiding audience may have breathed a sigh of relief at their necessary downfall, but in the meantime, they were the ones giving orders, the ones who could take care of their own.

As a critic, Gold admired this ability of gangsters to be guardians; in an appreciative essay on Upton Sinclair, he wrote that Sinclair was "as loyal to his friends as a gangster."[39] By using the word "gangster" to applaud Sinclair, Gold underscores the relevance of the outlaw-savior figure to the literary realm. Similarly, in *Jews without Money* Mikey's father's favorite play, he recalls, is Friedrich Schiller's *The Robbers* (1761), which tells the story of a noble bandit who ultimately gives his life so that an innocent man can be spared.

As one of the very few of Gold's myriad of intertexts and subtexts that the narrator mentions by name—twice, at that—the Schiller play deserves some attention. Mikey recalls that his father, Herman Gold, had dreamed of this play in steerage on his way to America, and while on the ship had laboriously translated it into English. These initial ironies are manifold: an immigrant Jew, crammed into unsanitary quarters where he must "shit on the ocean" (as Aunt Bertha in *Call It Sleep* so pithily put it),[40] en route to what he thinks will be "American fun" (104) but what turns out to be a night spent sleeping in a dismal room for immigrants known as the Nigger House, hopes that his contribution to American culture (and the making of his fortune) can be the introduction of a sentimental literary treatment of criminals. Of course, when Herman, after considerable maneuvering, finally obtains an interview with the popular Yiddish actor Mogelescu, he learns that he has been scooped: the play has long been known "even in America" (60).

Although he continues to feel cheated out of *The Robbers*, Herman retains a close connection to his favorite play. He shares his first name with a pivotal character, a pliant old servant who is bribed and deceived into selling out the good (gangster) brother for the sake of money provided by the bad one. The servant uses the money to support his family; however, he lives to regret bitterly his part in the scheme. Also, there is a Jewish gangster in Schiller's play, Moritz Spiegelberg, who is engaged in what Paul Breines calls "a definite if unusual project of Jewish deghettoization and assimilation, namely, crime."[41] The fact that Gold makes so much of this subtext while insisting that there were no Jewish gangsters in Europe (as mentioned above) sets up a necessary uneasiness regarding his enterprise of appropriation; he acknowledges as he undercuts, plunders as he ridicules, invokes as he denies.

The enterprise of uneasy appropriation foregrounds the passage of *Jews without Money* that is most dismissively treated by critics as superfluous: the closing. Even within the parameters of a conversion narrative, which by definition is at least somewhat abrupt, the novel's final page, in which the depressed Mikey suddenly discovers organized politics in general and socialism in particular, is almost unanimously considered to have a tacked-on quality that undercuts or is irrelevant to any narrative power the bulk of the novel might command. Barbara Foley calls *Jews without Money* "the *locus classicus* of troublesome closure in the proletarian novel," while James D. Bloom asserts that "what most readers find compelling in *Jews without Money* is at odds with the book's didactic, apocalyptic closure." Marcus Klein agrees that Gold has provided "the merest formality of an ending for a book," and Walter Rideout admits that "one might accept it as logically possible . . . but not as psychologically or artistically necessary."[42] A few critics, including John Pyros and Marcus Klein, take pains to locate as much thematic foreshadowing of the novel's revolutionary ending as possible, citing passages that refer to the Messiah, or to politics, or to collectivity. But there is a far more compelling surge toward the exultant conclusion of the book, one that takes place on a formal level. Gold's intertextual literary assessments have run a historical gamut from Shakespeare and Schiller to Twain and Emerson. Finally Gold needs to address "new" options for the future of literature in "a skyscraper America."[43]

As Klein has pointed out, every ambitious writer of the 1920s or 1930s was forced to contend with what is now usually called "high modernism," exemplified by the work of T. S. Eliot or Ezra Pound. Klein goes so far as to assert that the classical modernists provided Gold with "the basic tactics of his own thought" in addition to a useful rhetorical enemy.[44] Indeed, Gold frequently positions himself relatively to certain literary modernists; for instance, the title of his book, *Hollow Men*, acknowledges Eliot's imposing stature as much as it rejects his example. But conventional criticism has tended to con-

struct communist aesthetics and literary modernism as mutually exclusive—
if not downright hostile—categories.[45] Of course, the major problem with this
sort of analysis, as Cary Nelson, Barbara Foley, and others have pointed out,
is that it prescribes an extremely narrow and circular definition of what constituted literary modernism, excising not only the proletarians such as Gold
but also the American-vernacular poets such as Carl Sandburg and "ethnic"
writers such as Langston Hughes, despite structural and thematic concerns
they shared with the high modernists, such as attention to language-as-arti-
fact, radical formal experimentation, and incorporation of ambient city noises
into the language of poetry, thereby capturing the term "modernist" for a small
group of writers and limiting its usefulness in terms of understanding literary history or poetic strategy. At the very least, defining literary proletarianism
and literary modernism at each other's expense elides the murkier mutually
defining roles these categories played for each other as positive and negative
examples.[46] One of the modernist writers Gold could neither like nor leave
alone was James Joyce, whom he considered "the supreme expression of the
bourgeois individualist" and accused (among other things) of "the lack of
human feeling" that is the certain result of "the unbridled individualism of
capitalism."[47]

In his frequently disparaged ending to *Jews without Money,* Gold glosses
Joyce's ending to *A Portrait of the Artist as a Young Man,* which perhaps constitutes the most well-known modernist musing upon national identity and
art:

> Welcome, O life! I go to encounter for the millionth time the reality of experi-
> ence and to forge in the smithy of my soul the uncreated conscience of my race.
> . . . Old father, old artificer, stand me now and ever in good stead.[48]

In his own portrait of the proletarian artist as a young man, Gold mimics the
prophetic energy of Joyce's ending but invests his own closure with the antithesis of the "unbridled individualism of capitalism":

> O workers' Revolution, you brought hope to me, a lonely suicidal boy. You are
> the true Messiah. You will destroy the East Side when you come, and build there
> a garden for the human spirit.
> O Revolution, that forced me to think, to struggle and to live.
> O great Beginning!
> THE END. (309)

The swift pullback from the brink of suicide and advance forward into the dawn
of growth and struggle is the answer to Joyce's problem as Gold saw it: Joyce
and his ilk are bound to be "proved inadequate" despite formal achievement.[49]

As an artistic comment, Gold's ending to *Jews without Money* is as pointed and fitting as the message of a drawing that appeared in *New Masses* in 1929, during the same period when parts of *Jews without Money* were being serialized. The drawing, by William Siegel, portrays an orator addressing a demonstration in the streets; the audience carries banners and signs and the speaker exhorts them with raised arm. The caption reads "Proletarian Art."[50] Gold's infamous ending works the same territory: in the picture of activism, in the figure of the street-corner speaker, lies the new definition of modern art. Ultimately, Gold's metaliterary journey directs the reader to a simultaneously hopeful and confounding finale: an ending cry of "Beginning!"

"And Here, Ladies, Is a Spring Poem"

"We were actually kind of proud that Jews could gangster as well as other guys. It seemed only fair."
—former East Side resident at a Boston Workman's Circle forum on "The Day of the Jewish Gangster"

My love, my fragrant, blue-eyed sweetheart, child of
the morning, and of the sun and the moon;
Laughter of my dark days, fragile darling, friend of my
deep heart, listen! the spring is here, the sky is shining
like a butter-fly's blue wing; the tropics are flowing to
our dreary north; it will be summer soon;
And soon, dear, I hope, the coal miners will call their
nation-wide strike; they will raise a black hard fist under
the noses of the arrogant bosses, and shake it there, beloved.
—Mike Gold, "And Here, Ladies, Is a Spring Poem" (1922)

This sarcastic poem, tacked onto the end of a rambling, chatty *Liberator* editorial titled "Thoughts of a Great Thinker,"[51] is nothing so much as a "workerist" attempt to accomplish what James Joyce credited T. S. Eliot with doing in *The Waste Land*: ending "the idea of poetry for ladies."[52] Like the metapoetically modern ending to *Jews without Money,* Gold's concern with abolishing "poetry for ladies" suggests that he has more in common with the modernist project than is generally allowed. Accordingly, he recasts the (feminine) nostalgia and domesticity implicit in his chosen form for *Jews without Money*—the memoir—by means of a brilliantly effective locution, promising to rely upon the "newsreel of memory" to write his book (84). Gold thereby renders public, factual, and contemporary his largely interior account.

This line drawing by William Siegel of a street orator is provocatively titled "Proletarian Art" (*New Masses,* March 1929). Gold's ending to *Jews without Money* makes the same point: the picture of activism contains the new definition of modern art.

In the poem above, the performance of physical defiance—"they will raise a black hard fist under the noses of the arrogant bosses, and shake it there"—distinguishes Gold's new spring poem from the pallid verse the "ladies" expect. At the same time, it separates the (speaking) male body from the (spoken to) female body of the "fragile darling."

The valorization of the male working body, graphic images of which date from the beginning of the industrial revolution, served by the time Gold was writing as a recognizable sign for several binaries: Jewish and gentile; homosexual and heterosexual; female and male; sickly and healthy. As Sander Gilman has impeccably illustrated, one of the most historically available images of Jews was as possessed of a "natural" predisposition to weakness, emaciation, and effeminacy. The ways in which Jewish men have been feminized include myths of Jewish male menstruation, speculations about circumcision, and descriptions of them as "hysterical."[53]

Just as Gilman insists upon the necessity of reading the Zionist leader and physician Max Nordau's well-known call in 1902 for Jews to become "Muscle Jews" within this context of alleged deficiency, so Gold's preoccupation with the writer/fighter/lumberjack manifests an eagerness on his part to craft a working-class Jewish masculinity. According to Paul Breines's formulation, Jews like Gold faced a widespread *double* stereotyping of the Jew: "Modern, postreligious, racial anti-Semitism presented a double image of the Jew: first, as the wielder of immense economic power . . . and second, as physically weak, repulsive, and cowardly."[54] It is easy to see that the title of Gold's book speaks directly to the first part of this double image; his figuration of the Jewish gangster speaks, albeit ambivalently, to the second. Gold's introduction to the book's fifteenth printing in 1935 speaks explicitly to Jew-as-millionaire and Jew-as-weakling, repudiating both through an ideal of masculine proletarianism.

Gold's well-documented masculinism is in Gilman's terms "yet another attempt from within the Jewish community to co-opt the underlying premises of anti-Semitic rhetoric and use its strong political message for [his] own ends." In this regard, an echo can be heard in Gold of Nordau's "cry that we have killed our bodies in the stinking streets of the ghettoes and we must now rebuild them";[55] even Gold's ostensibly admiring observation that Jews have long been known as the people of the book is curtailed by the immediately following explanation for such commitment to literacy: "Shut for twenty centuries from the life of deeds, the broken Jewish nation learned to revere its writers and men of thought" (87).

Gold's connotation—that Jewish bookishness is implicated in Jewish victimization—comes in the context of widespread belief that while Jews excel in higher learning, they are lacking in physical prowess. Dr. A. Meyerson, a Jewish doctor from Boston State Hospital, in his 1920 essay "The Nervousness of the Jew," explained Jewish male weakness by positing that Jews were

a race of inferior physique, in that all those occupations that tend to develop strength of the body and hardihood were forbidden. . . . They lived in small towns, perhaps, but in crowded, dirty, disagreeable towns. In this urban life not only was a sedentary life necessary, but the race developed a curious antipathy to exercise and even to play. For centuries the Jews were a race that despised sports and discountenanced play. . . . [A]nd the children of the race grew up to be very serious, very earnest, too early devoted to mature efforts, excessively cerebral in their activities, and not sufficiently strenuous physically. *In other words, the Jew, through his restrictions, was cheated out of childhood.*[56]

Gold responds defensively to accusations of Jewish weakness. He takes pains to portray Jewish boys as just like any other little boys, citing their play in particular: "Our gang played the universal games, tag, prisoner's base, duck on a rock. Like boys in Africa or Peru, we followed the seasons religiously for kites, tops and marbles" (38). He is careful to qualify his own position as a typical Jewish prodigy, assuring the reader that "I was a precocious pupil in the public school, winning honors *not by study, but by a kind of intuition*" (303, emphasis added). The word "intuition" ties Gold as a writer and as a male to the young hero of his famous essay "Go Left, Young Writers!" who produces brilliant work precisely because "it is all instinct with him."[57]

The problem, then, is not Jewish male intellectualism per se, but rather that thought has been separated from physical labors. One of *Jews without Money*'s most astute and sympathetic characters, the honest intellectual Dr. Solow, avers that "there should be more Jewish farmers in the world" (234) and that the traditional Jewish ideal of study cannot "cure" the East Side. Solow's sentiment refers to early Soviet policies (beginning in 1924) of returning Jews to the land by setting up a Jewish Land Settlement Society to create Jewish collective farms in the Crimea. Many Jewish American socialists found a workable socialist utopia in the notion of a Jewish collective farm. Leon Dennen, author of *Where the Ghetto Ends* (1934), was an American Jew who traveled to the Crimea as it was being colonized by Jewish farmers. He reported that "a new life is being forged by Jews on soil" following the death of the Russian Jewish ghetto during the Russian Revolution. The fictional Dr. Solow's confidence that farms would be the salvation of the Jews is corroborated by Dennen's enthusiasm for what he discovers in the Jewish settlements: "Indeed, the typical ghetto Jew, destroyed and demoralized, inspired very little confidence in his ability to work on the soil. It was necessary to have the daring inspiration of a revolution to transform these Jews into peasants. It was an experiment. It is now a reality. The ghetto Jew is gradually being transformed into a new man."[58]

American capitalism, by contrast, offers Jews brutal physical work without access to ideas and books; and this, as Mikey discovers during his first humiliating job hunt, also leads to despair and squelched ambitions. Mikey's childhood friend, Joey Cohen, a "dreamy boy in spectacles . . . [who] was always reading books" (49), dies under the wheels of a horse car. When his body is recovered, Mikey recalls, "O what a horrible joke happened. The head was missing" (49). As well as underscoring the everyday carnivalesque in his brutal urban gothic (Gold calls East Side life a "carnival" in the first section), in which a child's decapitation is not out of place, Gold means quite literally a horrible joke on his own part: in a book that is obsessed with the cutting off of body from mind, a bespectacled, book-reading, gentle Jewish male's head is severed from his skinny body.

A much less touching instance of this severing is the repulsive immigrant Fyfka the Miser. Fyfka is described with hyperbolic disgust: "This thing, this Fyfka the Miser, this yellow somnambulist, this nightmare bred of poverty, this maggot-yellow dark ape with twisted arm and bright, peering, melancholy eyes; human garbage can of horror; fevered Rothschild in a filthy shirt; madman in an old derby hat" (76). The portrait of Fyfka's repulsiveness crescendos to a revelation that the "monster" suffered from "a horrible conflict between body and mind" (76) that he cannot resolve: he wants to sleep with a woman, but he is too miserly to pay the usual price of fifty cents. By the time Mikey meets him, Fyfka is diseased in both mind and body.

Unlike the damaged Fyfka, the book's "muscle Jews"—youthful or adult gang members—realize they must take history into their own hands. They instinctively recognize their need to shed physical meekness and inhibition; as Paul Breines notes, "Jewish toughness, like the anti-Semitism it abhors, is literally a body politics, a politics of ideal bodily images and the moral virtues that supposedly inhere in them: courage, dedication to the national-racial cause, loyalty, self-discipline, readiness for self-sacrifice, robustness, manliness, and so on."[59] So when Mikey's gang, the Young Avengers, confronts the Irish boy who has forbidden Mikey to sell newspapers in the neighborhood, they are able to defend their persons and their group honor by surprising the gentile world with an act of violence:

> I was the first member to be avenged. A big Irish boy who sold newspapers at Houston Street and the Bowery beat me up several times, and tore up my papers. "I'll murder you, kid, if yuh peddle around here again," he said.
> The Young Avengers trailed me one afternoon. The big Irish boy, as usual, rushed at me like a bulldog. But the five of us fell upon him with whoops and cries, punching and clawing in a pinwheel of gory excitement. We defeated him. It was the first victory for the Young Avengers. (261)

In a letter to Jewish left-wing poet Edwin Rolfe in 1938, who was fighting in the Spanish Civil War as a member of the voluntary Lincoln Brigades, Gold seeks literary potential in the increased "manliness" of the American men who return from the war: "Ed, I envy you your present experience. It must be a hard life, but one that arouses epic feeling in a man. I would not recommend war as a stimulus for writing, yet I am sure that many of the boys who come back from Spain will be the organizers, writers and leaders of the next decade in America. The ones I have met here seem to my impressionable mind to have acquired a certain manliness and quiet power that is impressive in youth."[60]

Gold's chain of reasoning, which links martial experience, manliness, and creativity, results in a gendering of the entire question of revolutionary literature. Recent feminist revisionist literary histories of American proletarian literature, most notably by Paula Rabinowitz and Barbara Foley, have amply demonstrated the infusion by Gold and his colleagues of the rhetoric of proletarian culture with masculinism. (Indeed, Rabinowitz ventures that by now Gold's sexism and heterosexism are "commonplace knowledge.") Rabinowitz writes: "During the 1930s, class struggle in the United States was metaphorically engendered through a discourse that represented class conflict through the language of sexual difference. The prevailing verbal and visual imagery reveled in an excessively masculine and virile proletariat poised to struggle against the effeminate and decadent bourgeoisie."[61] Gold's decidedly obnoxious masculinism stems from an eagerness to distinguish his own position from that of the traditionally feminized intellectual as much as from the (sometimes overlapping category of) traditionally feminized Jew—in short, the bookish Jew he is so concerned with in *Jews without Money*. Thus *as a rhetorical device* the category of "worker" is potently male for Gold, although his writings (including *Jews without Money*) occasionally portray "factory girls" and other working women, thereby betraying the author's own device to some extent. In 1921 Gold produced a celebration of workers that is Whitmanesque in its catalog:

> Who make up the unemployed? Workers. Workers: three giant American lumberjacks from the Maine woods, standing proudly and somberly like dying trees. Sailors, in rough, wrinkled clothes. Battered, emaciated factory hands. Dazed old derelicts with white, unshaven chins and doggish eyes. Young Huskies, veterans of the war, usually slangy and cheerful, but hanging their heads in shame. Stokers, cooks, waiters, mechanics, farmers, drivers, clerks and longshoremen, useful citizens of the world, creators of wealth, the hard-handed architects of society.[62]

Gold's appreciative list leaves out women workers. Howard Lee Hertz, who addresses this passage in his dissertation on Gold, refers accurately but without comment to the workers as "these men." As Foley points out, the language "reveals a marked tendency to associate lefties with broad strides and muscled shoulders—as if physical strength were not simply a metaphor for, but an actual carrier of, revolutionary politics."[63]

In 1929 Gold articulated an often-cited ideal for the new socialist writer in America. In his essay "Go Left, Young Writers!" he explicitly counterpoises powerful, working-class, male-identified writing to effete, bourgeois, female-identified writing: "A new writer has been appearing; a wild youth of about twenty-two, the son of working-class parents, who himself works in the lumber camps, coal mines, and steel mills, harvest fields and mountains camps of America. He is sensitive and impatient. He writes in jets of exasperated feeling and has no time to polish his work. He is violent and sentimental by turns."[64] In other words, Gold would have proletarian writers accomplish in narrative exactly what James D. Bloom astutely notes that the gangster Nigger accomplishes in illicit deed: the "wedding [of] sympathy and defiant . . . violence."[65] The ejaculatory "jets" of unfettered creativity represent a return from a metaphor of masculinity to a full-fledged biological essentialism.

Walter Kalaidjian, in his discussion of "Left Androcentrism and the Male Dynamo," locates the dominant masculinist metaphorical systems of the Communist Party of the United States back in the actual male body through "the typical symbols of proletarian solidarity—the vertical red banner of class brotherhood, the assertive upraised fist (often clenching a weighty tool such as wrench, sledgehammer, or sickle), the contractual handshake, the muscle-bound torso." Kalaidjian asserts that "vanguard [graphic] artists . . . were especially prone to such male-gendered visual codes."[66] Indeed, the cover art of *New Masses,* in which *Jews without Money* was first published serially, abounded with drawings by the likes of Fred Ellis, Rockwell Kent, or Hugo Gellert, depicting hugely muscled workingmen, with exposed chests, thighs, and even genitals.

The six woodcuts by Howard Simon that illustrate the original issue of *Jews without Money,* like Gold's conversion narrative itself, strain toward the masculine code as a concluding ideal. Simon's first illustration is of a nursing mother, surrounded by other children and elders. The second shows a child, mouth agape, watching as a scantily clad woman (presumably a prostitute) conducts her business amid the pushcart trade on the street. The next two plates show Orthodox Jewish men in traditional beards and clothing, carrying the Torah scroll in one and praying over the corpse of Mikey's sister Esther in the other. These five dark woodcuts, each poignant and affecting, represent the tragic and the old, even down to the fact that each depicts either in the foreground or the background elderly Jews in traditional garb. But the last woodcut, which in the first edition faces the verbal account of Mikey's conversion to socialism, is shot through with angular bolts of sunlight. The sunbeams point to and illuminate a male body held aloft—the male speaker on the East Side soapbox who tells Mikey of "a world movement . . . to abolish poverty" (309). The speaker, defiant arm raised, is surrounded by a group of strong, young-looking men.

To consider "autobiographical" fiction in terms of its degree of correspondence to the biographical details of the author's life is likely to be unsatisfying for several reasons. Gold's literary executor, Michael Folsom, warns that although "Gold often lacked a clear sense of the distinction between fiction and autobiographical fact," he nonetheless manages to convey to the reader "the inescapable sense that we are reading fact."[67] But in some cases it is precisely the departure from "fact" that signifies. In the spirit of Mikey's salvation, Gold claimed an epiphanic moment in his own youth, from which he dates his involvement with organized revolutionary politics. That moment was hearing Elizabeth Gurley Flynn address a May Day rally in Union Square.[68] The impetus for turning one of the Communist Party's most famous and effective speakers (and eventual national chairperson)—and an Irish American woman—into an anonymous man on a soapbox seems evident in the attractively powerful male body represented in Simon's woodcut. Gold not only protects the notion of manly "jets of feeling"; he also allows the possibility that the speaker was a Jew, a Messiah who looks like Buffalo Bill and who offers a strong alternative to the book's defeated Jewish intellectual, Reb Samuel.

Thus, conversion to socialism becomes a triumph of manhood. Correspondingly, a writer's willingness or failure to confront the realities of class struggle becomes for Gold a test of masculinity. Although he is usually tagged as rejecting all writers he called "bourgeois," Gold actually differentiates among these writers. What appears categorical is Gold's tendency to evaluate other writers in terms of their level of masculinity. Thorton Wilder was a homosexual, and by extension, womanly: "a daydream of homosexual figures in graceful gowns moving archaically among the lilies." Robinson Jeffers was "fearful . . . of women." Gold's colleague Jack Conroy, expressing his admiration for Gold's literary potency, wrote that "the stale bohemian writer, recognizing the vigor of the new proletarian literature, sadly contemplates his own wilted phallus, and howls that the Goddess of Pure Art is being raped by barbarians."[69]

If the virile gangster Nigger embodies the creatively defiant Jew, the female teacher he strikes embodies the derivative gentility of a Wilder or a Jeffers. By having Nigger punch the teacher, Gold assails what Ann Douglas has called the feminization of American culture. In *No Man's Land: The Place of the Woman Writer in the Twentieth Century,* Sandra Gilbert and Susan Gubar explore literary modernism as a result and expression of male panic at the entry of women in large numbers into the literary marketplace. Gilbert and Gubar marshal a remarkable array of evidence of anxiety about female literary power among Gold's contemporaries, which was thought to be eroding and diluting American letters. For instance, Van Wyck Brooks determined in 1922:

The last of the six woodcuts by Howard Simon that illustrated the original edition of *Jews without Money* (1930) equates angular, male imagery with hope, strength, and modernity (facing page). This comes in sharp contrast to the much darker and busier first five woodcuts, which foreground female bodies, children, and Jews in traditional clothing and beards, as in this marketplace scene (above).

"Samson had lost his virility. The American writer who 'goes wrong' is in a similar state." Harold Stearns fretted the same year that "hardly any intelligent foreigner has failed to observe and comment upon the extraordinary feminization of American social life, and . . . the intellectual anemia or torpor that seems to accompany it. . . . The men have been feminized."[70] Meanwhile, the sexual incapacity of female writers—along the lines of Gold's characterization of the teacher as a childless virgin—was to become a common refrain among modern and postmodern men of letters.

According to Leslie Fiedler, the high-culture modernist felt himself to be under assault by a culture simultaneously commercialized and feminized.[71] In this regard Gold's doggedly populist aesthetic proved not always to be a competing discourse with modernism; the gendered language of his attacks on bourgeois decay reveals a significant congeniality to the cultural horror experienced by the modernists. A vivid instance is Gold's story "Love on a Garbage Dump" (1928). The plot, insofar as there is one, deals with romantic love; the story's moral vision revolves around cultural politics. The story opens with Gold's adamant (and inaccurate) denial that he ever attended Harvard College, the existence of "slander" to that effect slightingly explained by the admission that he once lived and worked in "Boston, city of Harvard."[72] The joy of working on a garbage dump is that the job allowed Gold to trample, spit upon, and contemptuously shovel newspapers (printed lies) all day. The story ends with the young narrator's affirmation of "proletarian realities" as he imagines marching with the Communist Party, which had not yet been founded in the United States when the story takes place.

Gold's youthful travails are schematized in the story as a choice between two women: Concha, a young Portuguese beauty who works with him on the garbage dump, and a stranger, whose silhouette he has glimpsed bent over a piano while the strains of Mozart float down from a Beacon Hill window. The embarrassingly hot-blooded Concha finally invites the narrator to her house, only to make him feel that "physical love had betrayed [him] again" by asking for a dollar. The disillusioned narrator complies, but leaves to walk the streets in gloom, and again hears the piano-playing aristocrat. It is at this moment that the heartbreaking commercialization of culture (Concha, the "melodious lark" of the dump asking for pay for her favors) is linked to its feminization: "It is that lazy, useless parasite who plays Mozart who forced Concha so low!"[73] The vision of Concha "forced . . . so low" and the pianist up high "on Beacon Hill" also represents the coercive nature of the high culture–low culture split,[74] a split Gold as cultural critic addresses in a theater review for *New Masses* that he called "High Brow vs. Low Brow." Commenting that if he had to choose between high brow and low brow, he would prefer the vulgarity of the low to the phony elitism of what is considered high, Gold holds out for the day when "great playwrights will yet rise out of the mass-life of America, out from the workers, and they will have guts, brains and imagination. They will tell us what America is really like, and where it is going."[75] In the story, the narrator arrives at the same revolutionary conclusion and rejects the "high" pianist and the "low" Concha for the "harsh, strong, clean anger" of his masculine revolutionary fantasy of marching to the communist barricades.[76]

The same feminizing of commercial culture that this story accomplishes orders *Jews without Money*: Mikey recalls the sentimental song-sheets—"The Rabbi's Daughter," "She's Only A Bird in a Gilded Cage"—his mother and his aunt weep over.[77] These tearjerkers are at once baldly commercial and distinctly feminine:

> My mother shook her head again, and tears were in her eyes.
> "*Ai,* how sad that is, how sad and beautiful!" she said. "It is just like life."
> I look back at that moment. I know a cynic or a Broadway clown must have written those songs, with tongue in cheek, maybe, for money. (134)[78]

The restaurateur Moscowitz, plays music that by contrast is "soulful and wild" for Mikey and his father. Moscowitz, Mikey tells us, "is a real artist—after twenty years he still makes restaurant music with his heart, and has never saved any money" (115–16).

Any mention of money is immediately loaded, given the book's title. Gold's sole outright repudiation of criminals seems lukewarm and perfunctory at first glance, but ultimately serves a powerful metaliterary purpose by connecting the figure of the gangster to the figure of the writer through their economic vulnerability. Gold writes, "One must hate gangsters, as one hates all mercenaries" (125), cementing the parallel even further in the *New Masses* version by continuing, "One buys them the way one buys journalists."[79] He goes on to observe that sometimes gangsters work against the police (the gangsters in his book do), but sometimes they work for them. Of all the writers treated in this study, Gold regards his gangsters in the most ambivalent manner; their audacious masculinity has creative potential, but the question is still, Which side are you on?

Gold's preoccupation with masculinity, of course, bespeaks anxiety as well as ambition. As a vigorous literary model, the male gang is vexed. These interactions among men or boys are without question the novel's source of masculine activities, the masculine activities Gold insisted writers required; he purportedly sneered to Sinclair Lewis that literary humanists were nursing a "mad jealousy" because they had been "deprived of masculine experience."[80] Mikey can never resist taunting his sister when she must stay home and be "good" while he is out garnering oppositional boyish experience. Esther's eventual death under the wheels of a cart connects her to Joey, the overly dreamy, girlish boy.

But although it does stake off tough male terrain, the male gang is by definition passionately homosocial, if not downright homoerotic, and this tension must be reconciled with Gold's well-documented critical homophobia. Mikey experiences an attraction/revulsion dialectic for the gang expressed in highly sexualized terms. He is sickened by his own small participation in the gang rape that takes place in a hideout known as the Camp:

"Barlow, just say Barlow to Shorty, Truck, Fat, and the others," he once commanded me. I did not know what it meant. When I said "Barlow" to the gang, their exuberant comments made it clear. I was ashamed of myself. I refused the nickel one of them offered me, and ran away.

Kid Louie would take a girl's clothes from her, and lock her in the "Camp." Then the other men went in, one after the other. Sometimes all of them went in together; this was a "line-up." (28)

The vision of "all of them . . . together" has homosexual overtones that are at least as repellent to Mikey as is the cruelty toward the helpless girl.

But at the other end of the spectrum are more compelling (less repulsive) homosexual erotic moments. There is only one instance in the novel in which Mikey's sexuality is expressed as anything other than sordid. This is his necessarily pure, unconsummated infatuation with his beautiful, young Aunt Lena.

"Aunt Lena," I said, "you'll be sure to marry me when I grow up, won't you?"
"Yes, Mikey, dear, it's you I'll marry."
"Do you swear it?"
"Yes, see, Mikey, I kiss my little finger and swear it. You'll grow up and be a famous rich doctor, and then I'll marry you. You, only you, Mikey!"
She kissed me, and my heart beat wildly. (133)

The fact that Lena is Mikey's aunt and his elder establishes her as merely a formal, not an actual, object of desire. She becomes a chaste displacement of the eroticized attraction the vital world of the gangsters commands; in a highly charged scene, Mikey and Louis One-Eye compete on the rooftop for possession of Lena's revealed body.

Louis bent over, and touched my aunt's hair with his hot stubby hand. She sat there paralyzed.
"Run along, Mike, I want to talk to your aunt."
I stared at him. I couldn't move. In a moment I felt that I would fling myself at his legs, bite them, do anything to save my aunt. He put his hands on my aunt's kimono and tried to tear it open." (138–39)

At this moment, Lena, who has never been a real sexual option, has become decidedly redundant. Mikey overlaps with her identity in the scenario: she is "paralyzed," and he likewise "couldn't move." Instead, he has an oral fantasy about Louis's legs.

Louis One-Eye, by contrast, remains hypermasculinized. His nickname alone is crassly phallic. As Eve Kosofsky Sedgwick points out (reading through Freud and Girard), "in any erotic rivalry, the bond that links the two rivals is as intense and potent as the bond that links either of the rivals to the beloved." If Mikey's attraction/revulsion for the gang is located on Sedgwick's "homosocial continuum," then Gold's masculinism—and its critical legacy in communist cultural rhetoric and modernist letters—is fruitfully considered in terms of the questions she poses: "Why should the different shapes of the homosocial continuum be an interesting question? Why should it be a *literary* question?"[81]

In the case of *Jews without Money*, it is a literary question because a struggle between competing masculinities is one way to characterize what James D. Bloom calls Gold's "Kulturkampf."[82] Gold established his criticism on these grounds and, as Paula Rabinowitz has written, thereby "set the tone for the homophobic and antifeminine rhetoric of literary radicals."[83] He establishes the same sense of male contest in *Jews without Money* by presenting pairs of masculine alternatives. Joey, the dreamy boy with no stomach to kill (he feels guilty when he squashes a butterfly) is symbolically castrated when he is beheaded; earlier, he had been the victim of sexual assault by a male pedophile. Joey is introduced in the same chapter as the grammar-school teacher, who plays the mannish woman to his girlish boy: described as a "ruptured virgin" (37), she recalls a man whose testicles have burst. The gangster Nigger triumphs over both; first he punches the teacher, and then he steals a ride on a streetcar the very day Joey is killed by one to show he is not afraid. Finally, the male gang emerges as the most perfect presentation of competing masculinities. From the turf battles of ghetto children to the turf battles of adult racketeers to the turf battles of culture warriors, Gold helped to naturalize a large-scale story of cultural contest and artistic heroism.

The level of success of Gold's macho pyrotechnics is measured by the kinds of critical attention he has—or has not—received over the years. As the first section of this study posits, Gold's extensive intertextuality has been overlooked to a remarkable degree. To pay attention to it would lift Gold into the category of the studious Jew, a category he strenuously resisted. The extreme literariness of Gold's work would seem to indicate that writing is not "all instinct with him." Nonetheless, Gold's critical reception indicates an unspoken willingness to take him on his own masculinist terms—a willingness that stretches from the first review of *Jews without Money* in *New Masses* to the present feminist treatments by Paula Rabinowitz and Walter Kalaidjian; a willingness that unites (with few exceptions) Gold's admirers with his detractors; a willingness that often paradoxically coexists with strong moves to question the terms of Gold's organized, rather than sexual-linguistic, politics.

"Talk. Jewish Talk."

Jews and thieves were both worldly dangers to the Christian order. They both spoke related (if not identical) languages, at least as perceived by the Christian world.

—Sander Gilman, *Jewish Self-Hatred*

To me, Yiddish is the Robin Hood of languages.

—Leo Rosten, *Hooray for Yiddish!*

We are in the direct, legitimate line, we are people based in English as our mother tongue, and we do not abuse it or misuse it, and when we speak a word, we know what it means. These others . . . have fallen into a curious kind of argot, more or less originating in New York, a deadly mixture of academic, guttersnipe, gangster, fake-Yiddish, and dull old worn-out dirty words—an appalling bankruptcy in language, as if they hate English and are trying to destroy it along with all other living things they touch.

—Katherine Anne Porter, "A Country and Some People I Love"

From the writings of Martin Luther, who alleged that Jews used a "hidden" language to cheat vulnerable Christians, to present-day television cop shows, where tough guys and hit men still speak an obviously Jewish-inflected Brooklynese, a discussion of Jewish talk *is* a discussion of Jewish criminality, and vice versa. Jewish talk and criminality have long been understood as mutually constitutive; as Sander Gilman explains, a "systematic Christian interest in Yiddish" as the key to Jewish conspiracy followed the Protestant appropriation of Hebrew. Citing (among other documents) Johann Christoph Wagenseil's *Instruction in the Jewish-German Manner of Reading and Writing* (1699), Johann Andreas Eisenmenger's *Discovered Judaism* (1700), and Johann Christoph Gottfried's *Jewish Lies* (1714), Gilman discovers "an important Christian tradition of seeing the Jews and their evils as embodied within their writings and their language":

> By the beginning of the eighteenth century the idea that the Jews possessed a language in which they were able to conceal their evils had come to refer to Yiddish. Yiddish was the means by which Jews were able to undermine the authority of the Christian state. Thus the language of the Jews and the thieves' cant, both made up of German with elements of Hebrew and Aramaic, both written in Hebrew (or pseudo-Hebrew) characters, had come to be identical. The language of the Jews was the language of thieves, for the Jews were quintessential thieves.[84]

Yiddish did not so obsess American Protestants during the eighteenth and nineteenth centuries. But starting around the turn of the twentieth century, the influx of Eastern European Jews in mass numbers gave rise to a concern akin to the interest Gilman traces in Enlightenment Europe. Henry Adams imagined a "furtive Yacoob or Yssac . . . snarling weird Yiddish"; Henry James was dismayed by the sordid Jewish East Side cafés he called "torture-rooms of the living idiom"; Henry Ford's popular *Dearborn Independent* warned about perceived Jewish types whose speech as well as appearance gave them away as gangsters.[85] Even police commissioner Theodore A. Bingham's notorious report in 1908, which estimated that 50 percent of all New York criminals were Jews, posits an inevitable Jewish criminality connected to Jewish language: "Wherefore it is not astonishing that with a million Hebrews, mostly Russian, in the city . . . perhaps half of the criminals should be of that race, when we consider that ignorance of the language, particularly among men not physically fit for hard labor, is conducive to crime."[86] Drawing upon old notions of Jews as unable to work the land—and therefore inclined to live, be it as middlemen or thieves, as parasites—Bingham introduces a "logical" connection between the mysteries of Jewish physique, Jewish language, and Jewish contravention.

As I noted above, in the classic gangster movies Jewish actors defined screen toughness through a barely disguised Jewish affect. The Jew is not particularly marked as criminal (a gangster identified explicitly as Jewish did not make a film appearance until the 1960s); rather, qualities of the "criminal" are frequently figured through Jewishness (particularly Jewish speech), by Jews. Thus, although Neil Gabler has said (and it has been generally accepted) that the first sound movie, *The Jazz Singer* (1927), represented the first—and last—moment when Jewishness was explored on screen until after World War II,[87] the gangster subject provided a way for Jewishness to be explored in the movies. For Jewish audiences, even a certain amount of interethnic exploration was made possible through the figures of the gangsters. For instance, although the protagonist of *The Public Enemy* (1931) is an Irish American gangster named Tommy Powers, when Powers becomes "big enough," he is able to join forces with a gangster who is never explicitly identified as Jewish, but who introduces himself as "Nails Nathan—born Samuel." A crucial scene in the movie has various gangsters, including Powers and Nathan, in a business meeting with a "legitimate" businessman, a liquor manufacturer. This stiff, hypocritical character is a German Jew—his name is Lehmann—whose spoken English is proper and clipped. The energy of the scene derives from how much more vibrant, honest, and self-assured the Russian Jew is, whose English is cast as criminal slang in the mouth of Nails Nathan. Jewish talk accomplishes a lot here: through it, the shifting and overlapping categories of criminal and legitimate, German Jew and Slavic Jew, standard and vernacular, resistant and accommodationist, are investigated and judged. This exploration occurs just below the surface, at a moment in film history when Jewishness is generally believed to have been kept off screen.

Since Jewishness is not named in this movie or is sublimated in much the same way as when Edward G. Robinson uses familiar stage-Jew gestures to play an Italian mobster in *Little Caesar* (1930), recognizably Jewish affect—most notably speech—becomes naturalized as criminal. In the scene described above, the German Jew/East European Jew split is transposed onto the businessman/gangster split. Through such processes of transposition, American popular culture has followed the tradition limned by Sander Gilman, in which Jewish speech and criminality are conflated.

The ability of a Jewish actor to use his Jewishness to define and contain what would come to be known simply as tough urban sensibility is conveyed by an animated Little Audrey cartoon, *Mother Goose* (1947). In the cartoon, the child protagonist—who seems to live somewhere in the country, probably the South—encounters a modern, urban, and hip Mother Goose. The criminal in the strip, whose name is Boid-Brain ("bird" spelled b-o-i-d), has ambitions of being "the sensational foist criminal at Fort Knox." Edward G. Robinson, with his tendency toward stage-Jew gestures (such as talking with his hands), is invoked to represent generic criminality: Little Audrey meets a modern Humpty-Dumpty, drawn as the stocky Robinson, and when he falls off his wall he jumps up and snarls, "I'm hardboiled, see? Can't crack me up." In another cartoon, *Racketeer Rabbit* (1946), Bugs Bunny dresses as the handsome gangster Bugsy Siegel and flips a quarter in the trademark gangster gesture of the Jewish actor and gambler George Raft (who plays an Italian gangster in *Scarface*), a close friend and associate of the real Bugsy. In the same cartoon, Bugs Bunny, like Little Audrey, comes up against an Edward G. Robinson look-alike. Both drawl in Jewish-inflected talk. In this scene, as in all Bugs Bunny cartoons, Bugs's humorous transgressiveness is partly defined through his speech; he declares, "It's coitins for you, Rocky, coitins," before hanging a pair of drapes around the cartoon Robinson's neck. Mel Blanc, the Jewish vocalizer who provided the voice for Bugs Bunny, claimed in his autobiography to have been trying to characterize Bugs as a tough Brooklynite because "Brooklynites were associated with con artists and crooks. Without a doubt the stereotype was derived from the many motion-picture gangsters who always seemed to speak in Flatbush Avenue-ese. Consequently . . . Bugs Bunny wouldn't say *jerk*, he'd say *joik*."[88] These cartoons are slapstick treatments of police commissioner Bingham's notion that Jewish speech is synonymous with criminal speech—a notion that entered the mainstream of American popular culture through the wild popularity of the gangster movie coinciding with the introduction of the talkies.

In *Jews without Money* Gold tackles wholeheartedly the charge that in talk lies the secret identity of the Jews:

> Talk has ever been the joy of the Jewish race, great torrents of boundless exalted talk. Talk does not exhaust Jews as it does other people, nor give them brain-fag; it refreshes them. Talk is the baseball, the golf, the poker, the love and the war of the Jewish race.
>
> The whole tenement was talking and eating its supper. The broken talk came through the airshaft window. The profound bass of the East Side traffic lay under this talk. Talk. Talk. Rattle of supper dishes, whining of babies, yowling of cats; counterpoint of men, women and children talking as if their hearts would break. Talk. Jewish talk. (113)

His narrator apparently accepts the readily available terms of discussion—that Jews are revealed by their speech—only to revalue the assumption completely. By transforming the "weird Yiddish" into something venerable and profound, he crafts a collective identity wherein talk turns the whole tenement—and by extension the Jewish community—into a single sentient organism. Indeed, descriptions of people talking liberally pepper the pages of the book, the diction of which is conversational; through speech, Gold effects a powerful act of self-definition through self-expression.

New Yawk, New Yawk

Two kinds of Jewish talk inform *Jews without Money*. There are the Jewish languages—Gold represents both Hebrew, the ancient, sacred language of Jewish religion and law, and Yiddish, the vernacular spoken by Jews across Eastern Europe from about the thirteenth century. There is also Jewish-inflected English, which is really a dialectical process by which elements of Yiddish and Hebrew are continuously carried by Jewish speakers into English and vice versa; an example is Mikey's description of his mother as a "buttinsky" or Herman's reference to Baruch Goldfarb as a "real estatenik." Conversely, during this process American values are carried through speech acts into the life of the Jew; Mikey's father, kept overnight at Ellis Island, passes the time by shouting English words he knows: "Match! all right! go to hell! potato!" (104).

Writers of Gold's generation who attempted to reproduce the dynamism of this linguistic blending—either with horror or with appreciation—frequently grappled with the ways that the character of Yiddish could enter the English in which they wrote. For instance, in his masterpiece of the Jewish ghetto, *Call*

It Sleep (1934), Henry Roth renders spoken Yiddish into English in a fashion that lends it extraordinary grace and eloquence, in contrast to the harsh, broken English spoken by various characters on the street:

> "She looked so frail in death, in her shroud—how shall I tell you, my son? Like early winter snow. And I thought to myself, even then, let me look deeply into her face, for surely she will melt before my eyes."

> "Ow!" Yussie capered about for their further benefit. "Please, papa, lemme go! Ooh lemme go! Bang! Annudder smack he gabe 'im. Right inne ass!"
> "Wad 'e hitcha fuh?" They circled about him.
> "He hid 'im because he kicked me righd inna nose," crowed Yussie. "Right over hea, an' made blood."[89]

Through his mutually filtered representations of Yiddish and English, Roth seems to be making a polemic. The question is no longer only what the Jews are doing to English, as Henry James worried—in Roth's novel they cannot seem to help mangling it—but also what English is doing to the Jews, who speak with extravagant beauty in Yiddish but flounder or grate in English.

Because they are possessed of an adaptive power to create a hyphenated identity by violating boundaries, Jewish speech acts are inseparable (and sometimes indistinguishable) from Jewish criminal acts. In Reginald Wright Kauffman's *House of Bondage,* a spectacularly popular white-slavery novel published in 1910, anxiety about Jewish corruption of gentile women is intertwined with anxiety about Jewish corruption of English:

> Impulsively she had refused an answer to his first words; but the young man was a member of the persistent race, and speedily followed the first speech with a second.
> "Chust say the vord," he pleaded, "und I von' bother you no more. I only vanted to make myself *square* with you.[90]

In this passage, the young man has obviously attempted to master American slang—"*square* vith you"—for nefarious purposes, but the foreignness of his speech nonetheless reveals his true nature.

In *Jews without Money,* the speech of Mikey's father, the master storyteller, is marked by Yiddish syntax as well as occasional Yiddish words.[91] For instance, at one point in his coming-to-America narration, Herman uses the English word "so" eight times in sixteen lines (108). The repetition of the word is designed to reflect not a corresponding Yiddish conjunction but rather Yiddish word order. According to the rules of Yiddish grammar, the verb must occupy the second position in a sentence. ("I have a brother" could be "Ikh hob a bruder" or "A bruder hob ikh.") When the verb appears as the first word in a

Yiddish sentence, there is an implication that a summary of everything previously related actually fills the first semantic position; Gold is therefore replacing
the work done by the *absence* of a first word in Yiddish with the summarizing
"so." In this fashion Gold establishes his text as a dialogue between two languages that merges the shape of both.

The Jewish gangsters occupy the same space as Gold's miscegenating text.
Although they tower above other characters as more ominous or more heroic,
they are awarded fewer lines to speak in their own voices than other major
characters. They are silent except insofar as voices speak about and around
them, and thus through them. Rather than being actual speaking people, they
become an arena wherein different voices swirl, meet, debate, and define,
reflecting the plethora of public opinion that surrounded the doings of the
actual Jewish gangsters of Gold's day. The gangsters function as an aural vari-
ant of Gold's play on Emerson's invisible eyeball that sees all without being
seen. Indeed, they acquire a degree of transparency akin to natural forces; they
are likened to the rain, which falls at one point "like a gangster's blood" (61),
and to the sun, which "in the hot summer turns gangster" (126).

Because of their virtual silence, the few words the gangsters do utter acquire
an unusual portentousness. Nigger's only spoken lines describe to Mikey "the
way babies are made" (25), invoking the process of cultural as well as biological birth and establishing the gangster as generative, particularly vis-à-vis the
Jewish writer, Mikey, to whom Nigger teaches the facts of life before beating
him up. And in his own frightening way, the sullen Louis One-Eye reinserts a
violent linguistics into the mating process, saying, "Run along, Mike, I want
to talk to your aunt" (138) when what he wants to do is rape her, so that "talk
to" becomes equivalent to "sexually penetrate."

Thus, while the overly gentle are consistently silenced (Joey and Esther
through early death, and Reb Samuel by literally losing his ability to speak after
suffering his great disappointment), the gangsters, bums, and saloon-keepers
achieve a linguistic plurality that allows them to transcend social boundaries.
According to standard immigrant wisdom, the assimilation necessary for success is contained in language. A number of immigrant narratives, ranging from
the heartrending (as in Anzia Yezierska's *Bread Givers* [1925]) to the slapstick
(as in Leo Rosten's *Education of H*Y*M*A*N K*A*P*L*A*N* [1937]), pivot
upon language acquisition as Americanization; a familiar setting is the adult
education English class (which even figures in Kauffman's *House of Bondage*).
An emotionally intensified example of this attitude is found in *Early Life of a
Seamstress* by the Yiddish-influenced English-language poet Charles Reznikoff
(in the voice of his mother, Sarah Reznikoff). The narrator recalls her response
when her husband brings a Yiddish newspaper home to their New York apart-

ment: "He was still reading a Yiddish newspaper. 'You will never learn English, if you do that,' I said. But he kept on. At last I said, 'If you bring a Yiddish newspaper home again, I'll tear it up.' Next night he brought his newspaper with him and after supper settled down to read. I snatched it out of his hands and tore it to bits. He was furious, of course. 'I'll do it again,' I said. But I did not have to. The very next night he had an English newspaper, and soon knew more English than I."[92]

In *Jews without Money* this traditional motto of "Learn English, become an American" is preached by one of the neighborhood's two models of business savvy, Harry the Pimp:

> Harry was considered handsome. He was pleasingly fat and shiny, and had a curly mustache. He wore good clothes, clean linen, and smoked good cigars. . . . Next to Jake Wolf, the saloonkeeper, he was our pattern of American success. People envied him. He had a big pull with Tammany Hall. He owned a gambling house, and spoke perfect English.
>
> His favorite advice to the young and unsuccessful was to learn English.
>
> "America is a wonderful country," Harry would say, "really a wonderful country. One can make much money here, but first one must learn to speak English.
>
> "That is what I am always preaching to our Jews; learn English, become an American. Is it any wonder you must go on slaving in the sweatshops? Look at me; if I hadn't learned English I myself would still be buried in a shop. But I struggled—I fought—I learned English." (29)

Learn English, lectures a pimp, and be like me: an American success. Obviously Gold is turning on its head, or at least problematizing, the idea of "civilizing" Jews by teaching them the language of the nation in which they live—an idea Alfred Kazin remembers troubling him as a boy in Brooklyn during the 1920s: "[A] 'refined,' 'correct,' 'nice' English was required of us at school that we did not naturally speak, and . . . our teachers could never be quite sure we would keep. This English was peculiarly the ladder of advancement. Every future young lawyer was known by it."[93] An irreverent impulse on Gold's part has a pimp talk about how study lifted him out of the sweatshop. Through Harry, learning English, with all its attendant benefits, is associated with a brand of assimilation manifested by the immorality of pimping and with the monolithic machine politics of Tammany Hall, and is only parodically linked to the Horatio Alger model of success.[94]

But the humorous edge is complicated by the fact that Harry is the one who gives Mikey his first book—Mikey who, according to the logic of first-person narrative, goes on to write the novel we are now reading. An affinity emerges between providing women and providing literature—and by extension, between being able to read and write and being able to perform sexually. (Gold's tendency to assess the work of other writers in sexualized terms is relevant here.) Besides speaking to the masculinizing of cultural privilege by Gold and many of his contemporaries both inside and outside of the Communist Party, this passage demonstrates the fate of language under capitalism. Sex and speech are aspects of human relations that Harry perceives in terms of monetary value; the process by which language becomes a commodity parallels the process by which sex becomes a commodity.

Gold finds in Marx's notion of commodity fetishism a metaphor for certain relations within traditional Jewish culture, exemplified by the Hebrew language. Gold mentions Hebrew in no less than five passages in the book, mostly through asides or anecdotes related by various characters. There are stories of a pious Jew who bought magic words from a rabbi to make devils retreat; of an elderly magic-maker paid to cure Mikey with magic words and designs smeared on his body; of children left in the care of a sadistic monster of a *cheder* teacher after their parents have scraped up fifty cents (incidentally the standard price of a prostitute) for the privilege; of a dybbuk who entered the body of a girl on Hester Street; of a girl whose belly shrieked and groaned although her lips did not move; of a dog who spoke with a human voice. For Mikey, each instance is shrouded in mystery and strangeness; most of them culminate in a business transaction. Eventually all that remains of the ancient language is a sense of alienation and a fetishized and fetishizing economy.

These apparently arcane instances are associated verbally with the worst kind of exploitation in East Side life. Mikey doesn't understand the "meaningless Hebrew" chanted in synagogue or the "meaningless sounds" (66) of the Hebrew prayers he learns in *cheder;* likewise, he and his gang cannot understand the "terrible meaning" of the taunt they hurl at the prostitute Rosie: "'Fifty cents a night!'" (17). In the same fashion, according to Mikey the old junk man's street call strikes the same chord as prayers recited on Yom Kippur, the Jewish day of atonement and a High Holiday. In the junk man's voice, Gold blurs Hebrew scripture and economic oppression into one alienated cry: "I cash clothes, my god, why hast thou forsaken me?" (56). One lesson is that ridding society of one part of the pair (the old man's degradation) may necessitate ridding society of the other (the religious tradition). Thus while Gold finds beauty in the ancient sounds, like Babel he asserts that religious Judaism cannot provide a lasting answer; as Reb Samuel's disappointment proves, it promises yet another false Messiah.

Learning to Curse

In his autobiography *Love and Revolution,* Max Eastman recounts an anecdote about a visit from the socialist writer H. G. Wells. Commenting on the relative rigidity of American and British class systems, Wells reportedly remarked that a wonderful thing about America was that anyone could become a gentlemen. To which someone muttered, "You don't know Mike Gold."[95]

Of course, the vociferous Gold's inability to act the gentleman had more to do with what he *would* not do than what he *could* not do. As suggested earlier, Gold tended to seek the verbal equivalent of the garbage his childhood gang threw in the faces of "liars with megaphones" (55). Toward this end, outright cursing is perhaps the most important component of Gold's contemplation of what James D. Bloom calls the power of subjugated language.

Jewish culture is particularly rich in creative cursing, as books ranging from the novelty paperback *How to Curse in Yiddish* to the linguist James Matisoff's *Blessings, Curses, Hopes, and Fears* attest. Whether it is because, as Leo Rosten suggests, Yiddish "rests on a rueful past" or because, as I. B. Singer observes, Yiddish is perhaps the only language that has never been spoken by people of power, cursing has long been a trademark of *yiddishkeit.*[96] (In his autobiography Sholem Aleichem cites an early compendium of his stepmother's curses as his first literary venture. The stepmother herself was won over rather than offended by this gesture; after all, the Yiddish word *klug* means either "curse" or "clever.") Furthermore, as Marcus Klein has astutely suggested, through a kind of rugged bad manners Gold insists upon his Americanness in the face of decorous Protestant attack.[97] (Klein's suggestion could be extended to connect Gold's cursing to Huck Finn's great moment of American moral assertion, which also pivots upon a curse: when Huck decides not to turn in the escaped slave Jim, he declares, "All right, I'll *go* to hell."[98]) Cursing becomes a crucial form of expression in *Jews without Money,* one that encompasses and loudly vocalizes the position of the outraged victim and the savage rebel, while identifying the curser as both Jewish and American.

The notion of the victim/rebel—for a writer, the Jew who curses—is enfleshed in the figure of the Jewish gangster. Mikey's friend Nigger is an exemplary case. He is the most long-suffering character in the book; yet he is also the most able to confront the gentile world unhindered by either fear or propriety. Tellingly, his very name is a curse.

Gold's discussion of cursing in *Jews without Money* draws heavily upon his appropriation of the monster Caliban from Shakespeare's *The Tempest.* Gold's reclamation of Caliban was part of his deep involvement with the works of Shakespeare. In his essays, Gold repeatedly describes the American Yiddish culture of his youth as saturated with various revisions of Shakespeare. Nahma Sandrow, in her book on the Yiddish stage, lists nearly a dozen plays by Shakespeare that appeared in "more or less recognizably Yiddish versions" between 1890 and 1905.[99]

Moreover, in 1916, during Gold's literary apprenticeship, New York (and indeed the entire country) was lavishly celebrating the three hundredth anniversary of Shakespeare's death. Among others, the writer Max Eastman—Gold's friend, colleague, and early mentor (until their traumatic split)—served on the board of directors of the New York City Shakespeare Tercentenary Celebration Civic Organization. The Mayor's Honorary Committee for the New York Shakespeare Celebration brought together academics and socialites, capitalists and socialists, labor advocates and religious leaders; this committee, fascinating for its expansiveness, included such disparate luminaries as Eastman, Jacob Adler, Nicholas Butler, Abraham Cahan, Morris Hillquist, Walter Lippman, Adolph Ochs, Ralph Pulitzer, Jacob Schiff, Louis Untermeyer, J. G. Phelps Stokes, Mrs. William K. Vanderbilt, and Rabbi Stephen Wise. In short, the literary atmosphere surrounding the maturing Gold amply prefigured and encouraged his fascination with Shakespeare.

According to James D. Bloom, Gold saw his calling as a revolutionary writer in giving voice to Caliban, who in Shakespeare's play performs the menial labor required by Prospero and his daughter Miranda. Told that he should be grateful to Miranda for teaching him language, Caliban utters one of the most famous and potent repudiations of linguistic oppression: "You taught me language, and my profit on't / Is, I know how to curse. The red plague rid you / For learning me your language!"[100]

Caliban takes multiple forms in Gold's novel. The Yiddish language in the text, like Caliban, is a monstrous hybrid whose shape was used to justify its own oppression. Historically scorned from outside and inside the Jewish community (at the expense of the loftier Hebrew), Yiddish has been called the "Caliban of languages."[101]

Shakespeare's monster surfaces in several characters in *Jews without Money*. The original Caliban is more beast than human; the major appearance of Caliban in Gold's book is literally in an animal's body. This is Mrs. Fingerman's parrot, whose first owner taught it to swear before he died. The parrot howls Yiddish curses down the airshaft all day, prompting Mikey's father to call it "a good Jew" (113). Gold's choice of a parrot invokes a stereotype of Jewishness that Sander Gilman considers central to both anti-Semitism and the reactionary Jewish self-hatred: that Jews are unable truly to command the languages of the places where they live and merely become somewhat skilled in the art of mimicry. According to Gilman, Jewish writers from the High Middle Ages to contemporary America have grappled with the charge that the true nature of the Jew is as imitator. For Gold, this charge was perhaps put forth with the most immediate relevance in Hitler's *Mein Kampf* (1925):

> For the sham culture which the Jew possesses today is the property of other peoples, and is mostly spoiled by his hands. . . . What he achieves in the field of art is either bowdlerization or intellectual theft. With this, the Jew lacks those qualities which distinguish creativity and, with it, culturally blessed races.
>
> But how far the Jew takes over foreign culture, only imitating, or rather destroying it, may be seen from the fact that he is found most frequently in that art which also appears directed least of all toward invention of its own, the art of acting. But here, too, he is really only the 'juggler,' or rather the ape; for here, too, he lacks the ultimate touch of real greatness: here, too, he is not the ingenious creator, but the outward imitator, whereby all the turns and tricks he applies cannot deceive us concerning the inner lack of life of his creative ability.[102]

Through cursing, the Jewish parrot inverts the image of derivativeness with Gold's characteristic floridity.

The name Caliban is applied by the narrator of *Jews without Money* to the degraded character Fyfka the Miser, of whom he sneers, "This Caliban was tortured, behind his low puckered forehead" (76). The narrator describes Fyfka chiefly through animal imagery: "He was squat, with a glum black muzzle, and nostrils like a camel. A thatch of black uncombed hair fell down his forehead, over small eyes, too bright and too morbid, like a baboon's. One arm was twisted, and he never smiled, he never said a pleasant word, he was always scratching himself, he never cleaned his nose" (74). Fyfka's basic ambitions correspond with those of Shakespeare's Caliban, who wants to usurp the magician Prospero and rape Miranda. Fyfka also yearns to occupy the place of his oppressors—he wants to become an American capitalist, and seeks to steal contacts with the neighborhood prostitutes. Fyfka only speaks in bursts of rage that approach cursing when Mendel the Bum challenges his miserly ways. According to James D. Bloom, Gold's presentation of Fyfka the Miser "tempts the reader to blame this miser-madman for his own misery," but ultimately insists that he is a social product.[103] Indeed, the disgusting Fyfka is only an unsuccessful double of Harry the Pimp, who has, after all, achieved Caliban's goal of mastering the magic book (he reads English) and Miranda (as a pimp he controls women sexually). In this way Gold keeps his focus on the economic system that produced Caliban rather on than the monster's own failings: the point is not so much Fyfka's inability to succeed but the immorality of the tasks set out for him.

The Fyfka/Caliban figure is ostensibly counterpoised to another character in the book, Mendel the Bum; the chapter's heading—"The Miser and the Bum"—positions the two as contrasting if not downright adversarial. On the contrary, however, Fyfka and Mendel can be said to represent two poles of the same American mercantile impulse—recalling, after Gold's intertextual fashion, the whalers Starbuck and Stubb in Melville's *Moby-Dick*. Fyfka and Starbuck personify the side of American business that is cautious, scheming, mean with capital, risking little; Mendel and Stubb embody the happy-go-lucky, freewheeling, bluff, pioneering American spirit—willfully good-natured, fearless, and self-assured.

But it is Fyfka's Caliban function that most significantly ties him to Mendel, who like the parrot turns out to be a good Jew because he curses. Mendel goes around town getting baptized repeatedly at various Christian churches, which then provide him with "money, sacks of potatoes, suits of clothes, various odd jobs, and a chance to learn the cornet" (78). At first the pious Jews, represented by Mikey's mother Katie, are horrified and even feel they will be tainted by ingesting Mendel's "Christian potatoes," for which he has shrewdly sold his Jewish soul. Mendel assures them that, on the contrary, he has fooled the recruiters, for under his breath he curses: "'Those Christians, a black year on them, are so crazy to have Jews baptized they even pay for it. So what do I do— I fool them. I let them sprinkle their water on me—and all the time, under my breath, I am cursing them, I am saying, to hell with your idol! to hell with your holy water! When they are through, I take my potatoes and go—but I am the same Mendel still, a Jew among Jews!'" (79). As a result, everyone winds up proud of Mendel, who "passed himself off as a real American, yet talked Yiddish and was loyal to his race" (80). This equation—"talked Yiddish" equals "loyal to his race"—is worth pausing over. By speaking English while retaining a Yiddish identity (like Mrs. Fingerman's parrot, largely through cursing), Mendel the Bum thwarts the cultural hegemony that English represents. English becomes a cloak he can put on or take off. Furthermore, Mendel's pseudological argument about whether the potatoes are kosher once they belong to him likens him to the writers of the Talmud, who often debated whether something—food, cookware—was kosher (for example, whether a chicken that hatches on the Sabbath may be eaten).[104] Mendel is definitely using the master's tools, whatever they might be: English to dupe the goyim, Talmudic logic to rationalize getting baptized.

By casting Mendel's linguistic fluidity as a kind of moral triumph, Gold seems again to be responding defiantly to Hitler's ponderous charges of Jewish immutabity: "One can change the language of a man without ado, that means he can use another language; but then he will express his old thoughts in his new language, his inner nature will not be changed. This is shown best of all by the Jew who is able to speak in a thousand languages and yet remains always the one Jew."[105]

◉

As James D. Bloom suggests, Gold's interest in the struggle for ownership of Shakespeare has much to do with identifying and giving voice to the curser, thereby making Shakespeare speak "for and to the masses."[106] Through a common Yiddish curse—"May bananas grow in your throat"—Gold creates in *Jews without Money* his own revision of another of Shakespeare's dramas, *King Lear.* Gold has Mikey's mother utter this curse at the family's heartless landlord, who doubles as the neighborhood pawnbroker.

> He recognized her in the pawnshop gloom.
> "You're my tenant, aren't you?" he asked, "the one that made all the trouble for me?"
> "Yes," said my mother, "what of it?"
> The landlord smiled bitterly.
> "Nothing," he said, "but you are sure to come to a bad end."
> "No worse than yours," said my mother, "may the bananas grow in your throat!"
> (257)

This exchange testifies chiefly to the boldness of Mikey's mother, who dares to curse her landlord in his own shop. But the bananas return in an exemplary instance of Gold's careful patterning of seemingly disparate detail; Mikey's father, after he is injured and can no longer work as a house painter, must attempt to scrounge a living peddling bananas. Mikey accidentally encounters his father on the street, unsuccessfully trying to sell his fruit, and offers to help by advertising the wares. The scene with the landlord has prepared the reader to interpret Mikey's shouting of "bananas" as cursing: "I yelled and yelled. My father, standing by, spoke occasional words of praise, and said I was a wonderful yeller. No one else paid attention. . . . elevated trains crashed; the Cooper Union clock burned above us; the sky grew black, the wind poured, the slush burned through our shoes. . . . I yelled and yelled, nobody listened" (300).[107] Of course, this scene recalls the betrayed King Lear, who stands in a storm and curses the wind.[108]

In Shakespeare's scene, the cursing king, who has been betrayed by his children, stands accompanied only by his wise fool, Edgar. Mikey is also accompanied by a wise clown: his father, whose face, upon seeing Mikey, lights up with "Charlie Chaplin's smile" (299).[109] This reversal of the oedipal drama indicates movement into Americanness; as I noted in chapter 2, a common

Yiddish saying ran that in America, it is the children who raise the parents. Mary Antin, for instance, articulates this notion in her introduction to *The Promised Land* (1912), asking, "And when I discovered my own friends, and ran home with them to convert my parents to a belief in their excellence, did I not begin to make my father and mother, as truly as they had ever made me? Did I not become the parent and they the children, in those relations of teacher and learner?"[110] Mikey rails against his father's immigrant fate—specifically, his emasculation in the capitalist marketplace where no one wishes to buy his limp, spotted bananas. Through cursing, Mikey is able to give voice to the "poor little Jew without money" (301).

This important ability—barring all else, he can still curse—simultaneously affords Gold an identity as a Jewish writer and as a son of his beloved Shakespeare. Describing his mother's speech, Mikey recalls with pride that she went about "cursing in Elizabethan Yiddish, using the forbidden words 'ladies' do not use" (158). Through the modifier "Elizabethan" Gold deftly associates his mother's utterances with the language of Shakespeare; but he immediately makes it known that what she does with that language is curse. This crucial sentence locates Gold's "funny little humble East Side mother" (158) in a remarkable linguistic position. Irreverent, eloquent, outspoken, and earthy, she possesses all the complex raw material the Jewish writer—her son—requires.

The Gangster's Mother and the Polyglot Kitchen

Although Gold finds grace and immediacy in the "Elizabethan Yiddish" of his "funny little humble East Side mother," his interest in the female tongue is primarily what he as a male writer can make of it. While acknowledging the mother (and by extension the mother tongue), Gold limits her linguistic power by placing her in a circumscribed milieu: the "polyglot kitchen" (245). Here she is soon known to all as Momma. The speech acts Katie cooks up in the kitchen have a kind of utopian American quality. But while she initiates the linguistic hybridization that marks the richness of hyphenated Americans like her son, the blending scares her; she learns to "mother the Poles, Germans, Italians, Irish and Negroes" who work there (245), but makes Mikey swear never to eat American hamburger in a restaurant—which we as readers know, of course, that he will be able to do once he comes of age (158).

Ivan Illich's discussion of women's work as "shadow work" provides a useful tool for clarifying the complicated linguistic work Mikey's mother does for the writer. Illich articulates an unrecognized area of female labor he calls "shadow work," which includes "the unpaid toil that adds to a commodity an incremental value that is necessary to make this commodity useful to the consuming unit."[111] This dynamic is demonstrated by the mastery implicit in the narrator's and the author's frequent exhortations, in the text and in the introduction—along the lines of "Momma, you taught me that!"—effectively turning his mother's recognized eloquence into shadow work for his own artistic accomplishment.

While Katie is necessary to preparing the language of the American Jew, it is something she, in her role as Momma, serves up to the Jewish men and boys, who are singularly equipped to apply Momma's lessons to modern America:

> My father sat one evening at the supper table, drinking beer and reading a Yiddish newspaper. In the hot kitchen my mother was washing the dishes, and humming a Hungarian folk song.
>
> "*Nu, nu!*" my father exclaimed, striking the table with his fist, "another railroad accident! Katie, I have always said it is dangerous to travel on these American railroads!"
>
> "What has happened?" my mother gasped, appearing from the kitchen with steaming hands and face.
>
> "What has happened, you ask?" my father repeated in the important tone of a pedant. "What has happened is that seventeen innocent people were killed in a railroad accident in New Jersey! And whose fault was it? The fault of the rich American railroads!"
>
> My mother was horrified. She wiped her boiling face with her apron and muttered: "God help us and shield us! Were there any Jews among the dead?" (163–64)

This passage is most interesting for its details of a communicative event. The words associated with the father—"reading a . . . newspaper," "important tone of a pedant," "rich American railroads"—contrast with those defining the mother—"humming a . . . folk song," "in the hot kitchen," "wiped her boiling face with her apron."

Paula Rabinowitz elucidates the verbal/artistic differences between Mikey's mother and his father: "His mama, whose 'female realism' made her a 'workhorse with proletarian instincts,' contrasts sharply with his papa, whose 'male dreams' stemmed from his skill as a 'storyteller' and love of the theater as well as his belief in the American version of the tale of the Golden Bear."[112] Thus, although Gold claims in an introduction he appended to the book in 1935 that his mother is the heroine of *Jews without Money*, he ends by positioning her three sons as fighters of fascism in defense of her memory, as she has died one month earlier.

> She lived, to the last, in the same East Side tenement street, and prayed in the same synagogue. This was her world; though her sons born in America were forced into a different world.

We could not worship her gods. But we loved our mother; and she loved us; and the life of this brave and beautiful proletarian woman is the best answer to the fascist liars I know; and it is in the bones of her three sons, and they will never betray their mother . . . but will honor her dear memory, and fight the fascists in her defense until the bitter end. (10)

The figure of Gold's mother emerges as transmitter. As Lévi-Strauss concludes about mothers, she is not only a sign ("brave and beautiful proletarian woman") but a generator of signs ("[her life] is in the bones of her three sons").

Although several mothers are seen—Mikey's saintly mother, Nigger's crazy one, the gentile woman who pays Mikey to play with her sick boy—the role of mother culminates in the chapter heading "The Gangster's Mother." This crucial chapter is located at the novel's center, and is one Gold chose to print in *New Masses* when he serialized part of the book. Despite its heading, the passage is more about the gangster than his mother, who is mentioned in only a few scant paragraphs. The reader learns briefly that Louis's mother cannot see—not only are her eyes literally dim, but she is unable to recognize that her son is not a "good boy." She is pathetic and blind, but in her way a good and loving mother. Louis has a bad mother as well: the state that also created him by "carefully teaching him to be a criminal, and by robbing him of his eye" (128). By the end of the chapter, the title "The Gangster's Mother" refers equally to the two.

The ultimate point, however, becomes how the author can usefully interpret and represent the ambivalent sign the mothers have generated. The chapter's closing passage encompasses both mothers and moves on to manifest the writer's special way of knowing:

She [his mother] took a handkerchief, and wiped blood from his eye, mumbling complaints against the bad world. The neighbors drifted away, looking a little ashamed, as if they were in the wrong. And Louis's pigeons, that he had neglected all this time, flew down in a great whir of wings on their coop, prisoners, like all of us, of the East Side.

Every one went on hating Louis One-Eye, and I did too. Now I hate more those who took an East Side Boy and turned him into a monster useful to bosses in strikes, and to politicians on election day. (140)

Gold creates a division of consciousness, separating the adult writer from the child narrator. This division is conventional for retrospective first-person narratives; nonetheless, it serves here to emphasize the position of the writer as uniquely situated to interpret in a way that even his earlier self could not do.

In his own account, Mikey as a child hates and fears the gangsters. But Mike Gold the writer needs them anyway. The aggressive, ambivalent status of the gangster parallels and helps to inform the linguistic and literary boundary crossings—official versus unofficial, standard versus vernacular, Yiddish versus English—that preoccupy him. Although he was known occasionally to resort to fisticuffs himself, Gold's endeavor was to create a new literature (even a new vocabulary) that enjoys the same vitality and directness as the gangsters, being likewise born of American slums—a literature that is potent and communist, and that is equipped to silence with a verbal punch in the nose the "Ku Klux moralizers" (37) who see a Jew without money and call him a thief.

4

Business Is Business

The Death of the Gangster in Daniel Fuchs's Novels of the 1930s

> A philosopher produces ideas, a poet poems, a clergy-
> man sermons, a professor compendia, and so on. A
> criminal produces crimes.
>
> —Karl Marx, *Theories of Surplus Value*

The gangster-king Benya Krik robs an Odessa businessman, pausing to tell anecdotes about Jewish life while stuffing the loot into a suitcase. A New York street gang takes to the stage: by "violating" the classics and plundering African American music, its members create ragtime, America's new art form. A future gangster known as Nigger punches the mouth of a gentile teacher who calls a pupil "kike."

As these exemplary moments indicate, the intent of this study is to explore how the figure of the Jewish gangster has functioned as a metaliterary tool for experimental Jewish writers concerned with finding their artistic place in an era characterized by artistic and social experimentation. The works of Isaac Babel, Samuel Ornitz, and Michael Gold, written between 1921 and 1930, all fruitfully engage the transgressive figure of the Jewish gangster to interrogate the complex relationships among ethnicity, criminality, and linguistic power. But with his three novels of the 1930s—*Summer in Williamsburg* (1934), *Homage to Blenholt* (1936), and *Low Company* (1937)[1]—the Brooklyner Daniel Fuchs theorizes an end to the writerly gangster story, carrying the metaphors of violence and transgression that the writers of the twenties found so congenial to a point of irrelevance. As the Jewish gangster became fixed as a figure of creative transgression, it became easier to imagine that he, like other once-vanguard developments, could be incorporated easily into the state-business apparatus. With the mutually defining relationship between business and the mob an accomplished fact, Fuchs—unlike Babel, Ornitz, and Gold—can no longer inject into the gangster a transgressiveness useful to the revolutionary, the Jew, or the writer.

Like the earlier works, Fuchs's novels of the 1930s juxtapose gangsters and writers and consider what they have to offer each other. Philip, the protagonist of the first novel, contemplates his gangster uncle as a possible moral and aesthetic model, while he self-consciously sets about learning to be a writer. He attempts to follow the advice given to him by his chosen sage, Old Miller, who, like the elder Arye-Leyb in Babel's *Odessa Tales* (the chosen sage of Babel's writer figure), is a professional mourner most often found in the graveyard. Old Miller instructs him: "you must pick Williamsburg to pieces until you have them all spread out on your table, a dictionary of Williamsburg. And then select. Pick and discard. Take, with intelligence you have not and with a patience that would consume a number of lifetimes, the different aspects that are pertinent. Collect and then analyze. Collect and then analyze" (*SW*, 13).[2] But the novel's end finds Philip suffering from a headache, unable to read or even to imagine the value of writing.

In the second novel, the aspiring writer is the eccentric Coblenz, who plans a cynical masterpiece, the first chapter of which is called "Life's a Bowl of Cherries—All Rotten." His dreamy neighbor, Max Balkan, seeking in the gangster a new literary hero on the level of Tamburlaine, finds instead that there is no "hero in this flat age" (*HB*, 80).

By the third novel, even Philip's accumulated wisdom—that a writer must collect and then analyze—circles back to the dead end of the deflated gangsters. Theodore Dreiser's novel of crime and modernization, *American Tragedy* (1925), which he based upon newspaper accounts that he studied as Old Miller might have suggested, provides nothing more than a morbid pleasure for a washed-up racetrack gambler: "'They burned him in nineteen seven. The *American Tragedy* feller. Man wrote a book about him once. Well,' he spoke with easy nonchalance for all his importance, 'I sat in the very same electric chair a couple of hours after they burned him. Yes, just for the hell of it'" (*LC*, 173). A headache, a flat age, and a cheap thrill for a gambler: life according to gangsters turns out to be a tepid offering for a young writer searching for answers.

The gangster, it seems, has lost his earlier function as literary critic. Instead, he has commenced work as a social critic, commenting directly in these novels upon the path of American industrial capitalism. Taken together, Fuchs's novels chronicle the ongoing incorporation of crime in the first part of the twentieth century. In the first novel, *Summer in Williamsburg,* the young protagonist and his brother choose between the moral economies of their pathetic but honest father, a failed Yiddish tragedian turned sandwich-board advertiser, and their ruthless and wealthy uncle, a rising gang leader engaged in solidifying his organization and establishing a bus monopoly in Williamsburg through the hands-on methodology of beating up the competition. By the second novel, *Homage to Blenholt,* which centers on the funeral of the dead gangster Blenholt, a new level of criminal organization has been reached. Blenholt had held the colorful title of commissioner of sewers; here Fuchs portrays gangsters who are involved in politics, have legitimate business interests, control large amounts of capital, and mingle freely with high society (however sarcastically, Blenholt is truly "King of the Underworld"). The third novel, *Low Company,* revolves around the forced takeover and elimination of the gangster Shubunka by a huge national combination that simply does not leave room for small fish like Shubunka.

The advent of the combination that forces out Shubunka parallels the National Crime Syndicate formed after the repeal of Prohibition in a series of meetings spearheaded by Frank Costello and his associates Meyer Lansky, Lucky Luciano, and Joe Adonis. The plan was to establish a national commission with members from each crime family, thus putting crime on a more businesslike level. The climactic meeting occurred in the spring of 1934, in New York's lavish Waldorf Towers, and was attended by almost every major Italian and Jewish underworld leader from New York, Boston, Detroit, New Jersey, Cleveland, Minneapolis–St. Paul, and other cities. By the time the evening was over, according to George Walsh, "the Syndicate was firmly rooted in American society."[3]

Fuchs's meticulous and relentless attention to the increasing syndication of crime operates as social commentary through metonymy: his brutal gangsters are continually associated in one way or another with "regular" commerce, causing the criminal progression that unfolds to signal the expansion and consolidation of capital in the business world. As Ernest Mandel points out, "there is a fascinating parallel between the laws governing the concentration and centralization of capital in general and the logic of organized crime's takeover of bootlegging, prostitution, gambling and the numbers game, and its achievement of dominance in cities like Las Vegas, Havana, and Hong Kong."[4] Fuchs's novels investigate this parallel with increasingly eschatological tone, the final volume opening with an epigraph from the Jewish prayer of atonement and closing with newspaper accounts of death.

As I argue in earlier chapters, an important function of the interwar literary gangster figure was to probe the muddy question of what principles can be relied upon to separate criminal practices from legal business practices. Mike Gold, for instance, refers in *Jews without Money* to the capitalist state as the biggest gangster of all; Venyamin Kaverin's gang leader in *End of the Gang* convenes board meetings and appropriates the language of international commerce; Ornitz's crooked judge learns every trick in his book from his Uncle Philip, a wealthy sweatshop boss. But in Fuchs's novels of the 1930s, the threads of legitimate business and criminal activity are even more entangled; indeed, as Marcelline Krafchick has correctly noted, "this continuum between criminals and businessmen makes the problem of capitalism the backdrop for the dramas of individual lives" in these novels.[5]

In *Summer in Williamsburg,* Harry Hayman, who has been working as a *shtarker* (strong-arm man) for his Uncle Papravel, finally decides to reject Papravel's promise of material success in favor of what he perceives as his father's moral purity. It turns out, however, that the ethics in question are not so simple. Papravel insists that there is a straightforward equation between capitalism and gangsterism. He tells Harry that if he leaves crime for honest business, someone will still be required to live in poverty because of his success:

> "Everybody who makes money hurts people. Sometimes you can't see the people you are hurting, but you can be sure all the time there is always somebody who gets squeezed if he is not ruined. That's the kind of a world it is, and who am I to change it? Only, in my business you can see the people you hurt and that's what makes you hate it. I don't blame you, you're not like me maybe. But remember this, Harry, no matter where you go, no matter what business you'll be in, remember there will always be people who will live in rotten houses, who will have no money for a good time and who will die ten years earlier on account of you." (*SW*, 252)

The alternative story at which Papravel hints—a fortune made from a legitimate, yet exploitative, haberdashery—had already been written by the Jewish socialist Abraham Cahan, whose novel *The Rise of David Levinsky* (1917) portrays a former Talmudic scholar who sacrifices his Jewish ethos to amass millions of dollars in the cloakmaking industry. Harry can think of no rejoinder to Papravel's words; indeed, the novel never offers anything to refute them. On the contrary, Harry goes on to repeat his uncle's homily as truth to his younger brother Philip.

Through the character of Papravel, Fuchs takes the gangster to a new level of self-consciousness: the gangster not only illustrates but critiques in his own voice the workings of capitalism. In the third novel, *Low Company,* shop owner Herbert Lurie confirms Papravel's thesis from the legal point of view. The gangster Shubunka has revealed his true occupation to Lurie for the first time, and Lurie responds with understanding:

> He told Lurie of the girls who begged him for work . . . how they were ignorant, young in years but old, deserving a better life, but abused and exploited because

they were ignorant and helpless. Shubunka went on with the stories of their inevitable sicknesses, the casual medical treatment they received, their frequent
recourse to drugs and to perversion, the courts and the jails in their wretched short
lives. He did this to them, he affirmed, he was a monster. . . .

"I'm not a hypocrite," Lurie said, depressed. "I'm not angry and I don't hate
you. Business is business. It's the same goddammed thing in my line, only a little
less lousy." (*LC*, 181)

One of the knee-breakers who threatens Shubunka insightfully likens the new
criminal combination to "a chain-store system" (*LC*, 78).

The inseparability of crime and business is *Homage to Blenholt*'s structural
given. Their intrinsic connectedness is reified in the gangster funeral around
which all activity revolves, for the dead Blenholt is being laid to rest by representatives of the most respectable segments of the Williamsburg business
community and by the roughnecks who worked for him: Blenholt's associates from the Williamsburg Board of Business Trade and the Ladies Aid Aux-
iliary rub shoulders with individuals called Thickneck, Firpo, Pip, and Amchy.
Blenholt's funeral is a far cry from the gangster funeral that forms the occasion for Jacob Glatshteyn's poem "Sheeny Mike" (1929), in which the mourners, the sullen members of Mike's gang, are called orphans because their
criminal association has so severely compounded their social alienation. At
Blenholt's funeral, criminality has facilitated a ceremonial, public inclusion
in reputable institutions.

As their alliance with legitimate business continually attests, Fuchs's gangsters may have succeeded by breaking laws, but they have followed rules—rules
establishing the primacy of capital and the acceptable ruthlessness of business
practices. In short, the gangster of Fuchs's novels of the 1930s is not an outsider; rather, he is the perfectly adapted modern man.

Fuchs's assessment prefigures a quite radical essay by a later chronicler of
gangster life, Mario Puzo, author of *The Godfather* (1969). In an essay titled
"How Crime Keeps America Healthy, Wealthy, Cleaner, and More Beautiful"
(1966), Puzo writes:

> How are we to adjust to a society that permits cigarette manufacturers to cram
> cancer down the throats of 100,000,000 Americans? . . .
> How are we to adjust to a society in which industrialists sell deforming drugs
> and then, to protect their investment, use powerful lobbies to prevent government
> interference?
> How are we to adjust to a society that drafts human beings to fight a war, yet
> permits its businessmen to make a profit from the shedding of blood? . . . [A]s
> society becomes more and more criminal, the well-adjusted citizen, by definition,
> must become more and more criminal. So let us now dare to take the final step.[6]

The "final step" of which Puzo speaks is to present the top American criminal as the best-adjusted American citizen. Daniel Bell, in his essay "Crime as an American Way of Life" (1960), agrees that the criminal rackets touch upon issues at the heart of the American ideal of open society: "such 'normal' goals as independence through a business of one's own, and such 'moral' aspirations as the desire for social advancement and social prestige." Organized crime, Bell contends, has a "functional" role in American society as "one of the queer ladders of social mobility."[7]

The gangster in *Summer in Williamsburg,* Uncle Papravel, has indeed "worked himself up" in Horatio Alger fashion, and he often repeats this assertion with pride: "'America,' he repeated with conviction through the smoke, 'I don't care what anybody says, America is a wonderful country. Seriously, seriously, I mean it. Look at me, look how I worked myself up in four short years. In America everyone has an equal chance'" (*SW*, 380). His young nephew, Philip, is attracted to precisely this American self-reliance and ingenuity in Papravel and his gang, reflecting, "Call them what you want . . . they are grown-up" (119). It is not hard to see why young men might consider Papravel to be an example of an immigrant success story.

Fuchs's use of gangsters to savage the practices and rhetoric of legitimate capitalism is not out of keeping with the overall paradigm of this study. By now one is prepared to envision the ways in which the gangster figure, through his ambiguous relationship to the system, provided many writers with a congenial means to position art within a political economy. I have argued that Babel, Gold, and Ornitz have all used the figure of the Jewish gangster to explore what the role of the writer in general, and the Jewish writer in particular, will be under socialism, or in the struggle for socialism, which they all supported. Despite the stridency of his attack on the capitalist system, however, the usual critical stance on Daniel Fuchs is that he was definitively different from the radical writers who dominated the pre–World War II era.[8] For instance, Richard Pells maintains that Fuchs's works "were in no way dependent on radical ideas of any kind"; more recently, Gabriel Miller writes that "Fuchs stands out among the writers of his time as one of the few who did not write 'doctrine' literature."[9] There is no mention of Fuchs in Daniel Aaron's still-standard account of literary leftism, *Writers on the Left* (1961). Although some contemporary critics faulted Fuchs for being insufficiently political—for instance, the then-Trotskyist Irving Howe—the vision of Fuchs as apolitical tends to operate as a kind of redemptive mission: whatever he was, Daniel Fuchs was no Michael Gold. Miller, Marcelline Krafchick, and others make this negative comparison with Gold explicitly, despite the fact that there is compelling textual evidence that *Jews without Money* served as an important originary work for Fuchs, whatever distance between their moral or aesthetic visions might have eventuated. For instance, the comment on modernity that Miller calls Fuchs's "favorite image"—the panicked butterfly that has somehow, incongruously, blundered its way into a crowded subway—is borrowed directly from *Jews without Money*. Fuchs uses several additional images that seem indebted to Gold's novel, including Philip's story about boys throwing dead cats at slumming tourists (*SW*, 275) and Mrs. Balkan's comparison of her failed husband to Charlie Chaplin (*HB*, 209).

It is true that Fuchs (as far as is known) was never a communist (unlike Babel, Gold, and Ornitz); it is not true that he was either inactive or conservative politically. Fuchs joined the communist-founded League of American Writers in 1936. In his memoir of the league, Franklin Folsom finds no evidence of a hostile break on Fuchs's part—in fact, Fuchs signed his name to the league's call to its 1939 congress (Gold and Ornitz both signed in both 1935 and 1941).[10] Along with virtually every writer queried by the league in 1938, Fuchs supported the elected government in Spain and contributed to a pamphlet on the subject called *Writers Take Sides*.[11]

It does not seem that Fuchs was politically quiescent. Indeed, his work demonstrates as accessibly as Gold's a society suffocated by oppressive capitalists. But Fuchs takes a shrewd look at the vision of the gangster as implicitly critical of the status quo, a vision most plainly and famously summed up in 1948 by the *Partisan Review* critic Robert Warshow: "The gangster is the 'no' to that great American 'yes' which is stamped so large over our official culture."[12] Fuchs contradicts this gloomily: the ruling class is quite capable of containing these "rebels" and adapting them to its own needs. This is nowhere as evident as during Papravel's creation of a bus monopoly in Williamsburg, when Fuchs treats the historical role of Jewish gangsters in trade union struggles. Particularly in the garment industries, manufacturers hired gangsters to break strikes and discourage organizing, and union organizers brought in gangsters to protect pickets; the thugs generally sold their services to anyone who would buy them. This arena was so lucrative that by the 1920s some of the biggest gangsters were involved in union affairs and, as Papravel's bus station war indicates in *Summer in Williamsburg*, they could not easily be dismissed at their employers' whims. Gangsters played key roles on both sides of one of the most famous and dramatic strikes of the 1920s, the International Ladies Garment Workers Union (ILGWU) suit and cloak strike of 1926.[13] Papravel organizes the United Bus Drivers Association so that he can use the union as a tool to smash the competition. When Papravel sarcastically lists the very real needs of the drivers—"better pay, shorter hours, good working conditions" (*SW*, 164)—he is actually undercutting the drivers' ability to turn to a union for meaningful representation.

Among the few critics who discuss the political content of Fuchs's novels, there seems to be an almost eager consensus on one point in particular: that the communists figure buffoonishly, if at all. In *Summer in Williamsburg*, for instance, the protagonist's downstairs neighbor Cohen, who, as Irving Howe has aptly noted, "rac[es] through postures as if he were bolting bad food,"[14] goes through a stage as a communist writer. Cohen attends meetings and plans literary works, but what unfolds is that he wishes to sleep with Shura, the young woman who recruited him. In fact, when Shura rebuffs him, Cohen loses enthusiasm and doesn't join the Party. (Oddly enough, Gabriel Miller and others take this as a reflection on the Party rather than on Cohen.) There are several small, abortive references like this one to the Communist Party in the three novels; in each case, I would argue, the failure of the communists stems not from a flaw in ideology per se, but rather from the characters' lack of the drive and optimism necessary to challenge the system—the lack of which the novels are, furthermore, sharply critical. In *Homage to Blenholt*, in the central funeral scene, one man stands up and shouts out what the reader by then knows is the truth: that the honored Blenholt was a leech who became rich by sucking the blood of pushcart peddlers like himself. This man—so distraught that he gives no thought to the imprudence of disrupting a gangster's funeral—is hissed down by the crowd as a communist agitator. In short order the gangsters haul the truth-shouting "communist" out of the building.

Max, before even arriving at the funeral, has quarreled with his girlfriend, Ruth, and inwardly bemoaned the deficiency of idealism that means she can only perceive communists in a negative light:

> "It's all right when you're in high school, adolescence is the time for crazy ideas, but now you're a man! Any one of these days, you're so crazy, I wouldn't be surprised if you walked in and told me you decided to become a communist."
>
> See, all communists were crazy. No idealism whatever. (*HB*, 72)

These treatments of the Communist Party by Fuchs represent not so much a rejection of the revolutionary sentiment to which Gold, Babel, and Ornitz subscribed as they do pessimism about the willingness or ability of people to challenge the power and appeal of the state and its representatives, including the gangsters. Edward Anderson, writing at the same time as Fuchs, has his protagonist sum up the dilemma in his novel *Hungry Men* (1935): "Would the revolutionists say that all men who lived in houses that cost more than ten thousand dollars were their enemies? But men in ten-thousand-dollar houses needn't worry about bums revolting. They don't have the guts."[15] As the soap-box communist speaker says in *Summer in Williamsburg*, "I come here night after night. . . . I give you fact after fact. . . . What are you going to do?" (*SW*, 209). Far from the surge of response in the heart of Gold's young protagonist as he encounters a similar soapbox oration at the end of *Jews without Money*, the people gathered on Fuchs's corner answer with their feet.

Crime and the American Way

The literary gangster, as discussed above, could be markedly ethnic and yet defiantly deghettoizing. His shifting insider-outsider status spoke to the ob-session with ethnicity and polyvocality that occupied Russia (following its civil war) and the United States (following its great waves of immigration) in the first part of the twentieth century. Following in the footsteps of Babel's Benya Krik, Gold and Ornitz demonstrate that the Jewish gangster was well situated to play a special role as the bridger of many worlds, thereby bringing to light the intersection of the ethnic question with social reorganization: what would be the fate of Jewishness in America?

Fuchs does not depart entirely from this earlier notion that the gangster does important ethnic work. Instead, he writes that saga into a kind of exhaustion. Fuchs's Jewish gangsters do get themselves out of the ghetto—in *Summer in Williamsburg* Harry Hayman's "work" at least takes him to the Catskills, and the big bosses in *Homage to Blenholt* and *Low Company* have expanded their horizons to include the whole city of New York. These criminals do not, how-ever, manage to bridge Jewish and gentile worlds. They enter the mainstream by casting off their Jewishness—the destabilizing functions of the Jewish gang-ster proposed by Babel, Ornitz, and Gold are not envisioned as possible.

Participation in the criminal organization, then, stands for the process of Americanization. For Fuchs, an important part of adjustment to Americanism is the shedding of ethnicity, which represents a complete capitulation to the so-called American way. Fuchs repeats for emphasis the "melting-pot" makeup of Papravel's group of "boys": "the Irishman Gilhooley, two Jews, one Negro and three Italians" (*SW*, 19). This organization seems at least partially to be based upon the notorious Murder, Inc., the name given by newspapers to a band of professional killers assembled by the Brooklyn gang leader Louis "Lepke" Buchalter. Murder, Inc. was made up of Jewish and Italian executioners and "finger men," and was headed by the notorious Kid Twist Reles on the Jewish side and Albert Anastasia on the Italian side. Its mandate was to eliminate any-one suspected of cooperating with Special District Attorney Thomas A. Dewey, and from 1936 to 1939 the group killed between sixty and eighty people.[16]

Likewise, the gangster Blenholt, whose funeral forms the backdrop of the second novel, is described, to the bemusement of the protagonist's mother, as being essentially without ethnic character; for one thing, he attended both synagogue and church according to what might be useful to him. Thus, by "doing business" their way, Jewish gangsters become perfect representatives of their multinational society—and appear less Jewish.

Fuchs's vision of crime as a route to assimilation parallels a shift in the central concerns and tropes in gangster movies made after the first big wave in the early 1930s. As I argue in chapter 3, when the screen gangster burst onto the scene in the late 1920s and early 1930s, many viewers were able to find new ethnic heroes in these powerful figures. Although the gangsters were doomed to eventual failure, they succeeded, at least for a while, in taking control of their own fates and acquiring material rewards along the way. The gangsters in these movies dress the best, drive the nicest cars, and eat in posh restaurants. When they pick up their weapons—and even the guns are increasingly efficient and modern as the gangsters climb the underworld ladder—they are seizing control of their own fates as well as mastering the technologies of the New World. Through the visual economy of the 1930s gangster movie, which establishes the conventions of the criminal's style and upward mobility in the face of the Great Depression, the immigrant crook slips from being a collective processing site for immigrant marginalization and becomes a statement on crime as an efficient form of assimilation. As the decade progressed, screen gangsters appeared increasingly successful as businessmen, and were decreasingly associated with the ethnic slums from which they came. For an example of this progression, it is useful to compare the opening scene of *The Public Enemy* (1931) with the opening scene of *A Force of Evil* (1948). In the earlier movie, the birthplace of crime is shown to be an Irish neighborhood bar, where residents dressed in work clothes are shown buying beer in buckets while children (the future gangsters) slink around in patched knickers and slouched caps, trying to sell for "two bits" some watches they have just snatched.

In *A Force of Evil*, the gangster (played by John Garfield, who was born Julius Garfinkle) finds his inspiration on Wall Street; the movie's opening scene is a shot of well-dressed crowds hurrying purposefully along in New York's famous business district. A voice-over announces that the day is July 4, the metaphorical birthday of America. The protagonist, we learn, is a lawyer to the mob, referred to in the movie as "the corporation." His goal is to secure a monopoly on the numbers racket, to "reduce the overhead" and make the illegal lottery "legal, respectable and very profitable." The lawyer spends all his energy trying to convince his older brother, who has a much more prounced Jewish accent, syntax, and manner, that joining him in the numbers combine will finally take him away from the neighborhood they grew up in. According to the narrative logic of the movie, it is Garfield's speeches, in which he invokes corporate principles, his own advanced education, and American capitalist ideals, that are convincing to the viewer—certainly not his sloppy brother's ineffectual, weakly moralizing protestations. Like Fuchs's gangsters Papravel, Blenholt, and Shubunka, Garfield's Joe Minch insists that he is a businessman like any other. "What do you mean, gangsters? It's business!" he declares, voicing a kind of credo for his moment.

Far from being resistant, gangsterism has become the most logical form of accommodationism.[17] Even the violence of these criminal enterprises is entirely fitting. In his study of New York underlife, Luc Sante proposes an intrinsic violence to the American melting-pot ideal:

> If the process involved is one of taking a varied assortment of people of very different national backgrounds, mostly paupers and peons from semifeudal societies with an admixture of victims of prejudice and persecution, and dropping them into a kettle where they will be subjected to brand-new indignities and discomforts, but with the alleviating promise that such treatment will eventually stop and that they will emerge from this stewpot as equally functioning standard-issue Americans, does the cooking not require an awesome heat, a fire of such volatility that it could easily erupt and blow the kitchen to smithereens?[18]

Rather than challenge anti-Semitic narratives, Fuchs's gangsters merely literalize the violence of assimilation. Years after Fuchs published his novels, Meyer Lanksy remarked in his memoirs that he became a criminal and committed acts of violence in order to move into the American mainstream.[19]

Within Fuchs's novels of the 1930s, this movement into the mainstream is articulated through the slang that dominates speech acts. In the first book, *Summer in Williamsburg,* characters are given to Yiddish or Yiddish-inflected expostulation like "Gevalt" or "It stinks out loud." But the third book, *Low Company*—in which the gangster activity is the most vicious and the most syndicated—is instead dominated by standard American vernacular such as "B'gee" and "My heavens." Fuchs's most successful gangsters indulge in neither linguistic nor social transgressiveness. They smooth down their difference rather than offering up an outlaw body of poetic material. An example of this is the semantic positioning of the syndicate workers who threaten Shubunka. Under orders to get him out of town so the combination can take over, they do little theorizing; rather, they tell Shubunka that they "can't do no talking" (*LC,* 148). Their silence is quite a departure from the prodigious verbalizers of earlier books: Benya, known for his speechifying; Meyer Hirsch, writing books, contemplating poetry, and declaiming from the bench; Kaverin's Baraban, repeatedly invoking his rabbinical training.

Depictions of meals or cooking commonly serve as shorthand to invoke tradition or difference, or both, in ethnic literature. Furthermore, dietary regulations are central not only to the practice of Judaism, but also to early debates around the Jewish immigrant dilemma. Many examples of ordinary immigrant Jews confronting dilemmas relating to Jewish food practices as they tried to adapt to their new American home can be found in the letters addressed to the advice column that ran in Abraham Cahan's *Jewish Daily Forward,* the "Bintel Brief" (bundle of letters) that Max Balkan's father is seen reading in *Homage to Blenholt.*[20] In *Summer in Williamsburg,* food, like language, maps a process of acculturation that is specifically linked to gangster activity. When Philip Hayman visits his gangster brother at Papravel's hideout, the food that the gangsters eat seems bland; he misses his mother's ethnic food at home: "Philip reached Williamsburg late that Friday afternoon. First his mother sat him down to dinner. After the flat smells and lifeless, unspiced Gentile cooking, he looked forward to his mother's warm tasty food and juicy meats" (*SW,* 173). The progression of criminal association Fuchs sets up here—from Yiddish to American English, from "tasty" Jewish food to "lifeless" gentile food— is the opposite of Babel's imagery in his Benya Krik stories, wherein the same combination of language and food imagery is used to demonstrate the vitality Benya Krik draws from his Jewish background. Benya's robust, Yiddish-inflected speech is described as spicy ethnic food in the central observation, "He may not say much, but what he says is tasty" (*smachno*).[21] The reason for this difference is simple: while Benya Krik represents challenge to the cultural mainstream, Papravel represents accommodation. Fuchs connects Papravel's ascendancy at the close of *Summer in Williamsburg* with his ability to assimilate: the landlady at Papravel's boardinghouse hideout, an elderly gentile who considers him a gentlemen because he pays her generously, weeps at a party celebrating Papravel's brutal victory in driving Morand's bus station out of Williamsburg. Papravel asks her why and she explains:

> "I'm crying because you're such a fine, upstanding, kind young man, and yet when you die you won't go to Heaven."
> "Why?" Papravel wanted to know. "Why should you say a thing like that?"
> "You've never been baptized, Mr. Papravel."
> "Oh," he said with great relief. "Don't you worry your little gray head over that." He didn't know whether this was a joke or what. "Just you leave this to me, Mrs. Van Curen, and everything will be all right," Papravel said, and he smiled happily. (*SW,* 380)

These lines constitute the novel's final words; Papravel's victory, in which we have great confidence, is assured because he has made his Jewishness moot and mute.

This equation—criminality with deracination—runs counter to the notion of gangsters as ethnic heroes that the capacity for gallantry of a Benya Krik or a Louis One-Eye supports. Fuchs's vision, of course, depends on the more romantic one established earlier. He invokes the story of the ethnic outlaw hero to write it into collapse. Criminal Jews do not defend Jewishness by violently demanding its place at the table; instead, they spell its end. Fuchs shows the whole trajectory of the collapse of the gangster as ethnic hero in his early essay "Where Al Capone Grew Up" (1931), which was the inspiration for *Summer in Williamsburg.* In this essay Fuchs recalls his own participation in juvenile street gangs whose chief occupation seemed to be defending their "territory" against the invasion of hostile gentile gangs. On more than one occasion, Fuchs remembers, the boys in his gang cooperated with adults from the neighborhood synagogue to defend its worshipers against assaults by gentiles. With this reminiscence Fuchs nods toward the idea of gangsters as possible cultural saviors. But as these boy gangsters come into criminal adulthood, gangsterism becomes nothing more than "a business colorlessly operated."[22] It is no surprise that Fuchs implies the bleaching out of particularities in his description of organized crime; furthermore, since it was during the 1930s that Jews became fixed as "white" in the bipolar American racial scheme, an implication of Fuchs's essay is that crime helped them to be able to become "colorless." The cultural work performed by Fuchs's gangsters is perhaps most succinctly captured by the recollection of a Jewish writer created by Ishmael Reed in his novel *Reckless Eyeballing* (1986). Reed's Jewish writer tells a friend, "my uncle . . . used to be a gangster. You can't get any more assimilated than that."[23] In his book *Tough Jews* (1998), Rich Cohen brings the commentary on crime and conformity full circle by dreaming of the Jewish mobsters of the interwar years as legendary heroes who might inspire him, through their past daring and virility, to transcend the sterility and blandness of the Chicago suburb in which he grew up. The very assimilation Cohen bemoans and wishes to escape has been generated, Fuchs maintains, by the success of these same legendary mobsters.

The collapse of the gangster's role as ethnic hero is accomplished by Fuchs on a stylistic as well as a thematic level. Fuchs makes an outlaw hero ridiculous through a piling on of bathos. In Babel's *Odessa Tales,* the effeteness of the overly intellectual writer-narrator highlights the potency of the vibrant gangsters. The writer-narrator will never be called "the King" as Benya Krik is called, for he has "spectacles on his nose and autumn in his heart."[24] This comparison allows the figure of the gangster to represent a potentially active Jewish masculinity. In *Summer in Williamsburg,* the effete would-be writer Cohen decides to commit suicide because "I have pimples on my face, and tears in my eyes" (*SW*, 155). Turning the crisis of Jewish masculinity into an adolescent's whine does not allow the gangster figure to present a very impressive alternative. Similarly, Philip and Harry's father does not manage to complete the bitter immigrant lament "America ganev" (America, the thief) or "A klug tsu Columbus" (a curse on Columbus)—exclamations of despair Gold raises in *Jews without Money* to the dramatic level of King Lear's soliloquy during the storm. Fuchs's character can only splutter impotently and fragmentedly, "Nu, nu! Columbus! America! Nu, nu!" (*SW*, 200). This is a defeated Jew: a Caliban who lacks the profoundly Jewish ability to curse. But in this world, unlike in Gold's, the gangster will not do it for him—rather, the gangster betrays the Jewish impulse to curse, declaring glibly, "I don't care what anybody says, America is a wonderful country" (*SW*, 380).

The Gangster and Mass Culture

The growing syndication of crime, together with its corollary, the mainstreaming of the American white ethnic, in Fuchs's novels is part of a related syndication of American culture. This motion toward homogeneity is heralded by a constant stream of tawdry images from popular culture that represent Americanization. In the face of this relentless rush of images, however, the gangster does not play the romantic anarchist or the rugged individualist who rejects the imposed morality of the system. On the contrary, his brutal ascendancy becomes the emblem of what Dwight Macdonald has called the "homogenized culture" of mass consumption.[25] Thus, the gangster figure becomes a trope for discussing the burgeoning mass culture in its relation to the loss of ethnic particularity and social idealism. These elements eventually came together concretely for Fuchs in his vexed move west to work in the gangster-influenced big-culture business of Hollywood; for Fuchs, the concordance of crime, big business, mass culture, and acculturation, as I indicate below, were not symbolic at all.

Fuchs limns the relationships among crime syndication, ethnic accommodationism, and the spreading of mass culture in two important ways. The most concrete is the presence within the novels of the gangster films that mirror and form a backdrop for the "real" gangster activity. In these books, movies are as much a part of reality as are live gangsters. Fuchs introduces a new element here: Gold claims that *Jews without Money* recounts his actual childhood; Ornitz writes *Haunch Paunch and Jowl* in the guise of nonfiction; Babel did research for the *Odessa Stories* in actual criminal dives. Fuchs, on the other hand, while he does recall knowing actual gangsters in his youth, devotes at least as much space in his autobiographical essays to describing the formative experience of watching movies (at least twice a week) as a child. In a *New York Times* article titled "The Silents Spoke to the Immigrants" (1971), Fuchs speaks of both gangsters and movies in the same fond remembrance; he writes in this article that there were at least seven movie theaters within a few blocks of his childhood home, and then adds that if children wandered more than a few blocks away from their home street, a gentile gang was likely to beat them up. Thus, he sets up a tightly drawn territory marked off by gangsters and inhabited by movies. Unlike the other writers in this study, Fuchs documents the cultural work of gangsters; his realism includes exposing how important they have become in art.

Fuchs's almost documentary treatment of mass culture is perfectly in keeping with an attitude common in the organized left during the Popular Front period of unified resistance to the rise of fascism. At this time there was wide recognition that mass culture was inescapable as a social force, and that it needed to be confronted and its potential interrogated as such. Although, like Fuchs, many writers (for instance, the poet Gwendolyn Brooks or the novelist Nathanael West) were frequently dubious in their assessment of the realities of mass culture, this approach still differed significantly from the one commonly credited to "third period" communism, in which "folk" or "proletarian" forms were proposed as viable and more progressive popular alternatives to industrial mass culture. In his novels of the 1930s, Fuchs does not try to sidestep or dismiss mass culture, as Michael Gold did earlier; instead, he offers a complex narration of its functionality, including both positive and negative possibilities.[26]

In Fuchs's novels, children gape at these popular movies as they pass through various coming-of-age experiences ranging from street fights to first dates. The result is that gangster movies exert formative power on the behavior of Americans. For example, in *Summer in Williamsburg,* an almost-pubescent Natie seeks to impress Yetta by describing to her a film that has made a deep impression upon him: "'This picture was swell. I don't see how a person can forget it so soon. It had James Cagney in it. He was swell. Like in one part, see, he walks out of a pool room with a violin case under his arm. A man says, "Where are you going, Jeff?" See, James Cagney's name in the picture is Jeff. So he says, "I'm going to give a guy a lesson." See, the violin case ain't got a violin, that's what racketeers use to hold machine guns in. It was swell'" (*SW,* 333). Natie is almost certainly describing the opening sequence of *The Doorway to Hell* (1930), the film that launched a vogue of gangster movies billed as "snatched from today's headlines." The deliberate blurring of life and art here is bitter: the gangster movies Natie watches invoke the activities of the real gangs that the reader is witnessing gradually taking over through a process of homogenization and faceless organization, begging the question of how this process relates to art. In other words, the reader observes that the same takeover is being achieved in and by the movies as in the city's criminal structure. A tommy gun concealed in a violin case may have become a gangster cliché, but it hardly seems accidental that the musical instrument has been replaced by a gun.

Other egregious overlappings of characters' lives with popular art forms make this same commentary about syndication at the movies. Tessie is called "low company" because of her habit of reading movie magazines in order to learn how to live; the description equates her acceptance of bland popular culture—her willingness to be "taken over" by it—with the offhanded violence of the gangsters in the third book, the title of which is *Low Company*. Likewise, the tragic life story of a minor character in *Summer in Williamsburg*, Mrs. Linck's youngest daughter, Julie, connects literally the uniform commodification native to popular culture with a criminal takeover. Julie, we learn, "lived on the tabloids and the movie fan magazines. The surest access to her favors was to take her to a show" (*SW*, 37). Julie in fairly short order makes the transition from movie theater to brothel, where she encounters Harry Hayman, the gangster. (This metaphor of prostitution to describe the commercialization of art—here represented chiefly by the movies—was introduced by Ornitz in *Haunch Paunch and Jowl*, wherein the gangsters make money simultaneously from pimping and from writing popular songs.)

In addition to the presence of movies as signifying internal texts, each of the books includes a constant overflow of pop culture references that invade every consciousness. While the gangsters busily "negotiate," adolescents read popular novels for instruction in love, radio broadcasts blare across airshafts, children and adults troop in and out of movie theaters, and New Yorkers cram subway trains headed for Coney Island. These nonstop eruptions of mass culture take on a life of their own that frequently interrupts the narrative flow. Fuchs makes a virtuoso performance of mass-culture collage midway through *Homage to Blenholt*, when Ruth is daydreaming in the beauty salon—a moment when, by preparing to be an object of gaze according to the commercial standards of beauty, she is being turned into a commodity herself. This remarkable passage is worth quoting at length:

> Bing Crosby, The Voice of the Masked Tenor, Don Novis, Rudy Vallee's Hour, Myrt and Marge, The Gibson Sisters, Block and Sully, The Showboat Hour, Hollywood on the Air, *True Stories, True Confessions, Love Story Magazine* (Shall I Tell My Husband? Twelve Nights in A Dope Fiend's Penthouse! I Married A Gay Lothario!). *Movie Classic, Photoplay, Modern Movie, Movie Allure* (Are There Any Happy Marriages in Hollywood? I Shall Always Be A Bachelor Girl Says Lovely Lili Mojeska! Myrna Loy—From Vamp to Modern Woman! I Kissed Valentino!).

Silverman's Lending Library—The Latest Books No Deposit Required. (*Valerie Valencia, The Story of a Lustful Woman!* A young woman's battle between flesh and the spirit. Sensational reading that holds you spellbound. Charging it with being immoral, reformers tried in vain to prohibit its publication. They Tried to *Ban* This Book!!!), Walter Winchell, Louis Sobol, Mark Hellinger, Ed Sullivan, Beatrice Fairfax, Antoinette Perry, Donna Grace, Irene Thirer, Garbo, Marlene Dietrich, Carole Lombard, Joan Crawford, Jean Harlow, Clark Gable, Franchot Tone, Gary Cooper and Robert Montgomery. Beauty Parlor, Monday to Thursday Reduced Prices on All Services. Hindu brown stockings, 59¢, bought too often in spite of stopping all runs promptly with soap. Brassieres with points, glove-silk panties light green in color or else orchid or tea-rose. Two-forty-eight girdles, Formflex (Slenderize—but no Bulges. Reduce While You Wear It!) E.Z. Hair Removing Glove (New Shammy Touch—Works Better, Lasts Longer). Naturelle Lipstick; Blue Donna face powder, rachelle color; La Nuit Pour L'Amour perfume, mascara, cold cream, astringent, all applied faithfully, night and day. (*HB*, 39–40)

This passage, which supposedly represents the unguarded, intimate daydreams of Ruth, is not as chaotic as it first appears. It is a deliberate if breathless portrait of consumerism, illuminating the connections among sales on cosmetics, sensationalism in "journalism," feminine movie daydreams, and the objectification of the female body. Such elements float intrusively into the thoughts of all Fuchs's American-born characters. Their uniform presence blurs everyone's personality, effecting a sort of consumerist version of Bakhtin's breakdown of character zones, thus bringing about a defeat of individuality already seen in the incorporation of crime and the attendant assimilation of American ethnics.

The loss of individuality is most vividly drawn in the protagonist of *Homage to Blenholt*, the luftmensch Max Balkan. Max has always been different from his neighbors; his girlfriend remembers a dreamy, sensitive child who in adulthood conceives of endless failed schemes to keep him from being just like everyone else. At the novel's close, Max's spirit is crushed—as his father puts it, we have "witnessed the exact point at which his son had changed from youth to resigned age" (*HB*, 302). Max's loss of idealism is effected by the twin victors of commerce and mass culture: "Twelve dollars a week. Pushing hand trucks with dresses through traffic from jobber to manufacturer, eight to five. Get up, go to work, the subway, wait for the hours to pass, home, the movies, sleep. There was no other way" (201). The movies seem more than just an opiate that gets workers through the drudgery of their days, the way Gold sees the popular song-sheets Mikey's aunt Lena sends him to buy in *Jews without Money*. Rather, they play an active role in the creation of the class system. This notion is consonant with the work on popular culture done by other left-wing intellectuals of Fuchs's generation, such as the Jewish critic Irving Howe (who reviewed Fuchs's works on more than one occasion). Howe bewails the fact that mass culture (he mentions the movies in particular) "is oriented toward a central aspect of industrial society: the depersonalization of the individual." According to Howe, such depersonalization is demanded by the American workplace:

> One thing seems certain: except during brief revolutionary intervals, the quality of leisure-time activity cannot vary too sharply from that of the work day. If it did, the office or factory worker would be exposed to the terrible dualities of feeling that make it so difficult for the intellectual to adjust his job to himself. But the worker wants no part of such difficulties, he has had enough already. Following the dictum of industrial society that anonymity is a key to safety, he seeks the least troublesome solution: mass culture.[27]

Max Balkan's dreary coming-of-age experience seems designed to support Howe's pessimistic thesis.

Clement Greenberg, in his essay "Avant-Garde and Kitsch" (1946), voices despair at what he considers the stagnancy of mass culture, but he proposes an alternative in nonrepresentational art. Fuchs, however, satirizes the avant-garde just as sharply as he does popular culture. The poets he pictures in New York's bohemian coffeehouses are phony and laughable, every bit as bloodless (and fey) as the obstreperous Mike Gold feared being:

> In the small room a collegian acted pertly as master of ceremonies. He peered through the smoke and said, "We are very fortunate to have among us this evening the well-known poet Homer Quixby. Come up, Homer."
> And Homer came, his face glazed with profundity and anemia. . . . All in all it was a very abrupt performance, and four or five persons in the place caught their wind hurriedly and turned to their neighbors to say, "Homer is a soinso, did you know that? O yes, it certainly shows too." Homer, very proud that he was a soinso, disregarded the applause, carried his hips wide and high and took his place with three other soinsoes. (*SW*, 269)

These rarefied efforts at art simply cannot withstand the onslaught of the combination: even smug avant-gardists like the coffeehouse set are also influenced and subsumed by popular culture. Fuchs provides a glimpse of the callow and pretentious character Cohen's bedroom walls, upon which modernist painting and experimental magazines quickly give way to mass-marketed art: "A few pictures, cut out from *transition* and backed with beaver board, hung above the bed. They were some reprints of Picasso, the long faces and wavy guitars, a print of Epstein's Mother and Child, and, placed among them, a cover of the *Saturday Evening Post* by Norman Rockwell" (*SW*, 62). The relentless advance of mass culture is represented here by Rockwell's *Saturday Evening Post* cover, which Clement Greenberg also locates as the ultimate, deplorable example of kitsch. And there is no real contestation of whose interests it serves. Ornitz, who pictures gangsters in charge of the creation and distribution of mass culture, maintains nonetheless that the real question is not the form but rather whose side in the class war it is serving. For Fuchs, however, neither the flashy gangster of popular films nor the alienated gangster of ethnic modernism will reinvigorate literature. That experiment is over, and once again, the gangsters' own ascendancy brings on the end. Fuchs adopts a stance similar to that of the Jewish writer Maurice Samuel, who in a nonfiction work (*King Mob*, published in 1930 under the pseudonym Frank K. Notch) envisions mass culture as a criminal gang.

A noticeably literary finality characterizes the scene of destruction in *Summer in Williamsburg* when Papravel and his boys wreck a local bus station. Fuchs has a visibly marked social outsider, the group's only "Negro," swinging on the "modernistic" light fixture as the gang tears the station apart. The cruelty and tawdriness of the whole affair suggest an ending to the romance of ethnic modernism that other writers attempted to craft through their language experimentation and their use of similar marginal figures: "The Negro, an elegant gentleman named Fleurie O'Johnson, made a running leap for the modernistic chandelier. He swung the length of the room like a monkey until it gave, dropping him on the floor with a loud boom. O'Johnson looked up at the hole in the ceiling ruefully and rubbed his backside" (*SW,* 19). This passage, with its blend of humor and violence, tragedy and slapstick, racist primitivism and elegance, is final; the ride on the modernist chandelier has dumped Fleurie O'Johnson on his ass. The dumped O'Johnson is ethnically marked as French, Irish, and African American, invoking the modernist Paris of the 1920s, the writings of James Joyce, and the role of Harlem (and Africa) as a modernist trope of the primitive. The image's coarsely sexual nature—suggested by a "flurry o'johnson"—confirms the emasculation Babel, Gold, and others sought to avoid through the gangster's masculinism: the visible ethnic, rubbing his backside, has been fucked by modernism.

Fuchs also ridicules the vision of the subway as "essentially poetic." The subway, a standard of New York modernism, appears in works by Moyshe-Leyb Halpern, Kenneth Fearing, Muriel Rukeyser, A. Leyeles, Langston Hughes, Rudolph Fisher, and others, besides figuring in the paintings of Louis Lozowick, Max Weber, and Joseph Foshko, to name a few. In *Summer in Williamsburg,* however, the idea of a poetic subway becomes inane:

> Cohen had been jammed against the door and had had a struggle before he was able to get in. When he finally rejoined Philip his breath was pretty much gone but he remained triumphant. "Did you see them squeeze me against the door?"

he asked. "I thought they'd crack something." He drew his jacket in place and composed himself. "I knew I'd lose something. A button got pulled off. And yet," he said exultantly, "how vital, how living, these people are. What force, what— how dynamic—the surge of the crowd. Essentially it is a poetic thing, Hayman. Believe me." (*SW,* 81)

Philip responds wryly by muttering something about horse excrement. If there ever was poetic potential in the subway, it has (like the clippings on Cohen's walls from *transition*) given way to the more vulgar aesthetic demands of advertising:

> It was a long ride to Coney Island. Cohen sat back in a sleepy haze trying to forget his headache. The jumping, jerking train, the dull lightness with the filter-patches of darkishness, the other persons hiding behind the *Daily News* and the *Journal* as they picked their noses, the dirty, red clay floor with swills of mouse-colored dirt, the enameled hand supporters, the signs above: All tea is economical . . . here's the finest . . . keep your hands soft and white . . . in crowds . . . in dusty streets . . . GUARD— . . . year in and year out . . . always the same flavor. . . PLEASE keep hands off doors. (70)

Fuchs lampoons the modernist aesthetic as a futile and irrelevant impulse in the face of mass culture and the bourgeois interests it represents; there is no reason to demand or even assess the place of the Jewish writer in a modernist aesthetic that has already collapsed.

In the face of Fuchs's biting satire of mass culture, it is important to note his paradoxical indebtedness to popular cultural forms and the vitality that is drawn from them. It is in the passages invoking popular culture that the language of the books is most fresh and most experimental; what Michael Denning has called the "ghetto pastoral"[28] is combined with explosions into non-literary languages, including bits of text from slick magazines, graffiti, snippets from radio broadcasts, billboard slogans, and advertisements that are quoted or even inserted, frame and all, into the narrative (see fig. 1). This kind of inclusion makes the text visual, like a movie. It also adds to the documentary quality of the novels, a quality that Richard Pells ascribes to the proletarian writers and specifically singles out Fuchs as having sidestepped.[29]

Thus, Fuchs's satirical employment of popular forms still manages to suggest the possibilities as well as the limitations of these forms. He invokes them, even uses them, while maintaining an authorial distance, generally through irony. This duality results in an ongoing tension between high and low forms that characterizes each of the novels and serves as a reminder of the gangster's multilayered metaliterary significance. For instance, Max in *Blenholt* likes to call his mother Mrs. Mackenzie. This name refers to a scheming character in

```
┌─────────────────────────────────────────────────┐
│                MADAME CLARA                       │
│        SCIENTIFIC BEAUTY TREATMENTS               │
│              By Skilled Experts                   │
│        ANY THREE ITEMS FOR ONE DOLLAR             │
│     Manicure               Eyebrows               │
│     Shampoo                Finger Waves           │
│     Henna Rinse            Facial                 │
│     Scalp Treatment        Marcel                 │
│          Haircuts To Fit The Face                 │
│        PERMANENT WAVE—3.50 and up                 │
│          Given By Licensed Beautician             │
│     Tel. STagg 5-8324        298 Roebling St.     │
└─────────────────────────────────────────────────┘
```

Figure 1

Thackeray's novel *The Newcomes,* but also makes a pun in marketplace Yiddish on the phrase *M' ken zi,* or "we know her," meaning that the woman in question will look and look but buy nothing. Leo Rosten explains, "This cryptic designation was once popular among Jewish retail clerks who would call a signal to each other: 'Mrs. McKenzie!' meaning 'Keep an eye on her.'"[30]

"Keep an eye on her" sums up Fuchs's approach to popular culture, which he represents as a gangster—insidious and forceful. The final pages of *Low Company* depict a crowd scene, a mad rush by "tramping, shouting millions" (*LC,* 312) for the cheap amusements of Neptune Beach (the name Fuchs gives to Coney Island). There is something sinister as well as inevitable about the faceless mob's desperation for release: there is no hope offered for defeating the combination. As Philip Hayman comes to realize, "Poetry and heroism did not exist, but the movies did" (377).

Fuchs at the Movies

Fuchs's three novels of the 1930s, drawing their satirical likenesses among crime, mass culture, and ethnic accommodation, were resoundingly unsuccessful in terms of sales. (According to Fuchs, *Summer in Williamsburg* initially sold four hundred copies, *Homage to Blenholt* sold four hundred copies, and *Low Company* sold twelve hundred copies.) The period leading up to the publication of *Low Company* (the last novel he would write for nearly thirty-five years) found Fuchs "angry, discouraged, and poor."[31] He had been working as a permanent substitute teacher in Brooklyn's Brighton Beach neighborhood for seven years, and later wrote that permanent substitutes "are permanently assigned, have the same duties as permanent teachers, but are paid by the day, each day we work, $6 per day. Yom Kippurs we fast, and Christmases, and all through the summer vacation months."[32]

In 1937, Fuchs accepted an offer from RKO to move to Hollywood for thirteen weeks and write screenplays. Delighted to leave his poverty behind, he went to work for a movie studio that he referred to as "an organization" (the same word Shubunka uses for the combination that forces him out in *Low Company*) and encountered a film executive he called "a thug."[33] He settled permanently in California during the Hollywood rise of the gangster Bugsy Siegel, another Williamsburg native only three years older than Fuchs himself. And when Fuchs adapted *Low Company* to the screen ten years after its publication (the movie version is called *The Gangster*) he removed any traces of Jewishness. All the recognizably Jewish names are changed—Louie Spitzbergen, for example, becomes Nick Jamey, and the gambler Moe Karty's first name is changed to Frank.

Fuchs's move to Hollywood has its own symbolic resonance in terms of the issues of syndication and assimilation that frame his novels of the 1930s. The gangster as an independent operator—previously perceived as a heroic individualist on the rise—is now subsumed into the mundane business world, even as he is consumed by the public that "buys" his story again and again in the increasingly tedious popular culture. Perhaps this across-the-board co-optation is part of the reason Fuchs's setting moves with his third novel (and his movie version) from the Williamsburg of his childhood to an imagined version of Coney Island, site of freak shows, fast-food stands, disposable entertainment, and organized leisure time. With this progression, Fuchs effects a dramatic shift away from the vision of the urban gangster as producer, either of daring acts or vernacular style. Instead, he moves toward a figure whose function in the city is to comment upon consumption even as he is consumed.

Conclusion:
The Gangster's Funeral

Flabby, bald, lobotomized,
he drifted in sheepish calm
where no agonizing reappraisal
jarred his concentration on the electric chair—
hanging like an oasis on his air
of lost connections.
—Robert Lowell, "Memories of West Street and Lepke"

In each of the chapters of this study, I have aimed to underline a different primary function of the fictional gangster. Isaac Babel's Odessa tales demonstrate the centrality of the gangster's spoken vernacular—in this case, the colloquial Russian of criminals and Jews—as modernist utopia. Samuel Ornitz's *Haunch Paunch and Jowl*, by contrast, fashions the gangster as a negative artistic model. Ornitz uses criminals to show not what a Jewish artist could be (if he were tougher, freer, and so forth) but what a Jewish artist should not be: a crook who exploits his own people to advance in business.

In *Jews without Money*, Mike Gold portrays the gangster as a positive model of Jewish masculinity, crafting that role against a traditional perception of the Jewish male as feminized and toward the author's conception of a virile proletarian ideal. Finally, Daniel Fuchs, in his novels of the 1930s, turns the project of literary gangsterism upon its head, longing for an artistic moment when there are no longer any gangster-artists. Fuchs stresses the "organized" part of organized crime to comment upon the banality of incorporation: in crime, in government, in business, and above all in mass culture, where the gangster, by now, is most at home—as a familiar character in the movies and on the stage, and as boss of the empires of Hollywood and Las Vegas.

Of course, several of these authors could be treated by emphasizing others among these points; it would be fruitful to consider more deeply Babel's role in the movies, or Fuchs's crafty and erudite invocation of literary subtexts. Furthermore, it would certainly be worthwhile to look at representations of Jewish criminals by non-Jewish writers—for instance, the many African American writers who depict the numbers rackets in Harlem, which were run by Jewish criminals[1]—or to consider the function of the Jewish gangster in the historical novel.[2] As David Singer and Joe Kraus have pointed out, the gangster is a uniquely loaded figure in the task of constructing a usable ethnic past.[3]

Although the heyday of the historical Jewish gangster has passed on both continents, the aesthetic experience of the Jewish gangster is still capturing the public imagination—particularly, it seems, in film.[4] On the American side we have recent offerings such as *Lansky* (1999), *Bugsy* (1991), *Billy Bathgate* (1991), *Miller's Crossing* (1990), and *Once upon a Time in America* (1984). In Russia, the era of glasnost, followed by the dissolution of the Soviet Union, has witnessed a spate of movies that deal with black-marketeers and other organized criminals, including such films as *Luna Park* (1994), *Taxi Blues* (1990), and *Jazzmen* (1983). But the focus has changed. The intense inner debate about what it means to be a Jew while crafting a new identity (Soviet or American) has evaporated. The metaphor of transgression—social, literary, linguistic, psychological—provided by the gangster no longer carries the same direct poignancy. For instance, in E. L. Doctorow's novel *Billy Bathgate* (1989), which re-creates the Jewish gangster Dutch Schultz, Schultz utters the same Yiddish-inflected English spoken by Fuchs's Shubunka and, for that matter, Fitzgerald's Wolfsheim: "Show her how you can't do certain things anymore in your life, Bo. Show her how the simplest thing, crossing your legs, scratching your nose, it can't be done anymore by you."[5] But Schultz (whose real name was Arthur Fleigenheimer) was a German Jew whose first language would not have been Yiddish. The point is not that Doctorow has made a mistake, but rather that his concerns are elsewhere: the relationships among Jewishness, criminality, and linguistic power have lost their immediacy, and Schultz's characterization as a Jewish criminal has become somewhat of a stylistic question of association for contemporary readers. To put it simply, Doctorow marks the thief as a Jew, rather than the Jew as a thief.

It is precisely this evolution in the imaginative economy of gangsterism that informs Jack Levine's painting *Gangster Funeral* (1952–53).[6] Levine, like the authors I have discussed, is the child of Russian Jews, but he is not concerned with interrogating the Jewishness of his gangster-subject. Levine's grotesque portrayal of bloated corruption reveals the fruition and the passing of the ambivalent sensibility introduced by the American Yiddish poet Jacob Glatshteyn's gangster funeral in his poem "Sheeny Mike," which served as the epigraph to my introduction. There have, in fact, been a number of gangster funerals mentioned in these pages: not only Sheeny Mike's, but also Commissioner Blenholt's in Fuchs's *Homage to Blenholt,* as well as the one Benya Krik hosts in Babel's story "How It Was Done in Odessa" and the one Meyer Hirsch arranges for Davie in Ornitz's *Haunch Paunch and Jowl.* The gangster funeral appears in the movies as well; in *Little Caesar,* for instance, Rico sends showy flowers to the gangster whose death allows his own ascendency, and in *The Public Enemy,* Tom Powers's "straight" brother figures out that Tom is a gangster based on who has sent flowers to his murdered companion's funeral. Philip Roth lampoons the motif in his novel *Zuckerman Unbound,* in which a writer

In Jack Levine's *Gangster Funeral* (1952-53), the figure of the dead gangster lacks force or particularity. Instead, the emphasis is on the complacent wealth of his legitimate and illegitimate former associates. (Photograph © 1999 by the Whitney Museum of American Art, New York)

ducks into a gangster funeral to avoid the intrusion into his life of a crazy reader.[7]

Levine, a painter of "social realism," was born in 1915 (making him a few years younger than Daniel Fuchs, the youngest writer treated in this study). He was the youngest son of an immigrant shoemaker; his older brother (who was twenty when Jack was born) gave him his name. Because this baby was born in America, he chose "Jack," which struck his Russian ear as typically American. *Gangster Funeral* was received by critics as a culmination of Levine's sensibilities, hinted at in earlier satirical works with underworld themes: *A Feast of Pure Reason* (1937) shows a meeting among a policeman, a gangster/capitalist, and a city boss; *Syndicate* (1939) shows a ward heeler, a gangster, and a millionaire; *Gangster Wedding* (1957) depicts the marriage of a portly gangster to a much younger woman. The importance of *Gangster Funeral* in Levine's oeuvre is suggested by the fact that a one-person show at the Alan Gallery in New York in 1963 was devoted to paintings and drawings related to *Gangster Funeral*, a large oil painting on which Levine had worked for at least two years.

Since Levine claimed during the planning stages of this painting that he intended to paint a narrative (denying that this work was better left to novelists and filmmakers), it is not irrelevant to try to piece together the story that is told by this picture.[8] *Gangster Funeral* depicts the viewing of an open coffin, attended by a half-dozen mourners. The dead gangster is being laid to rest by a prosperous crowd—they are fleshy, like Ornitz's Meyer Hirsch, to the point of caricature. In the front of the line of mourners stands a beribboned police chief, openly paying his last respects to his former business associate. Also present are the governor and the mayor, as well as a pin-striped business tycoon holding impeccable white gloves and sporting a heavy gold watch-chain. There are two women dressed in full mourning and expensive furs—"two widows," Levine called them, "one very very shapely."[9]

Strikingly, the only figure in the painting with no real particularities is the gangster himself. His coffin lies open for viewing, but his features are blurred. The point seems to be that as a figure who can stand for something, who has aesthetic meaning, he is terminated. It is true that the gangster, although dead, is the force that has united the interests of the group of mourners—officer, legitimate businessman, politician. But he retains no allure or audacity himself. This indistinct dead gangster marks the conclusion of a process that has run throughout this study: a shift away from production—the gangster's ability to perform creative acts—and toward consumption—meaning both the gangster's co-optation into the status quo and his position under a controlling public gaze as an overdetermined icon of mass culture. (Levine "dates" his painting relationally to gangster films. In the commentary he wrote for a retrospective exhibit in 1989, he stated, "I did a painting of a gangster funeral around 1952. Chronologically, in American art, it comes after the movies *Public Enemy* [1931] and *A Slight Case of Murder* [1938] but before *The Last Hurrah* [1958] and *Some Like It Hot* [1959]."[10])

The dead gangster's nondescript persona also registers a movement away from earlier identity-centered treatments of gangsters, an attitude illustrated most fully in the movie *Let 'Em Have It* (1935), in which a gangster coerces a plastic surgeon to change his features so that he can elude the agents of the newly formed Federal Bureau of Investigation. The film's horrifying climax occurs when the fugitive gangster removes the bandages to discover that the surgeon has carved the gangsters' initials into his cheeks: the gangster is literally marked, identified by his face. But a face (especially a distinguishing feature like a "Jewish" nose) is exactly what Levine's gangster does not have. Moreover, he is unnamed, and positioned at the bottom left corner of the painting, where the viewer's eye does not first go. Levine has imagined a very different death for his gangster than Jacob Glatshteyn did twenty-four years earlier for Sheeny Mike, whose name, ambitions, family life, Jewishness, and intimate character still dominate his funeral and the poem itself.

Not only are the gangster's features obscured, but there is nothing about the funeral service or the dead man's attire that denotes his ethnicity in any way; the traditional elements of a Jewish funeral are noticeably absent. The male mourners do not have their heads covered, the casket is not wooden, the coffin lid is not closed. Daniel Fuchs gave us gangsters whose criminality acted as a process of deracination; Levine's successful gangster has conformed so thoroughly that his death, which totally erases his features from the painting, becomes a final act of conformity.

Gangster Funeral is a painting of lubricousness. There is queasiness to the ostentatious wealth of all the mourners, a feeling encouraged by a heavy murkiness to the play of light and shadows in the picture; as James Thrall Soby puts it, Levine makes us "laugh before we gag."[11] Levine's painting suggests that crime does pay; in fact, Levine maintained that because he was a painter, this may have been his thesis, unlike in the movies, where the Hays Code insisted otherwise.[12] But the message really seems to be that when crime pays well enough, it is no longer defined as crime. There is no indication of struggle or transgressiveness anywhere in *Gangster Funeral*.

With the disappearance of the gangster as a signifying trope, *Gangster Funeral* is finally a painting about audience. We are looking at the people who are looking at the gangster and finding that there is nothing for them to see. In his study of crime movies, Carlos Clarens proposes that the classic gangster movie "taught us to look over our shoulders at night."[13] Isaac Babel,

Samuel Ornitz, Michael Gold, and Daniel Fuchs try to use the Jewish gangster to teach the literary establishment to do the same thing. But although a gangster funeral may provide occasion for Isaac Babel to think about nation and difference in the 1920s, for Jack Levine in the 1950s it is a study in cynicism. In *Gangster Funeral* the insubordinate Jew has demanded his piece of the mainstream pie, and gorged on it.

Notes

Introduction

1. Fearing, *New and Selected Poems*, ix.

2. Fearing, "St. Agnes Eve," 11.

3. Quoted in Harshav and Harshav, *American Yiddish Poetry*, 39–40.

4. On the influence of the Russian Revolution upon Americans, see Foner, *Bolshevik Revolution*. Examples of early Soviet writers who were deeply impressed by modern America include Vladimir Mayakovsky (see his poem "Brooklyn Bridge" [1925; in Mayakovsky, *"The Bedbug" and Selected Poetry*, 173–81]) and Ilya Ilf and Yevgeny Petrov (see *Little Golden America* [1937]).

5. I take the category "writers on the Left" from Aaron, *Writers on the Left*.

6. See Gilman, *The Jew's Body*, 53.

7. Joselit, *Our Gang*, 84.

8. Ibid., 77.

9. Ibid., 140–49.

10. "Jewish Gamblers Corrupt American Baseball," 50. A linchpin of Ford's argument is the common assumption that "Jews are not sportsmen" (ibid., 38). In a book-length essay called *You Gentiles*, Maurice Samuel attempts to use precisely this assumption to prove that Jews by nature cannot be gangsters. In a chapter entitled "Sport," Samuel declares that "there is no touch of sport morality in our way of life" (46) and insists that "the idea of a 'gentleman thief' is utterly impossible to the Jew: it is only you gentiles, with your idealization of sporting qualities, who can thus unite in a universally popular hero" (47).

11. Fitzgerald, *Great Gatsby*, 74.

12. Joselit, *Our Gang*, 142.

13. Fitzgerald, *Great Gatsby*, 74, 75, 76.

14. Quoted in Cohen, *Tough Jews*, 57.

15. Fitzgerald, *Great Gatsby*, 69.

16. Ibid., 74.

17. According to Salo Baron, fully one-third of Russia's Jewish population found itself "declassed" following the revolution (Baron, *The Russian Jew*, 187).

18. As translated and quoted by Maurice Friedberg in Friedberg, "Jewish Themes," 192.

19. Weinryb, "Anti-Semitism in Soviet Russia," 299.

20. Eastman, *Love and Revolution*, 255.

21. The term "ethnic modernist" is Werner Sollors's (see Sollors, *Beyond Ethnicity*).

22. Singer, "Jewish Gangster," 74. See also Cohen, *Tough Jews*.

23. Quoted in Ellen Schiff, "Shylock's *Mishpocheh*," 93; see also Reed, *Japanese by Spring*, 215.

24. A novel by Andrew Holleran, *Dancer from the Dance* (1978), extracts camp value from the butchness of the Jewish gangster. Two gay male characters have the following exchange while touring a block of the Lower East Side:

> "The biggest Jewish gangsters of the twenties, this was their block," he said. . . .
> "And who lives in them now?"
> But before the friend could answer, Sutherland replied himself. "Faggots!" he said.
> (122)

25. Howe, *Jewish-American Stories*, 17. The only other non-American writers for whom Howe claims such centrality are Sholem Aleichem and I. B. Singer, both of whom, unlike Babel, lived and wrote in the United States.

26. Pinkwater, *Chicago Days/Hoboken Nights*, 5–7; Havazelet, "To Live in Tiflis"; Cohen, *Tough Jews*, 79; Pinsky, *Poetry and the World*, 144–45.

27. Freidin, "Isaac Babel," 1907.

28. See Gabriel Miller's introduction to *Allrightniks Row*, the 1985 reissue of *Haunch Paunch and Jowl*.

29. According to Ornitz, his last novel, the cloying *Bride of the Sabbath* (1951), represents an idealistic alternative to the bitterness of *Haunch Paunch and Jowl*.

30. *Encyclopaedia Judaica*, s.v. "Ornitz, Samuel Badisch" (article by Milton H. Hindus).

31. Michael Gold, *Mike Gold: A Literary Anthology*, 234.

32. Ibid., 235.

33. Michael Folsom, introduction to Michael Gold, *Mike Gold: A Literary Anthology*, 7.

34. Eastman, *Love and Revolution*, 265.

35. Murphy, *Proletarian Moment*, 66.

36. McKay, *Long Way from Home*, 140 (emphasis added).

37. See Wixson, *Worker-Writer in America*.

38. Sklar, *City Boys*, 8.

Chapter 1: Imagine You Are a Tiger

1. Andrey Sinyavsky, "Isaac Babel," 92; Falen, *Isaac Babel*, 79; O'Connor, *Lonely Voice*, 190.

2. Four of these stories constitute the cycle anthologized as *Odessa Tales:* "The King" (1921), "How It Was Done in Odessa" (1923), "The Father" (1924), and "Lyubka Cossack" (1924). Three additional stories chronicle Benya Krik and his gang: "Sunset" (1928), "Froim Grach" (1933), and "Justice in Parentheses" (1921; throughout the text, I have Americanized McDuff's translation of Babel's title from "Justice in Brackets"). Soviet publishing history is complicated; frequently, three dates are relevant: the date a work was written, the date of its first publication (which may well have been abroad), and the date of its first Soviet edition. Babel apparently wrote the stories of the Odessa cycle between 1921 and 1923; the dates given above represent their first publication in Soviet literary journals. "Justice in Parentheses" was published in 1921 with the subhead "From the Odessa Tales," but it was not included by Babel when he put the four others together as a cycle in the early 1920s. "Sunset" was written four years later but seems not to have been published until 1964; the 1990 Soviet (Khudozhestvennaya literatura) edition notes that the last page is missing. "Froim Grach" was first published in New York in 1963. In May 1933, Babel wrote some relatives that three new stories, including "Froim Grach," were being considered by the editors of a literary anthology to be called *God XXVI* (Year 26). The stories were returned with a note from the writer A. Fadeev saying that they were being rejected for Babel's own sake, since they were "unsuccessful."

In addition to these seven stories, Babel wrote a film scenario called *Benya Krik* (1926) and a dramatic version of "Sunset," *Zakat* (Sunset; 1928).

3. Harold Bloom, *Isaac Babel,* 113.

4. Jeffrey Brooks's fascinating study of Russian kopeck novels at the turn of the century, *When Russia Learned to Read,* notes that popular chapbooks frequently featured Jewish villains and often chronicled the feats of well-known Jewish gangsters such as Misha Yaponchik ("Mike the Jap").

5. Pinsky, *Poetry and the World,* 144–45.

6. Trilling, introduction, 31.

7. Glatshteyn belonged to the Yiddish modernist literary movement called introspectionism (*in zikh*). He and his colleagues, although they were almost without exception multilingual, chose to write in Yiddish as a muscular cultural assertion; their goal, as they saw it, was to adapt Yiddish to the experience of the Jew in modern America.

8. For a fuller exposition of what Gregory Freidin calls "the whole complex of ideas, texts, and events that have come to be associated with Babel's name," see Freidin, "Isaac Babel," 1889.

9. Babel, "In the Basement," 293. This ploy recalls Fyodor Dostoevsky's *Notes from Underground* (Zapiski iz podpol'ya), in which the narrator immediately warns the reader that he has "lied out of spite" (91).

10. This chain of events in "Moi Pervyi Gonovar" (My first fee) also associates storytelling with prostitution as a profession—an association that later arose for Babel under circumstances outside of his artistic control in 1924, when Commander of the First Cavalry Army Semyon Budennyi accused him of libeling the First Cavalry.

Budennyi called Babel a whore in a newspaper article titled "Babizm Babelya iz *Krasnoy novi*" (The sluttishness of Babel from *Red Virgin Soil*). *Red Virgin Soil*—one of the most important and prestigious literary journals of the Soviet 1920s—was the original publisher of Babel's stories from both *Red Cavalry* and *Odessa Tales;* the title of Budennyi's article in Russian contains a pun linking Babel's name and the Russian word *baba*, a rude sobriquet for a woman.

11. See Friedberg, *How Things Were Done in Odessa.*

12. Baron, *The Russian Jew,* 67.

13. Herlihy, *Odessa,* 253.

14. Friedberg, *How Things Were Done in Odessa,* 1.

15. For instance, Babel frequently prefaces turns-of-phrase with the clarification "As they say in Odessa . . ." (see his letters in *Sochineniya v dvukh tomakh,* vol. 1).

16. Pirozhkova, *At His Side,* 85.

17. See Shklovskii, "Yugo-zapad" (Southwest).

18. Raymond Williams, *Politics of Modernism,* 45, 46.

19. Paley, foreword, viii. Paley also acknowledges that her own chosen form, the short short story, "probably couldn't have happened without Babel's work" (ibid., xix).

20. Babel, "Odessa," 26.

21. Babel, "Odessa," 62 (my translation from the Russian version; this passage is omitted in Hayward's English translation).

22. Zamyatin, "On Language," 180.

23. For a clear example of Babel's opinion of the value of "pure" Russian, see his short story "Guy de Maupassant" (1920–22). The narrator describes an attempt by a Russian Jew to translate de Maupassant from French into Russian, an attempt that is unsuccessful because it is too correct and carefully devoid of Jewish inflection: "Raisa Bendersky took pains to write correctly and precisely, and all that resulted was something loose and lifeless, the way Jews wrote Russian in the old days" (331).

24. In an interesting circular move, Max Hayward, in his translation of this essay into English, turns *chelovek vozdukha* back into *luftmensch* (Babel, *You Must Know Everything,* 28).

25. Examples of the literary *luftmensch* include Hershele in Babel's "Shabbos Nakhamu," Benjamin in Mendele Moykher-Sforim's *Travels of Benjamin III,* Munves in Daniel Fuchs's *Homage to Blenholt,* and Menachem-Mendl in Sholem Aleichem's *Adventures of Menachem-Mendl.* Israel Zangwill wrote a humorous short story entitled "The Luftmensch."

26. Babel, "Odessa," 30.

27. Quoted in Herlihy, *Odessa,* 128, 28.

28. Quoted ibid., 281.

29. Paustovsky, *Years of Hope,* 11. The jazz-band leader Leonid Utesov also writes about Odessa's gangsters (including Misha Yaponchik) in his reminiscence "Moya Odessa" (My Odessa; 1964).

30. Lunts to Gorky, 1922, quoted in Erlich, *Modernism and Revolution,* 118.

31. Babel's diaries (and some of his essays for publication) deal extensively with so-

cial reorganization in the early Soviet period; see, for instance, Babel, *1920 Diary;* and "Evacuees," "Premature Babies," "Palace of Motherhood," and "Blind Men," in Babel, *You Must Know Everything.*

32. Cowley, *Exile's Return: A Narrative of Ideas,* 77, 100. In a subchapter entitled "Historical Parallel," Cowley adds that Russian and American writers had in common a vision that "going to Europe" could mean aesthetic salvation. Babel did in fact make three long trips to France, and he wrote often of his admiration for the French short-story writer Guy de Maupassant (including the story named after the writer that deals with a search for artistic truth).

33. It is important not to apply Cowley's theory of modernism too broadly here; although Russia before the revolution was a huge empire often included on lists of the great powers, in practice it was an economic colony of the major capitalist nations. Moreover, as I discuss in detail later, Babel's position as a pure product of his country's dominant culture is dubious. Nonetheless, something of this impulse of self-denial is present in his work.

34. The need for Jews to become closer to the natural world was a major focus of the enlightenment (*haskalah*) movement among European Jews in the late eighteenth and nineteenth centuries. The founder of modern Yiddish literature, Mendele Moykher-Sforim (who was involved with the enlightenment movement for many years), frequently thematized the Jewish tendency to be cut off from nature in his novels; in order that Jews might have access to natural science, he published Hebrew translations of popular biology texts.

35. Falen, *Isaac Babel,* 62.

36. Stories by Babel that were my primary sources are cited in the text of this chapter with the abbreviations listed below. Russian-language quotations from these works are transliterated from Babel, *Detsvo i drugie rasskazy;* although supposedly accurate Soviet and post-Soviet Russian complete issues of Babel's work are now available, I find this émigré edition to be the most reliable and free of errors or changes, especially in terms of vernacular Russian forms. The English translations of these primary works are taken from Babel, *The Collected Stories of Isaac Babel* (trans. Walter Morison), with three exceptions: "Froim Grach" excerpts are from Babel, *Isaac Babel: The Lonely Years* (trans. Max Hayward); "Justice in Parentheses" excerpts are from Babel, "Justice in Brackets," in *Isaac Babel: Collected Stories* (trans. David McDuff); and "Sunset" excerpts are from Babel, *You Must Know Everything* (trans. Max Hayward). In several instances I made minor adjustments to these quoted translations, as I have noted in the citations.

F	"Froim Grach" (Russian)
FG	"Froim Grach" (English)
GM	"Guy de Maupassant"
H	"How It Was Done in Odessa"
Is	"Istoriya moei golubyatin"
JP	"Justice in Parentheses"
K	"The King"

Kak	"Kak eto delalos' v Odesse"
Ko	"Korol'"
O	"Odessa"
L	"Lyubka the Cossack"
LK	"Lyubka Kozak"
S	"Sunset"
SD	"The Story of My Dovecote"
Sp	"Spravidlivost' v skobkakh"
Z	"Zakat"

37. Paustovsky, *Years of Hope*, 141.

38. See Sicher, *Style and Structure*, 77.

39. Falen, *Isaac Babel*, 91; Pritchett, "Isaac Babel," 16.

40. Paustovsky, *Years of Hope*, 125.

41. Paustovsky, "Few Words," 279.

42. A satire by Ping-Pong entitled "Nashi Pozhelaniya k 10-Letiyu Oktyabrya" (Our wish for the tenth anniversary of the October revolution; 1927) focuses on Babel's long period without publication and makes a wry joke about the significance of Benya's name: "Just put out something, if only a yell, as long as it isn't Benya the Yell" (Izdai khot' chto-nibud', khot' krik, / No chtob on ne byl Benei Krikom). The extremely thorough bibliography in Efraim Sicher's *Style and Structure in the Work of Isaak Babel'* called my attention to this piece.

43. Falen, *Isaac Babel*, 106.

44. Figures are taken from Baron, *The Russian Jew*, 56–58.

45. Paustovsky, *Years of Hope*, 141.

46. Fuchs, *Summer in Williamsburg*, in *Three Novels*, 155; Philip Roth, *Ghost Writer*, in *Zuckerman Bound*, 30. Taking a further page out of Babel's book, Roth refers in an interview to the craft of writing as "a kind of gangsterism" (Brian D. Johnson, "Intimate Affairs," 256).

47. Marcus, "Stories," 407.

48. Gilbert and Gubar, *No Man's Land*, 253. Mendele Moykher-Sforim makes this writerly oedipal fantasy explicit in his "Notes for My Biography," where he describes his artistry as a sacred calling: the elevation of the mother tongue. Mendele describes his success at that calling this way: "I fell in love with Yiddish and bound myself to that language forever. I found for her the perfumes and fragrances that she needed, and she became a charming lady who bore me many sons" (42). Following this remarkable assertion is a list of his Yiddish works.

49. Gilbert and Gubar, *No Man's Land*, 260.

50. Ong, *Fighting for Life*, 36.

51. Mendele Moykher-Sforim, "Notes for My Biography," 41 (emphasis added).

52. Howe and Greenberg, *Treasury*, 73.

53. A similiar ritual slaughter accounts for one of the most famous moments of *Red Cavalry*: in "My First Goose," Lyutov kills his landlady's goose in a manner forbidden by Jewish law; shortly thereafter he sits down to a meal of pork with the Cossacks.

54. Babel, "V Odesse kazhdiy yunosha ..." (In Odessa every youth ...), 358 (my translation). Although the anthology Babel's one-page essay was intended to introduce never appeared, the essay itself was subsequently published in the Soviet Union in 1962 (*Literaturnaya gazeta*, January 1).

55. Shklovskii, "Isaac Babel," 12–14.

56. For a discussion of this concept of ethnic trilogies, see Boelhower, "Ethnic Trilogies."

57. Rosenthal, "Fate," 126.

58. Joyce, *Ulysses*, 12.

59. According to the Bible, Moses lived 120 years; wishing Aunt Pesya a life this long is not merely evidence of Benya's extravagance but in fact reflects a convention of conversational Yiddish.

60. Sholem Aleichem, *"Tevye the Dairyman,"* 47.

61. Pirozhkova, *At His Side*, 107.

62. In the following passages, Babel borrows from Sholem Aleichem, but makes his images violent:

> ... the bride looked at the groom with one eye, licking her chops like a cat who had swiped some sour cream. (Sholem Aleichem, *From the Fair*, 9)

> With both hands she was urging her fainthearted husband toward the door of their nuptial chamber, glaring at him carnivorously. Like a cat she was, that holding a mouse in her jaws tests it gently with her teeth. (Babel, "The King," 211)

63. Sholem Aleichem, *"Tevye the Dairyman,"* 40, 36.

64. Babel, "After the Battle," 186.

65. Babel, "Life and Adventures of Matthew Pavlichenko," 101, 106.

66. Ruth Wisse suggested this comparison to me.

67. See Eikhenbaum, "Illyuziya skaza" (The illusion of skaz; 1918), and "Kak sdelana 'Shinel' Gogolya" (How Gogol's *Overcoat* was made; 1919); Vinogradov, "The Problem of Skaz in Stylistics" (1925); and Bakhtin, *Problems of Dostoevsky's Poetics*.

68. Harshav, *Meaning of Yiddish*, 39.

69. Efraim Sicher points this out in his extremely useful book *Style and Structure in the Work of Isaak Babel'*, 77.

70. Lenin, "Critical Remarks," 92.

71. Falen, *Isaac Babel*, 82.

72. Wisse, *Schlemiel*, 23, 3. Evidence of how widespread this particular subject of humor was can be found in the fact that the formulation Babel uses about shooting into the air is repeated verbatim by Woody Allen in the duel scene in his comedy of Russian Jewish life *Love and Death* (1975).

73. Babel, "Story of My Dovecote," 251 (emphasis added).

74. Leiderman, "I ya khochu," 11.

75. Oulanoff, *Serapion Brothers*, 134 (transliteration made consistent).

76. Friedberg, "Jewish Themes," 196. Some examples of satiric literature of this period portraying Jews under the NEP are Mikhail Kozakov's *Povest' o karlike Makse* (Tale

about Max the dwarf; 1926); Yulii Berzin's *Ford* (1928); and Matvei Roizman's *Minus shest'* (Minus six; 1931). Other works about criminality under the NEP (but not necessarily Jewish criminality) are Valentin Kataev's novel *Raztrachiki* (The embezzlers; 1928); Leonid Leonov's *Vor* (Thief; 1927); and Ilya Ilf and Yevgeny Petrov's *Dvenadtsat' stul'ev* (The twelve chairs; 1928) and its sequel, *Zolotoi telyonok* (Little golden calf; 1931).

77. My translation of Kaverin, *Konets khazy* (End of the gang), 268. No English version of this work has been published; subsequent translations are also my own.

78. Some critics refer outright to Bender as a Jew or a half-Jew, and some skirt the issue; in fact, there is no hard evidence in the novel to prove it. One of the authors—Ilf, whose real name was Faizelburg—was Jewish. The name Ostap could be a corruption of the Jewish name Osip, and Bender is believable as a Jewish name, but it could also be German. The fact that the Jewish American comic filmmaker Mel Brooks made a movie version of *The Twelve Chairs* probably indicates that Brooks, at least, had some sense of Jewishness in the novel.

79. Kaverin, *Konets khazy,* 241.

80. Ibid., 286.

81. Pirozhkova, *At His Side,* 107.

82. Ibid., 113.

83. Freidin, "Isaac Babel," p. 1911.

Chapter 2: A Sordid Generation

1. Throughout this chapter, page citations in the text refer to Ornitz, *Haunch Paunch and Jowl.*

2. The term "Jewface" is used by Robert Dawidoff in his essay "Some of Those Days" (277); Federal Writers Project, *New York City Guide,* 109.

3. Wiener apparently assumed that this name would be somehow more popular and therefore sell more books (see Melnick, *Right to Sing,* 80).

4. Ornitz's earliest social activism involved working with incarcerated juvenile delinquents; perhaps this experience made it harder for him to romanticize the creative potential of the criminal.

5. For more on Tim Sullivan's involvement with Jewish gangsters, especially Rothstein, Herman "Beansey" Rosenthal, and Monk Eastman, see Katcher, *Big Bankroll.*

6. See, for instance, Mary Antin's *Promised Land* (1912) or Israel Zangwill's *Melting-Pot* (1909).

7. See Alan Trachtenberg's *Brooklyn Bridge* for a detailed treatment of the structure's iconic, social, and technological significance.

8. See Michael Gold, *Jews without Money,* 41.

9. Melnick, *A Right to Sing,* 81.

10. Honors, "Guiding Spirit." As this interview suggests, Ornitz was entering an ongoing intellectual debate over the sources for musical innovation. Reisenfeld's vehement distinction between "jazzing up" classical music and elevating popular tunes

to the level of classical music is made almost identically by a German pianist in James Weldon Johnson's *Autobiography of an Ex-Coloured Man* (1912). The ex-colored man, visiting in Germany, has been "ragging the classics"; the German pianist shows him how he should be embellishing popular tunes instead, to elevate them to the level of classical music (see Johnson, *Autobiography,* 141–42).

11. Honors, "Guiding Spirit."

12. The character of Esther Brinn, who marries a millionaire settlement worker and becomes a well-known reformer, is quite possibly modeled on Rose Pastor Stokes, whom Ornitz knew.

13. Of course, this was an obsession of Eliot's; see for instance "Notes toward the Definition of Culture" (1948).

14. For additional discussion of goat imagery, see chapter 3 on Michael Gold's *Jews without Money.* It is likely that Gold's description of the gangster Nigger, which compares him favorably to a mountain goat, derives from Ornitz's earlier novel. See also the discussion of Ornitz in Melnick, *Right to Sing.*

15. Rubin, *Voices of a People,* 31.

16. Rideout, *Radical Novel,* 118.

17. See chapter 3 for a fuller discussion of Jewish language as the language of theft.

18. For details on Cahan's literary and journalistic contributions in English, Russian, and Yiddish, see Chametzky, *From the Ghetto.*

19. Rideout, *Radical Novel,* 118.

20. Shakespeare, *As You Like It* 2.7.139–66. Meyer's maturation follows Shakespeare's seven stages fairly closely. Shakespeare's Jaques first proposes the "infant, / Mewling and puking in the nurse's arms"; Meyer describes in his first period being nursed by a nanny goat. When Shakespeare moves on to the "the whining school-boy, . . . creeping like snail / Unwillingly to school," Meyer recalls his days as a reluctant student in *cheder,* or Hebrew school. Shakespeare's third stage is inhabited by the "lover, / Sighing like furnace"; Meyer, in the third period, discovers girls. And so forth, including, in both cases, an overweight judgeship.

21. I have taken the connection of Sterne to Locke from Cross, *Laurence Sterne.*

22. Quennell and Johnson, *English Literature,* 256. *Tristram Shandy* was issued by Ornitz's publisher, Boni and Liveright, in 1925.

23. A typical instance of comparing Ornitz with Cahan can be found in Sylvia Huberman Scholnick's article "Money versus *Mitzvot.*" Scholnick likens *Haunch Paunch and Jowl* to *The Rise of David Levinsky* by positing a shedding on the part of each protagonist of his Old World Jewish values—values, I would claim, that Meyer Hirsch never considered his own.

24. Ann Douglas uses "mongrel" to describe New York's cultural mixtures in her book *Terrible Honesty: Mongrel Manhattan in the 1920s.*

25. Joyce, *Ulysses,* 644. *Ulysses* was serialized in the United States in the *Little Review* from 1918 to 1920.

26. Dick, *Radical Innocence,* (photo insert following p. 120).

Chapter 3: A Gang of Little Yids

1. Throughout this chapter, page citations in the text refer to the 1942 reprint edition of Michael Gold, *Jews without Money.*

2. A 1965 Avon Books reissue of *Jews without Money* appears to have missed or disregarded Gold's internal admonition: the back cover screams in headline type "NEW YORK'S TENEMENT POOR" and goes on to promise "the anguished sound . . . of thieves, whores, pimps, gangsters, and the honest oppressed."

3. Michael Gold, *Mike Gold: A Literary Anthology,* 206 (emphasis added; hereafter cited in this chapter as *Anthology*).

4. For a detailed treatment of Gold's reworking of Caliban, see James D. Bloom, *Left Letters.*

5. Hoftstadter, *Anti-Intellectualism in American Life,* 293; Eastman, *Love and Revolution,* 268; Carlos Baker, *Ernest Hemingway,* 201; Rideout, *Radical Novel,* 154. For more, see John Pyros, "Miscellany of Views on Gold," in Pyros, *Mike Gold,* 168.

6. Michael Folsom, in *Anthology,* 7. The only published book-length work to treat Gold as a meritorious novelist is James D. Bloom's groundbreaking *Left Letters.*

7. Harrington, afterword, 227.

8. As I mentioned in the introduction, Gold later met Babel, at a 1935 meeting of the International Congress of Writers in Defense of Culture held in Paris. He writes about this meeting with Babel in Michael Gold, "Love Letter for France."

9. Ruth Rubin devotes a chapter of her study of Yiddish folk song, *Voices of a People,* to songs of the Jewish underworld in Western and Eastern Europe (see "Out of the Shadows," 310–41).

10. Ralph Ellison, in *Invisible Man,* and Ishmael Reed, in *Reckless Eyeballing,* indulge in similarly grotesque parody of Emerson's transparent eyeball. Gold frequently returns to Emerson in his discussions of American literary heritage. For instance, he calls Whitman, Thoreau, Twain, and Emerson "the spiritual forefathers of the proletarian writers of America, and the champions of the American people" (quoted in Murphy, *Proletarian Moment,* 134). He compares Thornton Wilder's words unfavorably to "the language of the intoxicated Emerson" (Michael Gold, "Wilder: Prophet of the Genteel Christ," 201).

11. Emerson, *Nature,* 189.

12. James D. Bloom, *Left Letters,* 37.

13. *Anthology,* 104.

14. See Michael Gold, "America Needs a Critic," 129–39; and Michael Gold, "Renegades: A Warning of the End," 58–96.

15. As James D. Bloom points out, this idiom has found (and continues to find) its way into the work of Jewish American writers ranging from Henry Roth to Philip Roth—including, I would add, the songwriter Bob Dylan (né Robert Zimmerman), whose lyric to "Bob Dylan's 115th Dream" ends, "I asked him what his name was and why he didn't drive a truck / He said, 'My name's Columbus,' and I just said, 'Good luck'" (Bob Dylan, "Bob Dylan's 115th Dream"). Nathanael West, in his harsh novel *A*

Cool Million (1934), not only participates in this idiom but attempts to give it histori-
cal substance: the "animate" part of a free traveling road show called "Chamber of
American Horrors, Animate and Inanimate Hideosities" is a pageant entitled "The
Pageant of America or a Curse on Columbus." The pageant consists of "a series of short
sketches in which Quakers were shown being branded, Indians brutalized and cheated,
Negroes sold, children sweated to death" (West, *Cool Million*, 366).

16. The left-wing cultural critics—energetically engaged in creating an American literary tradition by piecing together what Marcus Klein calls "random oddments of history" (Klein, *Foreigners*, 39)—were committed to finding broad creative opportunity
under the new rubric of "American culture." Furthermore, most called themselves socialists. These affiliations should have made them congenial to Gold's enterprise, and
indeed did so. But from Gold's stance there is a paradox implicit in even a populist separation of American culture from European culture. As Benjamin Harshav has pointed
out, Jewish American writers operated from a cross-cultural perspective that invigo-
rated their work as much as the hearty frontierism they loved and celebrated in Twain,
Whitman, Thoreau, and Emerson (see Harshav, "American Yiddish Poetry"). Van Wyck
Brooks, in particular, returns to an ultimately futile nostalgia for an ideal past that,
American or not, could not apply to Mikey. Even the more optimistic writer Constance
Rourke's *American Humor* posits ipso facto a "native" tradition that could not satis-
factorily explain the complicated cultural affiliations of Mikey's ghetto. What emerges
is a situation wherein twentieth-century immigrants become somehow different from
nineteenth- or eighteenth-century ones, whose Americanness is, after all, no "older" or
more fixed. This seems to be the point of Klein's *Foreigners*, which reads Gold as part
of "another idea of tradition" incipient in "the heritage of the ghetto" (37–38).

17. Van Wyck Brooks, *America's Coming of Age*, 134. In the version of this chapter published as a short work in *New Masses*, Gold pushes the comparison even further: "(Did
I hear the Mayflower mentioned so proudly? There have been thousands of Mayflowers;
my parents, too, were Pilgrims, daring for liberty to uproot themselves, and to con-
quer a wild dangerous land)" (Michael Gold, "Jews without Money," 11).

18. The nickname or variants of it were common among actual Jewish American
gangsters. A few examples are Benjamin "Nigger Benny" Snyder, who worked for Joseph Rosensweig, a hoodlum involved with the furriers' and bakers' unions; Joseph
"Yoski Nigger" Toblinsky, who worked for a gang of horse poisoners known as the
Jewish Black Hand; "Niggy" Rutman, a bootlegger in Newark; and Isadore "Nigger"
Goldberg, a member of Chicago's ferocious Twentieth Ward Group. Fictionalized accounts reflect the common occurrence of the nickname; in addition to Gold's portrayal,
the gangster Shubunka in Daniel Fuchs's novel *Low Company* is nicknamed "Nigger"
by rivals; in his historical novel *The Chains* (1980), Gerald Green creates a gangster
called Moishe "Nigger" Pearlberg. On the historical relationship of American Jews to
the category of "white," see Jacobson, *Whiteness*.

19. Harshav, *Meaning of Yiddish*, 39. Harshav writes that "each word has an aura of
connotations derived from its multidirectional and codified relations not just within
a semantic paradigm, as in other languages, but to parallel words in other source lan-

guages, to an active stock of proverbs and idioms, and to a typical situational cluster. . . . Since each word may belong to several heterogeneous or contradictory knots, ironies are always at hand."

20. During the 1930s, American communists adapted this into the slogan "Promote Folk Culture in Its Original Form, With Proletarian Content." See Smethurst, *New Red Negro,* 28.

21. *Anthology,* 292.

22. Michael Gold, "Jewish Childhood in the New York Slums," 306.

23. Ibid., (emphasis added). Mikey is placing a famous line into his father's mouth. Late in life, Twain met Sholem Aleichem and reputedly commented dryly, "It's an honor to meet you. I'm told I'm the American Sholem Aleichem, you know."

24. Ibid., 307.

25. Ibid.

26. Twain, *Huckleberry Finn,* 405.

27. Michael Gold, "Go Left, Young Writers!" 188.

28. Twain, *Huckleberry Finn,* 405.

29. A Buffalo Bill poster from 1900 with the caption "I AM COMING" is reproduced in Meisel, *Cowboy* (photo insert following p. 62).

30. Michael Gold, "John Reed and the Real Thing," 7.

31. Ibid.

32. Fitzgerald, *Great Gatsby,* 78.

33. In the version published in *New Masses,* this passage is given the subheading "U.S. Product" (Michael Gold, "Gangster's Mother," 3).

34. Quoted in Joselit, *Our Gang,* 78–79.

35. In a discussion of prewar Jewish criminals, Judge Jonah J. Goldstein wrote that "in one respect, they rendered a public service: they would take care of those who made fun of and attacked immigrant Jews with beards" (quoted in Joselit, *Our Gang,* 44).

36. Mumby, "'Art of the Weak,'" 102.

37. In *Little Caesar* (directed by Mervyn LeRoy), the gangster Rico Bandello is played by Edward G. Robinson, born Emanuel Goldenberg. In *Scarface* (directed by Howard Hawks and Richard Rosson), the gangster Tony Camonte is played by Paul Muni, born Friedrich Muni Meyer Weisenfreund. In his book *Hollywood's Image of the Jew,* Lester D. Friedman remarks that "America became aware of its Jews and its movies almost simultaneously" (3).

38. Ruth, *Inventing the Public Enemy,* 15, 13–14. Ruth is quoting *Scribner's* contributor Edwin Grant Conklin.

39. Quoted ibid., 168.

40. Henry Roth, *Call It Sleep,* 151.

41. Breines, *Tough Jews,* 109.

42. Foley, *Radical Representations,* 311; James D. Bloom, *Left Letters,* 35–36; Klein, *Foreigners,* 191; Rideout, *Radical Novel,* 187.

43. Michael Gold, "America Needs a Critic," 137.

44. Klein, "Roots of Radicals," 136–37.

45. A summary example of this determined division of modernist and proletarian writing can be found in the two versions of Malcolm Cowley's *Exile's Return*. In the original publication in 1934, Cowley juxtaposes the "enfeebled" and isolated world of the American modernist writers, which he calls the "lost generation" (303), with the "vivid effect" of "the cultural life of the American proletariat" (41)—effecting a separation that speaks favorably of cultural communism; but in the revisionist (and now standard) edition of 1951, Cowley insists on the same division, this time denigrating the "proletarians" as hacks: "Very few of the literary rebels [the experimentalists] were willing to march with others in disciplined ranks. Very few of them followed the current fashion by writing socially conscious poems or proletarian novels" (295).

46. For a detailed treatment of communist positions on Joyce and other modernist writers, see Murphy, *Proletarian Moment*, 133–47. Murphy, who thoroughly demonstrates a complicated and varied response to modernist literature on the part of communist writers, opens his section entitled "The Question of the Heritage and Modernism" with a polemic: "The contention of James Gilbert, Jack Salzman, and Alvin Starr that *New Masses* literary critics rejected the bourgeois heritage has no basis in fact. Among the critics in that magazine and in the *Daily Worker* in the mid-thirties, the position that proletarian writers had nothing to learn from bourgeois writers had no adherents" (133).

47. *Anthology*, 255.

48. Joyce, *Portrait*, 525.

49. *Anthology*, 245.

50. Siegel, "Proletarian Art."

51. Michael Gold, "Thoughts of a Great Thinker," 25.

52. Quoted in Ellmann, *James Joyce*, 510.

53. See Gilman, *The Jew's Body* and *Jewish Self-Hatred*.

54. Breines, *Tough Jews*, 126.

55. Gilman, *The Jew's Body*, 291, 53.

56. Quoted in Franklin, "Homosexual Jew(el)ry," 6.

57. Michael Gold, "Go Left, Young Writers!" 188.

58. Dennen, *Where the Ghetto Ends*, 63. For an official Soviet statement on the formation of Jewish collective farms, see Kalinin, "Evrei-zemledel'tsy v soyuze narodov SSSR" (The Jew and the farmer in the union of peoples of the USSR).

59. Breines, *Tough Jews*, 127.

60. "Letter from Mike Gold" (1938), in Nelson and Hendricks, *Edwin Rolphe*, 88.

61. Rabinowitz, *Labor and Desire*, 8.

62. Michael Gold, "American Famine," 88–89. Ornitz has a similar list in *Haunch Paunch and Jowl* (1923): "Sailors, stevedores, oilers, stokers, firemen, hobos and street walkers crowd the sidewalks. Country boys, threadbare and hungry-eyed, fortune seekers stranded in the big city, and tired-looking, jobless men from everywhere, wander in this land of the down and out" (138).

63. Hertz, "Writer and Revolutionary," 29; Foley, *Radical Representations*, 97.

64. Michael Gold, "Go Left, Young Writers!" 188.

65. James D. Bloom, *Left Letters*, 61.

66. Kalaidjian, *American Culture*, 138.

67. *Anthology*, 177.

68. Klein, *Foreigners*, 185. In his well-researched dissertation on Gold, Howard Lee Hertz claims that the speaker was not Flynn but the Jewish anarchist Emma Goldman: "Folsom assures me on the basis of papers in his possession that, despite Gold's many reports that the speaker was Elizabeth Gurley Flynn, the soap box orator was Ms. Goldman" (from "Recorded Letter" [1972], in Hertz, "Writer and Revolutionary," 147). If anything, this further complication indicates Gold's willingness to tailor his account of the event to suit his rhetorical needs.

69. *Anthology 200;* Michael Gold, *Hollow Men*, 69; Conroy, "Author's Field Day," 28.

70. Quoted in Gilbert and Gubar, *No Man's Land*, 143, 157.

71. Fiedler, "Literature and Lucre," 7 (also quoted in Gilbert and Gubar, *No Man's Land*, 143). This casting of mass culture as modernism's bane was characteristic of intellectuals of Gold's time; see Huyssen, "Mass Culture as Woman."

72. Gold attended Harvard in fall 1914 and left after one semester—not because he disliked the college, but because he was unable to maintain himself financially while studying full-time. His brief tenure at Harvard came during an outbreak of anti-Semitic rhetoric about the supposed invasion of the American university system by Jews. By 1922 Harvard's president, Abbot Lawrence Lowell (who not coincidentally served as vice president of the Immigration Restriction League), advocated quotas on admission of Jews to Harvard. The prevalence of this rhetoric—which also tended to emphasize that the presumed superior intelligence of Jews was at the expense of their physical capacity—no doubt contributed to Gold's bitterness about attending the university.

73. Michael Gold, "Love on a Garbage Dump," 184, 181, 185.

74. Ibid., 185.

75. Michael Gold, "High Brow vs. Low Brow."

76. Michael Gold, "Love on a Garbage Dump," 185.

77. "A Bird in a Gilded Cage" was cowritten by Harry von Tilzer, a Jew who changed his name so that it would sound more German than Jewish.

78. In Samuel Ornitz's *Haunch Paunch and Jowl*, the Jewish gangsters are the cynics writing these songs—indeed for money, as Gold's narrator supposes. See chapter 2.

79. Michael Gold, "Gangster's Mother," 1.

80. Quoted in Hofstadter, *Anti-Intellectualism in American Life*, 294.

81. Sedgwick, *Between Men*, 21, 5.

82. Bloom explains his usage: "Associated with Bismarck's consolidation and modernization of Germany in the 1870s, the term was actually introduced by a left liberal Bundesrat deputy to describe 'the great struggle for civilization in the interest of humanity.' Hence the ironic resonance of Kulturkampf when applied to Gold and [Joseph] Freeman recalls their will to progressive democratic change and to the transformation of a citizenry's consciousness thorough the adaptive appropriation of a culture's myths and icons" (*Left Letters*, 9).

83. Rabinowitz, *Labor and Desire*, 22–23.

84. Gilman, *Jewish Self-Hatred*, 71, 76.

85. Henry Adams, *Education of Henry Adams*, 238; James, *American Scene*, 139.

86. Bingham, "Foreign Criminals in New York," 383.

87. For an account of Jews in Hollywood movies before and after World War II, see Gabler, *Empire of Their Own*.

88. Blanc, *That's Not All, Folks!* 87.

89. Henry Roth, *Call It Sleep*, 68, 90.

90. Kauffman, *House of Bondage*, 19. A host of novels were published around this time in which pimps called "cadets"—frequently Jewish, "redskin," or "Oriental"—lure or kidnap girls into prostitution. The novels reflected and fanned a white-slave paranoia that peaked in 1910 and resulted in the notorious Mann Act, which made it illegal to transport women across state lines for illicit purposes. The popularity of white-slave novels and magazine serials was followed by a run of white-slave films— *What Happened to Mary, The Perils of Pauline, Exposure of the White Slave Traffic,* and many others (see Clarens, *Crime Movies*). These films were generally as titillating as they were admonishing; one, *Traffic in Souls* (1913), claimed to have been based upon the *Rockefeller White Slavery Report,* a document that is included as a kind of appendix to later printings of *House of Bondage.*

91. J. Q. Neets (Joshua Kunitz), who reviewed *Jews without Money* for *New Masses,* noted the conspicuous repetition of the Yiddish interjection *"Nu"* and objected to it as irritating: "One is somewhat annoyed, for instance, by the constantly reiterated italicized Jewish *Nu,* which is not infrequently tacked on to a sentence without any artistic or psychological function." Neets, Review of *Jews without Money*, 15.

92. Reznikoff, *Family Chronicle*, 98.

93. Kazin, *Walker*, 22.

94. For an account of the involvement of Jews in Tammany Hall, see Goren, *New York Jews.*

95. Eastman, *Love and Revolution*, 255.

96. Rosten, *Joys of Yiddish*, xviii; Singer quoted ibid., xix.

97. Klein, *Foreigners*, 248. Klein is referring especially to the debate surrounding Gold's verbal thrashing of Thornton Wilder.

98. Twain, *Huckleberry Finn*, 235.

99. Sandrow, *Vagabond Stars*, 137.

100. Shakespeare, *The Tempest* 1.2.363–65. Revisions and rereadings of the Caliban figure in various forms have become a fascination of postcolonial critics; see, for instance, Margaret Paul Joseph's study *Caliban in Exile* (1992), the scholarly journal of Native American writing *Caliban,* or Houston Baker's essay "Caliban's Triple Play" (1986). As James D. Bloom points out, the major success of Percy MacKaye's stage extravaganza *Caliban by the Yellow Sands* (1916) indicates the tropological importance of Caliban in Gold's time. MacKaye's play concludes with a subdued Caliban kneeling at the feet of Shakespeare; it was performed by a cast of more than a thousand to an audience of more than one hundred thousand.

101. Slobin, *Tenement Songs*, 24. For a discussion of Yiddish as "corrupt discourse" in the European context, see Gilman, *Jewish Self-Hatred*.

102. Hitler, *Mein Kampf*, 417.

103. James D. Bloom, *Left Letters*, 62. For a fuller discussion of Fyfka as Caliban, see Bloom's chapter "Caliban and the Police."

104. The Talmud, the chief object of Jewish religious education, is a lengthy collection of debates and commentaries of Jewish scholars dealing chiefly with the problems of everyday life, including not only food but also sex, marriage, law, worship, and so forth. Leo Rosten has a fairly energetic and just description of the Talmud in *Hooray for Yiddish!:* "The Talmud is not the Bible, not the Old Testament, not the Torah (the five books of Moses). It is the assembled, centuries-long analysis, debate and legal findings of Jewish scholars, jurists, philosophers and sages—from the fifth century before the Christian era until the second century after. I know of no body of seminars with which to compare it. It is a stenographic report of a millennial discussion of the Torah. It is majestic, profound, bursting with insights. It is also maddening: hair-splitting, superstitious, pedantic. Sophistry jostles reason, mythology confounds logic. But the intellectual totality is staggering" (322).

105. Hitler, *Mein Kampf*, 130.

106. James D. Bloom, *Left Letters*, 52.

107. The *New Masses* version reads, "So I yelled and yelled bananas." Michael Gold, "Jews without Money," 11.

108. Anzia Yezierska, in her novel *Bread Givers* (1925), also likens the protagonist's father in his moment of defeat to a modern King Lear wailing in the streets (284).

109. Charlie Chaplin was widely believed to be Jewish; Henry Ford's *Dearborn Independent* wrote that "Charlie Chaplin's name was, in all probability, Caplan, or Kaplan. At any rate, this is what the Jews believe about their great 'star'" ("Gentle Art," 115). Hannah Arendt mentions Chaplin in her essay "The Jew as Pariah" (79–81). Chaplin, a fellow traveler of sorts, was very popular in Gold's circle; Gold wrote an unsuccessful children's book on Chaplin (*Charlie Chaplin's Parade*), and in his autobiography Max Eastman recounts with evident pride the dinners he shared with Chaplin and his wife (Eastman, *Love and Revolution*, 172–74).

110. Antin, *Promised Land*, xii.

111. Illich, *Gender*, 45. For a discussion of how Illich can be interpreted as turning the feminist criticism upon which he heavily relies into shadow work, see Doane and Hodges, *Nostalgia and Sexual Difference*, 97–113.

112. Rabinowitz, *Labor and Desire*, 187.

Chapter 4: Business Is Business

1. These three novels are frequently lumped together as "The Williamsburg Trilogy," although they do not share characters, plot, or even a Williamsburg setting. According to Marcelline Krafchick's *World without Heroes*, Fuchs objected to his publisher's packaging of the novels as a trilogy—an apparent marketing ploy inspired by the large

"ethnic" trilogies being written at the time by influential novelists such as John Dos Passos and James T. Farrell (106 n. 31). For purposes of clarity, I refer to these novels collectively as Fuchs's "novels of the 1930s." (Fuchs published one additional novel, *West of the Rockies*, in 1971.)

2. Throughout this chapter, page citations in the text refer to Fuchs, *Three Novels*, and use these abbreviations:

SW   *Summer in Williamsburg*
HB   *Homage to Blenholt*
LC   *Low Company*

3. Walsh, *Public Enemies*, 62. For more details on the establishment of the National Crime Syndicate, see Walsh's discussion, ibid., 53–81.

4. Mandel, *Delightful Murder*, 31.

5. Krafchick, *World without Heroes*, 22.

6. Puzo, "Crime," 79.

7. Bell, "Crime," 129.

8. Alan Wald makes a passing mention of Fuchs in a list of "radical" writers whose works were reprinted during the 1960s (Wald, *Writing from the Left*, 17). Brian Neve also cites the effect of Fuchs's "radical" and "liberal" politics on the Hollywood films Fuchs scripted (Neve, *Film and Politics*, 147, 183). But with nominal exceptions, few critics consider Fuchs to be a radical writer.

9. Pells, *Radical Visions*, 194; Miller, *Daniel Fuchs*, 22.

10. See Folsom, *Days of Anger*. Other signatories in 1939 included Ben Appel (a communist novelist who also created Jewish gangsters), Van Wyck Brooks, DuBose Heyward, John Howard Lawson, Stanley Kunitz, Joshua Kunitz, Carey McWilliams, Dorothy Parker, and Muriel Rukeyser.

11. Fuchs's reply, as excerpted in the pamphlet: "The activities of Franco and his Italian-German allies in Spain make it impossible for me to have any doubt on the nature of fascism and its meaning to people who are concerned with peace, freedom and civilization. I am glad to list myself among those who are against Franco and fascism, and who are for the legal government of Republican Spain" (League of American Writers, *Writers Take Sides*, 26).

12. Warshow, "Gangster," 130.

13. For detailed historical accounts of Jewish gangsters' involvement in trade union struggles, see Foner, *Fur and Leather Workers Union*, Dubinsky and Raskin, *Life with Labor* (the autobiography of David Dubinsky, head of the ILGWU), and Fried, *Rise and Fall*. For fictionalized treatments, see Tax, *Rivington Street* (1982) and its sequel *Union Square* (1988); Gerald Green, *The Chains* (1980); and Levin, *The Old Bunch* (1937) and its sequel *Citizens* (1940).

14. Howe, "Daniel Fuchs' Williamsburg Trilogy," 100.

15. Anderson, *Hungry Men*, 22.

16. For more details, see Fried, *Rise and Fall*; Joselit, *Our Gang*; Fox, *Blood and Power*; and Walsh, *Public Enemies*.

17. As Jonathan Mumby astutely notes, the relationship of movie gangsterism to ethnic identity changed again with the gangster epics of the 1970s, when ethnic traits were emphasized and celebrated as marking "a clearer and less confusing American 'past' when men had an undiluted authentic and honorable 'identity'" (Mumby, "'Art of the Weak,'" 103).

18. Sante, *Low Life*, 341.

19. See Joselit, *Our Gang*, 169–70.

20. A selection of these letters has been translated by Moses Rischin and included in his anthology of Cahan's journalism, *Grandma Never Lived in America*.

21. Babel, "How It Was Done in Odessa," 213.

22. Fuchs, "Al Capone," 95.

23. Reed, *Reckless Eyeballing*, 16.

24. Babel, "How It Was Done in Odessa," 212.

25. Macdonald, "Mass Culture," 62.

26. As James Smethurst points out in his book *The New Red Negro*, few left-wing American critics of the 1930s and 1940s treated the subject of mass culture with any consistency. The more important theorizing work in this arena during the first half of the century was done within imaginative literature (for instance, in the poetry of Sterling Brown or Waring Cuney, or in the novels of Nathanael West or Fuchs).

27. Howe, "Notes on Mass Culture," 497, 496.

28. Denning, *Cultural Front*, 230.

29. On the documentary impulse in proletarian literature, Pells writes: "If some writers found it necessary to abandon fiction for journalism, there were others who tried to adapt the methods of the documentary to the traditional concerns of art. This is especially true of the 'proletarian' novel, which, whether or not it was written from a truly revolutionary perspective, exhibited many of the techniques of reportage: a preoccupation with the factual details of modern life, an emphasis on the function and relation of groups and classes, an interest in social types and external events" (Pells, *Radical Visions*, 202).

30. Rosten, *Hooray for Yiddish!* 212.

31. Miller, *Daniel Fuchs*, 17.

32. Fuchs, "Days in the Gardens," 2.

33. Fuchs, "Hollywood Diary," 131; also, Fuchs, "Days in the Gardens," 24.

Conclusion

1. See especially Meriwether, *Daddy Was a Numbers Runner*, and the movie *Hoodlum* (1997), directed by Bill Duke.

2. Singer, "Jewish Gangster"; Kraus, "Jewish Gangster." E. L. Doctorow's novel *Billy Bathgate* (1989), Meredith Tax's *Rivington Street* (1982) and its sequel *Union Square* (1988), Gerald Green's *The Chains* (1980), and Herbert Gold's *Fathers* (1962) are examples of historical novels that prominently feature Jewish gangsters.

3. See Singer, "Jewish Gangster," and Kraus, "Jewish Gangster."

4. The fact that the heyday of the Jewish gangster has ended does not mean that there are no more scares about Jewish gangsters. In the 1990s, the Jewish gangsters who make sensational news are all Russian Jews, whether they live in the former Soviet Union or have brought their criminal activity to Brooklyn's Brighton Beach neighborhood. An August 1992 article by Nathan M. Adams in *Reader's Digest* ("Menace of the Russian Mafia") shrills that "the world's fastest-growing crime network is now exporting its violence to the United States" (33). James Gray's movie about the Jewish mob in Brighton Beach, *Little Odessa* (1995), implies that these Russian-born Brooklyn thugs are the scattered grandchildren of Benya Krik: the protagonist's Yiddish-speaking grandmother is named Tsilya, which is the name of Benya Krik's wife.

5. Doctorow, *Billy Bathgate*, 27.

6. Levine's painting is held by the Whitney Museum of American Art, New York.

7. Philip Roth, *Zuckerman Unbound*, in *Zuckerman Bound*, 335–40.

8. Levine is quoted in Shapiro, *Social Realism*, 267.

9. Ibid., 266.

10. Levine, *Jack Levine*, 59.

11. Soby, "'Gangster's Funeral' (1953)," 58.

12. Shapiro, *Social Realism*, 267.

13. Clarens, *Crime Movies*, 14.

References Cited

In cases where I relied on the Russian version of a work but quoted an English translation in the text, the two versions are included here as a single entry. Unless otherwise indicated, page numbers cited throughout this book refer to the reprint editions listed below.

Aaron, Daniel. *Writers on the Left: Episodes in American Literary Communism.* 1961. Reprint, New York: Columbia University Press, 1992.

Adams, Henry. *The Education of Henry Adams: An Autobiography.* 1918. Reprint, Boston: Houghton Mifflin, 1961.

Adams, Nathan M. "Menace of the Russian Mafia." *Reader's Digest,* August 1992, 33–40.

Anderson, Edward. *Hungry Men.* 1935. Reprint, Norman: University of Oklahoma Press, 1993.

Antin, Mary. *The Promised Land.* 1912. Reprint, New York: Riverside Press, 1940.

Arendt, Hannah. "The Jew as Pariah: A Hidden Tradition." 1944. Reprinted in *The Jew as Pariah: Jewish Identity and Politics in the Modern Age.* Ed. Ron H. Feldman. 67–90. New York: Grove Press, 1978.

Asinof, Eliot. *Eight Men Out: The Black Sox and the 1919 World Series.* 1963. Reprint, New York: H. Holt, 1987.

Babel, I. E. [Isaac Emmanuelovich Babel]. "After the Battle." In *The Collected Stories of Isaac Babel.* Trans. and Ed. Walter Morison. 182–87. New York: New American Library, 1955. "Poslye boya." 1920. Reprinted in *Detstvo i drugie rasskazy.* 221–25. Jerusalem: Aliya, 1979.

———. "Avtobiografiya." 1932. Reprinted in *Detstvo i drugie rasskazy.* 7–8. Jerusalem: Aliya, 1979.

———. "Awakening." In *The Collected Stories of Isaac Babel.* Trans. and Ed. Walter

Morison. 304–14. New York: New American Library, 1955. "Probuzhdenie." 1930. Reprinted in *Detstvo i drugie rasskazy*. 68–75. Jerusalem: Aliya, 1979.

———. *Benya Krik: A Film-Novel*. Trans. Ivor Montagu and S. S. Nolvandov. Westport, Conn.: Hyperion Press, 1973. *Benya Krik: Kinopovest'*. 1926. Reprinted in *Sochineniya v dvukh tomakh* 2:406–46. Moscow: Khudozhestvennaya literatura, 1990.

———. *The Collected Stories of Isaac Babel*. Trans. and Ed. Walter Morison. New York: New American Library, 1955.

———. *Detstvo i drugie rasskazy* (Childhood and other stories). Jerusalem: Aliya, 1979.

———. "The Father." In *The Collected Stories of Isaac Babel*. Trans. and Ed. Walter Morison. 223–33. New York: New American Library, 1955. "Otets." 1924. Reprinted in *Detstvo i drugie rasskazy*. 270–79. Jerusalem: Aliya, 1979.

———. "Froim Grach." Trans. Max Hayward. In *Isaac Babel: The Lonely Years, 1925–1939*. Trans. Andrew R. MacAndrew and Max Hayward. Ed. Nathalie Babel. 10–15. New York: Farrar, Straus, 1964. "Froim Grach." 1933?/1963. Reprinted in *Detstvo i drugie rasskazy*. 292–97. Jerusalem: Aliya, 1979.

———. "Guy de Maupassant." In *The Collected Stories of Isaac Babel*. Trans. and Ed. Walter Morison. 328–37. New York: New American Library, 1955. "Gyui de Mopassan." 1920–22. Reprinted in *Detstvo i drugie rasskazy*. 81–89. Jerusalem: Aliya, 1979.

———. "How It Was Done in Odessa." In *The Collected Stories of Isaac Babel*. Trans. and Ed. Walter Morison. 211–22. New York: New American Library, 1955. "Kak eto delalos' v Odesse." 1923. Reprinted in *Detstvo i drugie rasskazy*. 246–55. Jerusalem: Aliya, 1979.

———. "In the Basement." In *The Collected Stories of Isaac Babel*. Trans. and Ed. Walter Morison. 293–304. New York: New American Library, 1955. "V podvale." 1929. Reprinted in *Detstvo i drugie rasskazy*. 58–67. Jerusalem: Aliya, 1979.

———. *Isaac Babel: Collected Stories*. Trans. and Ed. David McDuff. New York: Penguin Books, 1994.

———. *Isaac Babel: The Lonely Years, 1925–1939*. Trans. Andrew R. MacAndrew and Max Hayward. Ed. Nathalie Babel. New York: Farrar, Straus, 1964.

———. "Justice in Brackets." In *Isaac Babel: Collected Stories*. Trans. and Ed. David McDuff. 254–59. New York: Penguin Books, 1994. "Spravidlivost' v skobkakh." 1921. Reprinted in *Detstvo i drugie rasskazy*. 256–62. Jerusalem: Aliya, 1979.

———. "The King." In *The Collected Stories of Isaac Babel*. Trans. and Ed. Walter Morison. 203–11. New York: New American Library, 1955. "Korol'." 1921. Reprinted in *Detstvo i drugie rasskazy*. 239–45. Jerusalem: Aliya, 1979.

———. "The Life and Adventures of Matthew Pavlichenko." In *The Collected Stories of Isaac Babel*. Trans. and Ed. Walter Morison. 100–106. New York: New American Library, 1955. "Zhizneopisanie Pavlichenki, Matveya Rodionycha." 1924. Reprinted in *Detstvo i drugie rasskazy*. 152–57. Jerusalem: Aliya, 1979.

———. "Lyubka Cossack." In *The Collected Stories of Isaac Babel*. Trans. and Ed. Walter Morison. 234–44. New York: New American Library, 1955. "Lyubka Kazak." 1924. Reprinted in *Detstvo i drugie rasskazy*. 263–69. Jerusalem: Aliya, 1979.

———. "Moi pervyi gonovar" (My first fee). 1922–23/1963. Reprinted in *Sochineniya v dvukh tomakh* 2:245–53. Moscow: Khudozhestvennaya literatura, 1990.

———. "My First Goose." In *The Collected Stories of Isaac Babel.* Trans. and Ed. Walter Morison. 72–76. New York: New American Library, 1955. "Moi pervyi gus'." 1924. Reprinted in *Detstvo i drugie rasskazy.* 129–32. Jerusalem: Aliya, 1979.

———. *1920 Diary.* Trans. H. T. Willetts. Ed. Carol J. Avins. New Haven, Conn.: Yale University Press, 1995.

———. "Odessa." In *You Must Know Everything: Stories, 1915–1937.* Trans. Max Hayward. Ed. Nathalie Babel. 26–30. New York: Farrar, Straus, and Giroux, 1966.

———. [Bab-El, pseud.]. "Odessa." 1916. Reprinted in *Sochineniya v dvukh tomakh* 1:62–65. Moscow: Khudozhestvennaya literatura, 1990.

———. "Pervaya lyubov'" (First love). 1925. Reprinted in *Detstvo i drugie rasskazy.* 49–57. Jerusalem: Aliya, 1979.

———. "Shabbos Nakhamu." 1918. Reprinted in *Detstvo i drugie rasskazy.* 19–25. Jerusalem: Aliya, 1979.

———. *Sochineniya v dvukh tomakh* (Works in two volumes). Moscow: Khudozhestvennaya literatura, 1990.

———. "The Story of My Dovecote." In *The Collected Stories of Isaac Babel.* Trans. and Ed. Walter Morison. 251–64. New York: New American Library, 1955. "Istoriya moei golubyatin." 1925. Reprinted in *Detstvo i drugie rasskazy.* 36–48. Jerusalem: Aliya, 1979.

———. "Sunset." In *You Must Know Everything: Stories, 1915–1937.* Trans. Max Hayward. Ed. Nathalie Babel. 135–54. New York: Farrar, Straus, and Giroux, 1966. "Zakat." 1924–25/1964. Reprinted in *Detstvo i drugie rasskazy.* 280–91. Jerusalem: Aliya, 1979.

———. "V Odesse kazhdiy yunosha. . ." (In Odessa every youth . . .). 1923. In *Sochineniya v dvukh tomakh* 2:358. Moscow: Khudozhestvennaya literatura, 1990.

———. *You Must Know Everything: Stories, 1915–1937.* 1966. Trans. Max Hayward. Ed. Nathalie Babel. Reprint, New York: Farrar, Straus, and Giroux, 1969.

———. *Zakat* (Sunset). 1928. Reprint, Letchworth, England: Prideaux Press, 1977.

Baker, Carlos. *Ernest Hemingway: A Life Story.* New York: Charles Scribner's Sons, 1969.

Baker, Houston. "Caliban's Triple Play." In *"Race" Writing and Difference.* Ed. Henry Louis Gates Jr. 381–95. Chicago: University of Chicago Press, 1986.

Bakhtin, M. M. *Problems of Dostoevsky's Poetics.* Trans. and Ed. Caryl Emerson. Minneapolis: University of Minnesota Press, 1984.

Barlow, Joel. *Columbiad.* Baltimore: Conrad Lucas, 1807.

Baron, Salo W. *The Russian Jew under Tsars and Soviets.* 2d ed. New York: Macmillan, 1976.

Bell, Daniel. "Crime as an American Way of Life: A Queer Ladder of Social Mobility." In *The End of Ideology: On the Exhaustion of Political Ideas in the Fifties.* 127–50. 1960. Reprint, Cambridge, Mass.: Harvard University Press, 1988.

Berzin, Yulii. *Ford.* Petrograd: n.p., 1928.

Billy Bathgate. Dir. Robert Benton. Warner Bros./Touchstone, 1991.

Bingham, Theodore A. "Foreign Criminals in New York." *North American Review* 188, no. 3 (1908): 383–94.

References Cited

Blanc, Mel, with Philip Bashe. *That's Not All, Folks!* New York: Warner Books, 1988.

Bloom, Harold, ed. *Isaac Babel.* New York: Chelsea House, 1987.

Bloom, James D. *Left Letters: The Culture Wars of Mike Gold and Joseph Freeman.* New York: Columbia University Press, 1992.

Boelhower, William. "Ethnic Trilogies: A Genealogical and Generational Poetics." In *The Invention of Ethnicity.* Ed. Werner Sollors. 158–75. New York: Oxford University Press, 1988.

———. *Through a Glass Darkly: Ethnic Semiosis in American Literature.* New York: Oxford University Press, 1987.

Breines, Paul. *Tough Jews: Political Fantasies and the Moral Dilemma of American Jewry.* New York: Basic Books, 1990.

Brooks, Jeffrey. *When Russia Learned to Read: Literacy and Popular Literature, 1861–1917.* Princeton, N.J.: Princeton University Press, 1985.

Brooks, Van Wyck. *America's Coming of Age.* 1915. Reprinted in *Van Wyck Brooks: The Early Years.* Ed. Claire Sprague. 79–158. New York: Harper and Row, 1968.

Budennyi, S[emyon]. "Babizm Babelya iz *Krasnoy novi*" (The sluttishness of Babel from *Red Virgin Soil*). *Oktyabr'* 3 (1924): 196–97.

Bugsy. Dir. Barry Levinson. TriStar/Desert Vision, 1991.

Bullard, Arthur [Albert Edwards]. *Comrade Yetta.* 1913. Reprint, Upper Saddle River, N.J.: Gregg Press, 1968.

Bullets over Broadway. Dir. Woody Allen. Miramax, 1994.

Cahan, Abraham. *"Grandma Never Lived in America": The New Journalism of Abraham Cahan.* Ed. Moses Rischin. Bloomington: Indiana University Press, 1985.

———. *The Rise of David Levinsky.* 1917. Reprint, New York: Harper and Row, 1960.

Chametzky, Jules. *From the Ghetto: The Fiction of Abraham Cahan.* Amherst: University of Massachusetts Press, 1977.

Clarens, Carlos. *Crime Movies: An Illustrated History.* New York: W. W. Norton, 1980.

Clarke, Donald Henrick. *In the Reign of Rothstein.* New York: Grosset and Dunlap, 1929.

Cohen, Rich. *Tough Jews: Fathers, Sons, and Gangster Dreams.* New York: Simon and Schuster, 1998.

Conrad, Joseph. *Heart of Darkness.* 1902. Reprint, Ed. D. C. R. A. Goonetilleke, Orchard Park, N.Y.: Broadview Press, 1995.

Conroy, Jack. "Author's Field Day: A Symposium on Marxist Criticism." *New Masses* 12, no. 1 (3 July 1934): 27–32.

Cowley, Malcolm. *Exile's Return: A Literary Odyssey of the 1920s.* New York: Viking, 1951.

———. *Exile's Return: A Narrative of Ideas.* New York: W. W. Norton, 1934.

Cross, Wilbur L. *The Life and Times of Laurence Sterne.* 3d ed. London: H. Milford, Oxford University Press, 1929.

Dawidoff, Robert. "Some of Those Days." *Western Humanities Review* 41, no. 3 (1987): 263–86.

Dennen, Leon. *Where the Ghetto Ends: Jews in Soviet Russia.* New York: Alfred H. King, 1934.

Denning, Michael. *Cultural Front: The Laboring of American Culture in the Twentieth Century.* New York: Verso, 1996.

Dick, Bernard F. *Radical Innocence: A Critical Study of the Hollywood Ten.* Lexington: University Press of Kentucky, 1989.

Doane, Janice, and Devon Hodges. *Nostalgia and Sexual Difference: The Resistance to Contemporary Feminism.* New York: Methuen, 1987.

Doctorow, E. L. *Billy Bathgate.* New York: Harper and Row, 1989.

The Doorway to Hell. Dir. Archie L. Mayo. Warner Bros., 1930.

Dostoevsky, Fyodor. *Notes from Underground* (Zapiski iz podpol'ya). Trans. Mirra Ginsburg. New York: Bantam, 1974.

Douglas, Ann. *Terrible Honesty: Mongrel Manhattan in the 1920s.* New York: Farrar, Straus, and Giroux, 1995.

Dubinsky, David, and A. H. Raskin. *A Life with Labor.* New York: Simon and Schuster, 1977.

Dylan, Bob. "Bob Dylan's 115th Dream." *Bringing It All Back Home.* CBS, 1965.

Eastman, Max. *Love and Revolution: My Journey through an Epoch.* New York: Random House, 1964.

Eight Men Out. Dir. John Sayles. Orion, 1988.

Eikhenbaum, B. M. "Illyuziya skaza" (The illusion of skaz). 1918. In *Skvoz' literatura: Sbornik statei.* 152–56. Leningrad: Academia, 1924.

———. "Kak sdelano 'Shinel' Gogolya" (How Gogol's *Overcoat* was made). 1919. In *Skvoz' literatura: Sbornik statei.* 171–75. Leningrad: Academia, 1924.

Eliot, T. S. "The Hollow Men." 1925. Reprinted in *The Complete Poems and Plays, 1909–1950.* 56–59. New York: Harcourt Brace Jovanovich, 1971.

———. "Notes toward the Definition of Culture." 1948. Reprinted in *Christianity and Culture.* 79–187. New York: Harcourt Brace Jovanovich, 1988.

———. *The Waste Land.* 1922. Reprinted in *The Complete Poems and Plays, 1909–1950.* 37–49. New York: Harcourt Brace Jovanovich, 1971.

Ellison, Ralph. *Invisible Man.* 1952. Reprint, New York: Vintage Books, 1972.

Ellmann, Richard. *James Joyce.* New York: Oxford University Press, 1959.

Emerson, Ralph Waldo. *Nature.* 1836. Reprint, Boston: Beacon Press, 1991.

Erlich, Victor. *Modernism and Revolution: Russian Literature in Transition.* Cambridge, Mass.: Harvard University Press, 1994.

Falen, James. *Isaac Babel: Russian Master of the Short Story.* Knoxville: University of Tennessee Press, 1974.

Fearing, Kenneth. *New and Selected Poems.* 1956. Reprint, Bloomington: Indiana University Press, 1974.

———. "St. Agnes Eve." *New Masses* 1, no. 5 (September 1926): 11.

Federal Writers Project. *New York City Guide: A Comprehensive Guide to the Five Boroughs of New York.* New York: Random House, 1939.

Fiedler, Leslie. "Literature and Lucre." *New York Times Book Review,* 31 May 1981, 7.

Fielding, Henry. *The History of Tom Jones, a Foundling.* 1749. Reprint, New York: Washington Square Press, 1963.

Fitzgerald, F. Scott. *The Great Gatsby.* 1925. Reprint, New York: Charles Scribner's Sons, 1953.

Foley, Barbara. *Radical Representations: Politics and Form in U.S. Proletarian Fiction, 1929–1941.* Durham, N.C.: Duke University Press, 1993.

Folsom, Franklin. *Days of Anger, Days of Hope: A Memoir of the League of American Writers, 1937–1942.* Niwot: University Press of Colorado, 1994.

Foner, Philip Sheldon. *The Bolshevik Revolution: Its Impact on American Radicals, Liberals, and Labor.* New York: International Publishers, 1967.

———. *The Fur and Leather Workers Union: A Story of Dramatic Struggles and Achievements.* Newark, N.J.: Nordan Press, 1950.

A Force of Evil. Dir. Abraham Polonsky. Enterprise/MGM, 1948.

Fox, Stephen. *Blood and Power: Organized Crime in Twentieth-Century America.* New York: Penguin Books, 1989.

Franklin, Paul B. "Homosexual Jew(el)ry: Homophobia and Anti-Semitism in the Prosecution of 'Babe' Leopold and 'Dickie' Loeb." Paper presented at the annual meeting of the American Studies Association, Boston, 1993.

Freidin, Gregory. "Isaac Babel." In *European Writers of the Twentieth Century.* Ed. George Stade. 11:1885–1915. New York: Charles Scribner's Sons, 1993.

Fried, Albert. *The Rise and Fall of the Jewish Gangster in America.* New York: Holt, Rinehart, and Winston, 1980.

Friedberg, Maurice. *How Things Were Done in Odessa: Cultural and Intellectual Pursuits in a Soviet City.* Boulder, Colo.: Westview Press, 1991.

———. "Jewish Themes in Soviet Russian Literature." In *The Jews in the Soviet Union since 1917.* Ed. Lionel Kochan. 188–207. New York: Oxford University Press, 1978.

Friedman, Lester D. *Hollywood's Image of the Jew.* New York: Frederick Ungar, 1982.

Fuchs, Daniel. "Days in the Gardens of Hollywood." *New York Times Book Review,* 18 July 1971, 2–3, 24–25.

———. "A Hollywood Diary." In *The Apathetic Bookie Joint.* 131–39. New York: Methuen, 1979.

———. "The Silents Spoke to the Immigrants." *New York Times,* 17 October 1971, 1A.

———. *Three Novels by Daniel Fuchs: "Summer in Williamsburg," "Homage to Blenholt," "Low Company."* New York: Basic Books, 1961.

———. *West of the Rockies.* New York: Knopf, 1971.

———. "Where Al Capone Grew Up." *The New Republic* 9 (9 September 1931): 95–97.

Gabler, Neal. *An Empire of Their Own: How the Jews Invented Hollywood.* New York: Crown, 1981.

The Gangster. Dir. Gordon Wiles. Screenplay Daniel Fuchs, based on his novel *Low Company.* Monogram, 1947.

"The Gentle Art of Changing Jewish Names." In *Aspects of Jewish Power in the United States.* 109–20. Vol. 4 of *The International Jew: The World's Foremost Problem.* Dearborn, Mich.: Dearborn Publishing, 1922. Originally published in the *Dearborn Independent.*

Gilbert, Sandra M., and Susan Gubar. *No Man's Land: The Place of the Woman Writer in the Twentieth Century*. Vol. 1, *The War of the Words*. New Haven, Conn.: Yale University Press, 1988.

Gilman, Sander. *Jewish Self-Hatred: Anti-Semitism and the Hidden Language of the Jews*. Baltimore: Johns Hopkins University Press, 1986.

———. *The Jew's Body*. New York: Routledge, 1991.

Glatshteyn, Jacob. "Sheeny Mike" (Shini Mayk). 1929. In *American Yiddish Poetry: A Bilingual Anthology*. Trans. and Ed. Benjamin Harshav and Barbara Harshav et al. 241–46. Berkeley: University of California Press, 1986.

The Godfather. Dir. Francis Coppola. Based on the novel by Mario Puzo. Paramount, 1972.

The Godfather: Part 2. Dir. Francis Coppola. Paramount, 1974.

The Godfather: Part 3. Dir. Francis Coppola. Zoetrope/Paramount, 1990.

Gold, Herbert. *Fathers*. New York: Random House, 1962.

Gold, Michael. "America Needs a Critic." 1926. Reprinted in *Mike Gold: A Literary Anthology*. Ed. Michael Folsom. 129–39. New York: International Publishers, 1972.

———. "The American Famine." 1921. Reprinted in *Mike Gold: A Literary Anthology*. Ed. Michael Folsom. 86–95. New York: International Publishers, 1972.

———. *Charlie Chaplin's Parade*. New York: Harcourt, 1930.

———. "The Gangster's Mother." *New Masses* 4, no. 3 (August 1928): 3–6.

———. "Go Left, Young Writers!" 1929. Reprinted in *Mike Gold: A Literary Anthology*. Ed. Michael Folsom. 186–89. New York: International Publishers, 1972.

———. "High Brow vs. Low Brow." *New Masses* 3, no. 4 (August 1927): 27.

———. *The Hollow Men*. New York: International Publishers, 1941.

———. "A Jewish Childhood in the New York Slums." 1959. Reprinted in *Mike Gold: A Literary Anthology*. Ed. Michael Folsom. 292–319. New York: International Publishers, 1972.

———. *Jews without Money*. 1930. Reprint, New York: International Publishers, 1942.

———. "Jews without Money: From a Book of East Side Memoirs." *New Masses* 4, no. 1 (June 1928): 11–12.

———. "John Reed and the Real Thing." *New Masses* 3, no. 7 (November 1927): 7–8.

———. "A Love Letter for France." 1935. Reprinted in *Mike Gold: A Literary Anthology*. Ed. Michael Folsom. 231–42. New York: International Publishers, 1972.

———. "Love on a Garbage Dump." 1928. Reprinted in *Mike Gold: A Literary Anthology*. Ed. Michael Folsom. 177–85. New York: International Publishers, 1972.

———. *Mike Gold: A Literary Anthology*. Ed. Michael Folsom. New York: International Publishers, 1972.

———. "Renegades: A Warning of the End." In *The Hollow Men*. 58–96. New York: International Publishers, 1942.

———. "Thoughts of a Great Thinker." *Liberator* 5, no. 4 (April 1922): 23–25.

———. "Wilder: Prophet of the Genteel Christ." 1930. Reprinted in *Mike Gold: A Literary Anthology*. Ed. Michael Folsom. 197–202. New York: International Publishers, 1972.

Goldfaden, Abraham. "Rozhinkes mit Mandlen" (Raisins and almonds). In *Mir Trogn a Gezang.* Ed. Eleanor Mlotek. 4. New York: Workmen's Circle Education Department, 1972.

Goren, Arthur. *New York Jews and the Quest for Community: The Kehillah Experiment, 1908–1922.* New York: Columbia University Press, 1970.

Green, Gerald. *The Chains.* New York: Seaview Books, 1980.

Greenberg, Clement. "Avant-Garde and Kitsch." 1946. In *Mass Culture: The Popular Arts in America.* Ed. Bernard Rosenberg and David Manning White. 98–107. Glencoe, Ill.: Free Press, 1957.

Greenberg, Eric Rolfe. *The Celebrant.* Lincoln: University of Nebraska Press, 1983.

Hapgood, Hutchins. *The Spirit of the Ghetto: Studies of the Jewish Quarter of New York.* 1902. Reprint, New York: Schocken Books, 1966.

Harrington, Michael. Afterword to *Jews without Money,* by Michael Gold. 227–34. New York: Avon Books, 1965.

Harshav, Benjamin. "American Yiddish Poetry and Its Background." In *American Yiddish Poetry: A Bilingual Anthology.* Trans. and Ed. Benjamin Harshav and Barbara Harshav et al. 3–73. Berkeley: University of California Press, 1986.

———. *The Meaning of Yiddish.* Berkeley: University of California Press, 1990.

Harshav, Benjamin, and Barbara Harshav, eds. and trans. *American Yiddish Poetry: A Bilingual Anthology.* Trans. with Kathryn Hellerstein, Brian McHale, and Anita Norich. Berkeley: University of California Press, 1986.

Havazelet, Ehud. "To Live in Tiflis in the Springtime." *New England Review* 15, no. 3 (Summer 1993): 35–56.

Hawthorne, Nathaniel. *The Scarlet Letter.* 1850. Reprint, New York: Oxford University Press, 1990.

Herlihy, Patricia. *Odessa: A History, 1794–1914.* Cambridge, Mass.: Harvard University Press, 1986.

Hertz, Howard Lee. "Writer and Revolutionary: The Life and Works of Michael Gold, Father of Proletarian Literature in the United States." 2 vols. Ph.D. diss., University of Texas at Austin, 1974.

Hitler, Adolf. *Mein Kampf.* 1925. Trans. Ralph Manheim. Reprint, Boston: Houghton Mifflin, 1943.

Hofstadter, Richard. *Anti-Intellectualism in American Life.* New York: Vintage Books, 1962.

Holleran, Andrew. *Dancer from the Dance.* 1978. Reprint, New York: Plume Books, 1986.

Honors, L. "A Talk with the Guiding Spirit of Three Broadway Theatres." *Jewish Daily Forward,* 29 April 1923, 3.

Hoodlum. Dir. Bill Duke. United Artists, 1997.

Howe, Irving. "Daniel Fuchs' Williamsburg Trilogy: A Cigarette and a Window." In *Proletarian Writers of the Thirties.* Ed. David Madden. 96–105. Carbondale: Southern Illinois University Press, 1968.

———. "Notes on Mass Culture." In *Mass Culture: The Popular Arts in America.* Ed. Bernard Rosenberg and David Manning White. 496–503. Glencoe, Ill.: Free Press, 1957. Originally published in *Politics* 5 (Spring 1948): 120–23.

————, ed. *Jewish-American Stories*. New York: New American Library, 1977.

Howe, Irving, and Eliezer Greenberg, eds. *A Treasury of Yiddish Stories*. New York: Schocken Books, 1953.

Huyssen, Andreas. "Mass Culture as Woman: Modernism's Other." In *After the Great Divide: Modernism, Mass Culture, Postmodernism*. 44–62. Bloomington: Indiana University Press, 1986.

Ilf, Ilya, and Yevgeny Petrov. *Dvenadtsat' stul'ev; Zolotoi telyonok* (The twelve chairs [1928]; Little golden calf [1931]). Moscow: Khudozhestvennaya literatura, 1990.

————. *Little Golden America*. Trans. Charles Malamuth. New York: Farrar and Rinehart, 1937.

Illich, Ivan. *Gender*. New York: Pantheon Books, 1982.

Inside of the White Slavery Traffic. Dir. Frank Beal. Moral Feature Film Co., 1913.

Jacobson, Matthew Frye. *Whiteness of a Different Color: European Immigrants and the Alchemy of Race*. Cambridge, Mass.: Harvard University Press, 1998.

James, Henry. *The American Scene*. 1907. Reprint, New York: Horizon Press, 1967.

Jazzmen (My iz dzhaza). Dir. Karen Shakhnazarov. Mosfilm, 1983.

"The Jewish Degradation of American Baseball." In *Jewish Influences in American Life*. 51–63. Vol. 3 of *The International Jew: The World's Foremost Problem*. Dearborn, Mich.: Dearborn Publishing, 1921. Originally published in the *Dearborn Independent*.

"Jewish Gamblers Corrupt American Baseball." In *Jewish Influences in American Life*. 37–50. Vol. 3 of *The International Jew: The World's Foremost Problem*. Dearborn, Mich.: Dearborn Publishing, 1921. Originally published in the *Dearborn Independent*.

Johnson, Brian D. "Intimate Affairs." In *Conversations with Philip Roth*. Ed. George J. Searles. 254–58. Jackson: University Press of Mississippi, 1992.

Johnson, James Weldon. *The Autobiography of an Ex-Coloured Man*. 1912. Reprint, New York: Hill and Wang, 1960.

Joselit, Jenna Weissman. *Our Gang: Jewish Crime and the New York Jewish Community, 1900–1940*. Bloomington: Indiana University Press, 1983.

Joseph, Margaret Paul. *Caliban in Exile: The Outsider in Caribbean Fiction*. New York: Greenwood Press, 1992.

Joyce, James. *A Portrait of the Artist as a Young Man*. 1916. Reprint, New York: Viking Press, 1947.

————. *Ulysses: The Corrected Text*. 1922. Reprint, New York: Vintage Books, 1986.

Kalaidjian, Walter. *American Culture between the Wars: Revisionary Modernism and Postmodern Critique*. New York: Columbia University Press, 1993.

Kalinin, Mikhail Ivanovich. "Evrei-zemledel'tsy v soyuze narodov SSSR" (The Jew and the farmer in the union of peoples of the USSR). Speech delivered at the Congress of the Jewish Land Settlement Society, Moscow, 17 November 1926. In *Za eti gody: stati, besedy, rechi*. New Haven, Conn.: Yale University Library Photographic Services, 1975.

Kataev, Valentin. *Raztrachiki* (The embezzlers). 1928. Reprint, Moscow: Federatsya, 1933.

Katcher, Leo. *The Big Bankroll: The Life and Times of Arnold Rothstein*. New York: Harper, 1959.

Kauffman, Reginald Wright. *House of Bondage.* New York: Grosset and Dunlap, 1910.

Kaverin, Venyamin. *Konets khazy* (End of the gang). 1924. Reprint, Moscow: Khudo-zhestvennaya literatura, 1980.

Kazin, Alfred. *A Walker in the City.* New York: Harcourt Brace Jovanovich, 1951.

Klein, Marcus. *Foreigners: The Making of American Literature, 1900–1940.* Chicago: University of Chicago Press, 1981.

———. "The Roots of Radicals: Experience in the Thirties." In *Proletarian Writers of the Thirties.* Ed. David Madden. 134–57. Carbondale: Southern Illinois University Press, 1968.

Kozakov, Mikhail. "Povest' o karlike Makse" (Tale about Max the dwarf). 1926. Re-printed in *Chelovek padayushchii nits* (Man falling prostrate). 99–160. Leningrad: Priboi, 1930.

Krafchick, Marcelline. *World without Heroes: The Brooklyn Novels of Daniel Fuchs.* Rutherford, N.J.: Fairleigh Dickinson University Press, 1988.

Kraus, Joe. "The Jewish Gangster: A Conversation across Generations." *American Scholar* (Winter 1995): 53–65.

Lansky. Dir. John McNaughton. HBO, 1999.

League of American Writers. *Writers Take Sides: Letters about the War in Spain from 418 American Authors.* New York: League of American Writers, 1938.

Leiderman, N. "I ya khochu internatsionala dobrykh lyudei . . ." (And I want an inter-national of good people . . .). *Literaturnye obozrenie* 10 (1991): 11.

Lenin, V. I. "Critical Remarks on the National Question." 1913. Reprinted in *Lenin on Literature and Art.* 88–95. Moscow: Progress Publishers, 1967.

Leonov, Leonid. *Vor* (Thief). 1927. Reprint, Moscow: Khudozhestvennaya literatura, 1979.

Let 'Em Have It. Dir. Sam Wood. Reliance Pictures/United Artists, 1935.

Levin, Meyer. *Citizens.* New York: Viking Press, 1940.

———. *The Old Bunch.* 1937. Reprint, Secaucus, N.J.: Citadel Press, 1985.

Levine, Jack. *Jack Levine.* New York: Rizzoli International Publications, 1989.

Libedinskii, Yurii. "Nedelya" (A week). 1922. Reprint, Moscow: Gosudarstvennoe izdatel'stvo khudozhestvennoi literatury, 1934.

Little Caesar. Dir. Mervyn LeRoy. Warner Bros./First National, 1930.

Little Odessa. Dir. James Gray. Fine Line/New Line, 1994.

Love and Death. Dir. Woody Allen. Rollins and Joffe, 1975.

Luna Park. Dir. Pavel Lungin. Blyuz, 1994.

Macdonald, Dwight. "A Theory of Mass Culture." In *Mass Culture: The Popular Arts in America.* Ed. Bernard Rosenberg and David Manning White. 74–97. Glencoe, Ill.: Free Press, 1957.

MacKaye, Percy. *Caliban by the Yellow Sands.* Garden City, N.Y.: Doubleday, Page, 1916.

Mandel, Ernest. *Delightful Murder: A Social History of the Crime Story.* Minneapolis: University of Minnesota Press, 1984.

Man without a World. Dir. Eleanor Antin. 1991.

Marcus, Stephen. "The Stories of Isaac Babel." *Partisan Review* 23, no. 3 (1955): 400–411.

Matisoff, James A. *Blessings, Curses, Hopes, and Fears: Psycho-Ostensive Expressions in Yiddish.* Philadelphia: Institute for the Study of Human Issues, 1979.

Mayakovsky, Vladimir. *"The Bedbug" and Selected Poetry.* Trans. Max Hayward and George Reavey. Ed. Patricia Blake. Bloomington: Indiana University Press, 1973.

McKay, Claude. *A Long Way from Home.* 1937. Reprint, London: Pluto Press, 1980.

Meisel, Perry. *The Cowboy and the Dandy: Crossing over from Romanticism to Rock and Roll.* New York: Oxford University Press, 1999.

Melnick, Jeffrey. *A Right to Sing the Blues: African Americans, Jews, and American Popular Song.* Cambridge, Mass.: Harvard University Press, 1999.

Melville, Herman. *Moby-Dick, or, The Whale.* 1851. Reprint, Evanston, Ill.: Northwestern University Press, 1988.

Mendele Moykher-Sforim. "Notes for My Biography." 1889. Trans. Gerald Stillman. In *Selected Works of Mendele Moykher-Sforim.* Ed. Marvin S. Zuckerman, Gerald Stillman, and Marion Herbst. 31–46. Malibu, Calif.: Joseph Simon-Pangloss Press, 1991.

———. *Selected Works of Mendele Moykher-Sforim.* Ed. Marvin S. Zuckerman, Gerald Stillman, and Marion Herbst. Malibu, Calif.: Joseph Simon-Pangloss Press, 1991.

———. *The Travels of Benjamin III.* In *Selected Works of Mendele Moykher-Sforim.* Ed. Marvin S. Zuckerman, Gerald Stillman, and Marion Herbst. 353–74. Malibu, Calif.: Joseph Simon-Pangloss Press, 1991.

Meriwether, Louise. *Daddy Was a Numbers Runner.* 1970. Reprint, New York: Methuen, 1986.

Miller, Gabriel. *Daniel Fuchs.* New York: Twayne, 1979.

———. Introduction to *Allrightniks Row: Haunch Paunch and Jowl. The Makings of a Professional Jew,* by Samuel Ornitz. New York: Markus Wiener, 1985.

Miller's Crossing. Dir. Joel Coen. 20th Century Fox/Circle, 1990.

"Mother Goose." Dir. Bill Tytla. Famous Studios, 1947.

Mumby, Jonathan. *"Manhattan Melodrama*'s 'Art of the Weak': Telling History from the Other Side in the 1930s Talking Gangster Film." *Journal of American Studies* 30, pt. 1 (April 1996): 101–18.

Murphy, James F. *The Proletarian Moment: The Controversy over Leftism in Literature.* Urbana: University of Illinois Press, 1991.

Neets, J. Q. [Joshua Kunitz]. Review of *Jews without Money,* by Michael Gold. *New Masses* 5, no. 10 (March 1930): 15.

Nelson, Cary, and Jefferson Hendricks, eds. *Edwin Rolfe: A Biographical Essay and Guide to the Rolfe Archive at the University of Illinois at Urbana-Champaign.* Urbana: University of Illinois Press, 1990.

Neve, Brian. *Film and Politics in America: A Social Tradition.* New York: Routledge, 1992.

Notch, Frank K. [Maurice Samuel]. *King Mob: A Study of the Present-Day Mind.* New York: Harcourt, Brace, 1930.

O'Connor, Frank. *The Lonely Voice: A Study of the Short Story.* 1962. Reprint, New York: Harper Colophon, 1985.

Once upon a Time in America. Dir. Sergio Leone. Warner Bros./Embassy International/ PSO International, 1984.

Ong, Walter J. *Fighting for Life: Contest, Sexuality, and Consciousness.* Ithaca, N.Y.: Cornell University Press, 1981.

Ornitz, Samuel. *Bride of the Sabbath.* New York: Rinehart, 1951.

———. *Haunch Paunch and Jowl: An Anonymous Autobiography.* New York: Boni and Liveright, 1923.

Oulanoff, Hongor. *Serapion Brothers.* Paris: Mouton and Co., 1966.

Paley, Grace. Foreword to A. N. Pirozhkova, *At His Side: The Last Years of Isaac Babel.* Trans. Ann Frydman and Robert L. Busch. South Royalton, Vt.: Steerforth Press, 1996.

Paustovsky, Konstantin. "A Few Words about Isaac Babel." In *You Must Know Everything: Stories, 1915–1937,* by Isaac Babel, 275–83. New York: Farrar, Straus, and Giroux, 1966.

———. *Years of Hope.* Trans. Manya Harari and Andrew Thomson. London: Harvill Press, 1968.

Pells, Richard. *Radical Visions and American Dreams: Culture and Social Thought in the Depression Years.* New York: Harper and Row, 1973.

The Perils of Pauline. Dir. Louis J. Gasnier and Donald MacKenzie. Pathé, 1914.

The Petrified Forest. Dir. Archie Mayo. Warner Bros., 1936.

Ping-Pong [pseud.]. "Nashi pozhelaniya k 10-letiyu oktyabrya" (Our wishes for the tenth anniversary of the October Revolution). *Na literaturnom postu* 20 (1927): 128.

Pinkwater, Daniel. *Chicago Days/Hoboken Nights.* New York: Addison-Wesley, 1991.

Pinsky, Robert. *Poetry and the World.* New York: Ecco Press, 1988.

Pirozhkova, A. N. *At His Side: The Last Years of Isaac Babel.* Trans. Ann Frydman and Robert L. Busch. South Royalton, Vt.: Steerforth Press, 1996.

Pritchett, V. S. "Isaac Babel: Five Minutes of Life." In *Lasting Impressions: Selected Essays.* 16–19. London: Chatto and Windus, 1990.

The Public Enemy. Dir. William Wellman. Warner Bros., 1931.

Puzo, Mario. *The Godfather.* New York: Putnam, 1969.

———. "How Crime Keeps America Healthy, Wealthy, Cleaner, and More Beautiful." In *The Godfather Papers and Other Confessions.* 70–80. New York: Putnam, 1972.

Pyros, John. *Mike Gold: Dean of American Proletarian Literature.* New York: Dramatika Press, 1979.

Quennell, Peter, and Hamish Johnson. *A History of English Literature.* London: Weidenfeld and Nicolson, 1973.

Rabinowitz, Paula. *Labor and Desire: Women's Revolutionary Fiction in Depression America.* Chapel Hill: University of North Carolina Press, 1991.

"Racketeer Rabbit." Dir. Fritz Freleng. Warner Bros., 1946.

Reed, Ishmael. *Japanese by Spring.* New York: Atheneum, 1993.

———. *Reckless Eyeballing.* 1986. Reprint, New York: Atheneum, 1988.

Reznikoff, Charles. *Family Chronicle: An Odyssey from Russia to America.* New York: Markus Wiener, 1963.

Rideout, Walter B. *The Radical Novel in the United States, 1900–1954: Some Interrelations of Literature and Society.* Cambridge, Mass.: Harvard University Press, 1956.

Roizman, Matvei. *Minus shest'* (Minus six). Berlin: Kniga i Stena, 1931.

Rosenthal, Raymond. "The Fate of Isaac Babel, a Child of the Russian Emancipation." *Commentary* 3, no. 2 (1947): 126–31.

Rosten, Leo [Leonard Q. Ross, pseud.]. *The Education of H*Y*M*A*N K*A*P*L*A*N.* New York: Harcourt, Brace and World, 1937.

———. *Hooray for Yiddish! A Book about English.* New York: Simon and Schuster, 1982.

———. *The Joys of Yiddish.* New York: McGraw Hill, 1968.

Roth, Henry. *Call It Sleep.* 1934. Reprint, New York: Farrar, Straus, and Giroux, 1991.

Roth, Philip. *Zuckerman Bound: A Trilogy and Epilogue. "The Ghost Writer," "Zuckerman Unbound," "The Anatomy Lesson," "Epilogue: A Prague Orgy."* New York: Fawcett Crest, 1985.

Rourke, Constance. *American Humor: A Study of the National Character.* 1931. Reprint, New York: Doubleday, 1953.

Rubin, Ruth. *Voices of a People: Yiddish Folk Song.* New York: Thomas Yoseloff, 1963.

Ruth, David E. *Inventing the Public Enemy: The Gangster in American Culture, 1918–1934.* Chicago: University of Chicago Press, 1996.

Samuel, Maurice. *You Gentiles.* New York: Harcourt, Brace, 1924.

Sandrow, Nahma. *Vagabond Stars: A World History of the Yiddish Theater.* New York: Harper and Row and the Jewish Publication Society of America, 1977.

Sante, Luc. *Low Life: Lures and Snares of Old New York.* New York: Vintage Books, 1991.

Scarface. Dir. Howard Hawks and Richard Rosson. United Artists, 1932.

Schiff, Ellen. "Shylock's *Mishpocheh:* Anti-Semitism on the American Stage." In *Anti-Semitism in American History.* Ed. David A. Gerber. 79–99. Chicago: University of Illinois Press, 1987.

Schiller, Friedrich. *The Robbers.* 1761. Reprint, trans. from the German of Frederick Schiller [*sic*]. New York: Samuel Campbell, 1795. Microform, Early American Imprints, no. 29471.

Scholnick, Sylvia Huberman. "Money versus *Mitzvot:* The Figure of the Businessman in Novels by American Jewish Writers." *Modern Jewish Studies Annual* 6 (1987): 48–55.

Schulberg, Budd. *What Makes Sammy Run?* 1941. Reprint, New York: Random House, 1990.

Sedgwick, Eve Kosofsky. *Between Men: English Literature and Male Homosocial Desire.* 1985. Reprint, New York: Columbia University Press, 1992.

Shakespeare, William. *The Complete Works.* Ed. Alfred Harbage. Baltimore: Penguin Books, 1969.

Shapiro, David, ed. *Social Realism: Art as a Weapon.* New York: Frederick Ungar, 1973.

Shklovskii, Victor. "Isaac Babel: A Critical Romance." In *Isaac Babel.* Ed. Harold Bloom. 9–14. New York: Chelsea House, 1987.

———. "Yugo-zapad" (Southwest). *Literaturnaya gazeta,* 5 January 1933, 3.

Sholem Aleichem. *The Adventures of Menachem-Mendl.* Trans. Tamara Kahana. New York: Putnam, 1969.

———. *From the Fair: The Autobiography of Sholom Aleichem.* Trans. and Ed. Curt Leviant. New York: Viking, 1985.

———. *Shomar's mishpot, oder der sud prisyazshnikh oyf alle romanen fun Shemer.* 1888. Reprint, New York: Clearwater/YIVO, 1980.

———. *"Tevye the Dairyman" and "The Railroad Stories."* Trans. Hillel Halkin. New York: Schocken Books, 1987.

———. *Tevye's Daughters.* Trans. Frances Butwin. New York: Crown, 1949.

Sholokhov, Mikhail. *Tikhii Don* (And quiet flows the don). 1928–40. Reprint, Moscow: Khudozhestvennaya literatura, 1985.

Sicher, Efraim. *Style and Structure in the Work of Isaak Babel'.* Columbus, Ohio: Slavica Publishers, 1985.

Siegel, William. "Proletarian Art" (drawing). *New Masses* 4, no. 10 (March 1929): 4.

Singer, David. "The Jewish Gangster: Crime as 'Unzer Shtik.'" *Judaism* (Winter 1974): 6–16.

Sinyavsky, Andrey. "Isaac Babel." In *Isaac Babel.* Ed. Harold Bloom. 87–95. New York: Chelsea House, 1987.

Sklar, Robert. *City Boys: Cagney, Bogart, Garfield.* Princeton, N.J.: Princeton University Press, 1992.

Slobin, Marc. *Tenement Songs: The Popular Music of the Jewish Immigrants.* Chicago: University of Illinois Press, 1982.

Smethurst, James. *The New Red Negro: African American Poetry and the Left.* New York: Oxford University Press, 1999.

Soby, James Thrall. "'Gangster's Funeral' (1953)." *Saturday Review,* 5 December 1953, 57–58.

Sollors, Werner. *Beyond Ethnicity: Consent and Descent in American Culture.* New York: Oxford University Press, 1986.

Stearns, Harold E., ed. *Civilization in the United States: An Inquiry by Thirty Americans.* New York: Harcourt, Brace, 1922.

Stein, Harry. *Hoopla.* New York: St. Martin's Press, 1983.

Sterne, Laurence. *The Life and Opinions of Tristram Shandy, Gentleman.* 1759. Reprint, New York: Boni and Liveright, 1925.

Tax, Meredith. *Rivington Street.* New York: William Morrow, 1982.

———. *Union Square.* New York: William Morrow, 1988.

Taxi Blues. Dir. Pavel Lungin. Lenfilm/ASK Eurofilm, 1990.

Trachtenberg, Alan. *Brooklyn Bridge: Fact and Symbol.* 2d ed. Chicago: University of Chicago Press, 1979.

Traffic in Souls. Dir. George Loane Tucker. Independent Moving Picture Co., 1913.

Trilling, Lionel. Introduction to *The Collected Stories of Isaac Babel.* Trans. and Ed. Walter Morison. New York: New American Library, 1955.

Twain, Mark. *The Adventures of Huckleberry Finn*. 1884. Reprint, New York: Penguin Books, 1985.

The Twelve Chairs. Dir. Mel Brooks. Crossbow, 1970.

Utesov, Leonid. "Moya Odessa" (My Odessa). *Literaturnaya Rossiya*. 21 August 1964, 6–17.

Vinogradov, Viktor. "The Problem of Skaz in Stylistics." *Russian Literature Triquarterly* 12 (Spring 1975): 237–52.

Wald, Alan. *Writing from the Left: New Essays on Radical Culture and Politics*. New York: Verso, 1994.

Walsh, George. *Public Enemies: The Mayor, the Mob, and the Crime That Was*. New York: W. W. Norton, 1980.

Warshow, Robert. "The Gangster as Tragic Hero." 1948. Reprinted in *The Immediate Experience*. New York: Atheneum, 1970.

Weidman, Jerome. *I Can Get It for You Wholesale*. 1937. Reprint, London: Bodley Head, 1984.

Weinryb, Bernard. "Anti-Semitism in Soviet Russia." In *The Jews in Soviet Russia since 1917*. Ed. Lionel Kochan. 288–320. New York: Oxford University Press, 1972.

West, Nathanael. *A Cool Million*. 1934. Reprinted in *The Collected Works of Nathanael West*. 277–380. New York: Penguin Books, 1981.

———. *The Day of the Locust*. 1939. Reprinted in *"Miss Lonelyhearts" and "The Day of the Locust."* New York: New Directions, 1962.

What Happened to Mary? Writ. Horace G. Plympton. Edison, 1912.

Williams, Raymond. *The Politics of Modernism: Against the New Conformists*. New York: Verso, 1989.

Williams, William Carlos. *Spring and All*. 1923. Reprinted in *The Collected Poems of William Carlos Williams*. Ed. A. Walton Litz and Christopher MacGowan, vol. 1 (1909–39). 175–236. New York: New Directions, 1986.

Wisse, Ruth R. *The Schlemiel as Modern Hero*. Chicago: University of Chicago Press, 1971.

Wixson, Douglas. *Worker-Writer in America: Jack Conroy and the Tradition of Midwestern Literary Radicalism, 1898–1990*. Urbana: University of Illinois Press, 1993.

Yezierska, Anzia. *Bread Givers*. 1925. Reprint, New York: Persea Books, 1975.

Zakat. Dir. Aleksandr Zeldovich. Based on Isaac Babel's *Odessa Tales*. Goskino/Mosfilm/Slovo, 1990.

Zamyatin, Yevgeny. "On Language." 1919–20. Reprinted in *A Soviet Heretic: Essays by Yevgeny Zamyatin*. Trans. and Ed. Mirra Ginsburg. 175–89. Chicago: University of Chicago Press, 1970.

Zangwill, Israel. "The Luftmensch." In *Ghetto Comedies*. New York: Macmillan, 1907.

———. *The Melting-Pot*. 1909. Reprint, New York: Macmillan, 1932.

Index

Index

Index

Index

Rachel Rubin, an assistant professor of American studies at the University of Massachusetts at Boston, is a co-editor of *American Popular Music: New Approaches to the Twentieth Century* (forthcoming).

Typeset in 10.5/13 Minion
with Galliard display
Designed by Dennis Roberts
Composed by Jim Proefrock
at the University of Illinois Press
Manufactured by Thomson-Shore, Inc.

University of Illinois Press
1325 South Oak Street
Champaign, IL 61820-6903
www.press.uillinois.edu